The Visitor's Guide
to
HOLLAND

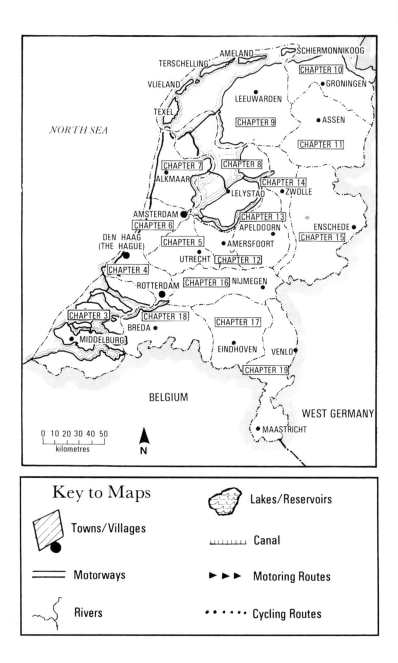

CHAPTER 10

SCHIERMONNIKOOG
AMELAND
TERSCHELLING
GRONINGEN
VLIELAND
LEEUWARDEN
TEXEL
CHAPTER 9
ASSEN
NORTH SEA
CHAPTER 11
CHAPTER 7
CHAPTER 8
ALKMAAR
CHAPTER 14
LELYSTAD
ZWOLLE
AMSTERDAM
CHAPTER 13
CHAPTER 6
APELDOORN
ENSCHEDE
DEN HAAG
(THE HAGUE)
CHAPTER 5
AMERSFOORT
CHAPTER 15
UTRECHT
CHAPTER 12
CHAPTER 4
CHAPTER 16
NIJMEGEN
ROTTERDAM
CHAPTER 3
CHAPTER 18
CHAPTER 17
BREDA
MIDDELBURG
EINDHOVEN
VENLO
CHAPTER 19
BELGIUM
WEST GERMANY
0 10 20 30 40 50
kilometres
N
MAASTRICHT

Key to Maps

Towns/Villages

Motorways

Rivers

Lakes/Reservoirs

Canal

► ► ► Motoring Routes

• • • • • Cycling Routes

THE
VISITOR'S GUIDE TO
HOLLAND

Pat & Hazel Constance

MPC

HUNTER
PUBLISHING INC

British Library Cataloguing in Publication Data

Constance, Pat
    The visitor's guide to Holland.
    1. Netherlands — Description and travel
    — 1978 — Guide-books
    I. Title II. Constance, Hazel
    914.92′0473   DJ16

ISBN 0-86190-168-1
ISBN 0-86190-167-3 Pbk

Published in the UK by
Moorland Publishing Co Ltd,
Ashbourne, Derbyshire DE6 1HD

ISBN 0 86190 167 3 (paperback)
ISBN 0 86190 168 1 (hardback)

Published in the USA by
Hunter Publishing Inc,
300 Raritan Center Parkway,
CN94, Edison, NJ 08818

ISBN 0 935161 16 3

Black and white illustrations have been supplied by:
De Efteling: p216; KLM: p90; Netherlands National Tourist Office: pp23, 75, 163, 198, 232; L. Porter: pp46, 70; the rest of the photographs were supplied by P. Constance.
Colour photographs were supplied by P. Constance (Kasteel de Haar, Haarlem, Hindeloopen, Dokkum, Amersfoort) the remainder were taken by L. Porter.
Cover: Windmill at Kinderdijk (Klaus Kerth, Zefa Picture Library).

Printed in Great Britain by
Butler and Tanner Ltd,
Frome, Somerset.

CONTENTS

FOREWORD

The Netherlands — the 'Low Country' — may be small in size, but it is a land of fascinating contrasts. To anyone visiting the country for the first time we would say explore with open eyes and an open mind. Do not be too ambitious. Small as it is, the country has so much to offer that it would be a sad mistake to attempt too much in a limited time. After all, what better excuse for a return visit than the fact that you have not seen it all?

Some understanding of the geography and the history of this land will show how each has affected the other, not least in the way man has changed the geography of the country we see today.

Modern developments, and the culmination of the latest achievements in man's struggle against the water surely merit the description 'dynamic'. However, that same element, water, brings a great feeling of peace and tranquillity, and gives rise to that special quality of light which so attracted Dutch painters in the past, and still exists today.

In this book many routes are described. The intention is not to lay down 'ready-made' itineraries, rather to point the way to getting off the beaten track, to be curious, to look around the next corner and down the side turnings, so to discover more than will be seen by the tourist in a hurry. It is a country for browsing, not for rushing.

You will find people willing to talk, to explain, to help. Over the years, we have made many friends, and it is they, maybe unknowingly, who have helped so much in the writing of this book. Our thanks to them all, also to many people in VVV offices and not least to those in the NBT office both in Holland and in London, who have contributed their time, advice and help.

If, like us, you find there is still much to see, do not say 'Goodbye' when you leave. Say '*Tot ziens*', and we will be satisfied.

Note:

Normally, the letter Y does not appear in Dutch, usually being written as IJ. It appears in indexes in the same position as an English Y. For example, IJsselstein may sometimes be written as Ysselstein. Also, for example, Vollenhove appears before Vijfhuis in a gazetteer, and Workum appears before Wijns. Usually, words beginning with these two letters, such as IJssel river, when proper names, are written with the two letters in upper case, as above.

1 AN INTRODUCTION TO HOLLAND

'God made the world, but the Dutch made Holland'. The truth of this saying may be realised when one looks back on the history of the country, with the struggles of the people against the sea from the very earliest times.

Strictly speaking, the term 'Holland' should apply only to the provinces of South and North Holland, in the west of the country, the correct name for the entire country being the Kingdom of the Netherlands. However, the term 'Holland' is becoming more widely used, even in official circles and by the Dutch themselves.

Land

Holland is a small country, with an area of about 40,000sqkm of which more than twenty-five percent has been reclaimed from the sea. This figure increases as yet more land is reclaimed. Two-fifths of the country is below sea level, and without the protection of the man-made dykes this would be covered by water at high tide. Except for the southernmost parts of the country, where the ground rises to a height of about 300m above sea level, hilly ground is almost unknown, and there are few places where the land exceeds 50m in height. The theory that, because it is flat, the country must therefore be uninteresting, is simply not true. The ever-present water gives a quality of light which the Dutch landscape artists recognised, and it is quite an experience to see quite large vessels gliding along amongst the fields and meadows!

The central part of Holland consists of the three great river plains, which are protected from flooding by a system of dykes, dams, locks and canals.

Further south, in Brabant and North Limburg, the land consists of bog peat and heathland, which is also found in Friesland and parts of Utrecht province. Here, great lakes have been formed by the flooding of the peat workings. The area known as the Veluwe, is one great heathland, stretching from the shores of the IJsselmeer in the north to Arnhem in the south. The east and far south of the country is 'old land' — more hilly and wooded than the rest of Holland, and where most of the traces of early civilisations are to be found.

As early as the seventh century AD, dykes were being constructed to hold back the sea, but the first real development of the polders, came in the sixteenth century with the development of the windmills, which enabled the land cut off from the sea by dykes to be drained and used for agriculture. From these early efforts, great strides have been made.

The first suggestion for draining the Zuiderzee was made as early as the seventeenth century, but was not considered feasible until two hundred years later. Work on the project actually started in 1919, since when more than 1,500,000 hectares (600,000 acres) have been reclaimed in that area alone! Modern technology is such that dykes and barriers can now be built in areas and in conditions which would have been unthinkable only a few years ago. The scale of such engineering has to be seen to be believed, and the Dutch are very proud of their achievements. By the time the present plans are completed, the coastline of the Netherlands will have been reduced by approximately 1,550km, of which more than 1,000km are in the 'delta' area around the former islands of the south-west. Although the original plans were intended to provide good defences against the sea, and give the inhabitants more agricultural land, the works have done far more than this. The drinking water supplies have been greatly improved, and large areas for recreation have been created. In addition, in the Flevo-polders, two new cities have been built, complete with every social and recreational facility, to allow people to move from the overcrowded cities to pleasant new environments.

Climate
The climate of Holland is very similar to that of Britain; temperate, but with seasonal extremes of temperature due to the continental influence. Strong winds are common, as there is nothing to stop them from sweeping across the flat landscape from the sea. This is particularly noticeable in Zeeland and the northern parts of the country. The prevailing wind is from the south-west, and there are about 150cms of rainfall in a year. The wettest months tend to be from July to November, and the coldest February, when the average temperature is -0.3°C, although, as elsewhere in Northern Europe, there can be no hard and fast rule about this.

Whatever the weather, Holland is worth visiting at almost any time of the year, as there is so much to see and do.

Flora and Fauna
There are many beautiful areas of Holland which abound with plants, birds and animals. Most are freely accessible to the public by road or path, but sometimes an admission charge is payable. The dunes in the west are particularly beautiful, with thorn bushes, brambles and roses growing in profusion beside the winding paths, giving colour at all times of the year. Tall pines and delicate silver birches offer restful shade for human and animal population alike, for the area abounds with small mammals, lizards, pheasants and sea birds. The paths enable the visitor to approach quietly and observe the beauty of the area without disturbing the natural habitat. Within the dunes are small lakes, offering safe breeding grounds for a variety of water birds, including spoonbills. Due to the effect of the sea breaking through in bygone days, great deposits of clay have built up and mixed with the sand. This has left large fertile areas which are ideal for growing bulbs and other market garden produce. The whole area from Den Haag in the south to Den Helder in the north is a blaze of colour when the bulbfields are in bloom. South of Den Haag is the area known as

Westland, famous for its greenhouses and such associated products as tomatoes, lettuces and grapes.

Small animals are also to be found in the many new forestry and nature areas of the Flevoland, even deer in a few places. Many migrating birds are found here also, and towards the end of May the whole area is ablaze with colour from the yellow rape-seed flowers which are grown in the region. These flowers also attract the bees, so hives are put out and another crop is produced — honey. Beehives can also be found beside the many paths which wind across the heathlands of the Veluwe, Drenthe and parts of Twente and Achterhoek, where deer, foxes, badgers and wild pigs may be seen. There are probably more nature reserves in Drenthe than in any other province, and strangely enough, despite its distance from the coast, the area is particularly well known for the breeding grounds of seagulls. Central Holland, along the three great rivers, is the main fruit-growing area, and it is a treat to visit the region when the apple, pear and cherry trees are in bloom.

The People

Holland has the highest population density of any other European country, averaging more than 2,000 people per square kilometre of land. More than fourteen million people live in the six major cities, and by far the largest part of the population lives within North and South Holland and Utrecht. Although these provinces cover only about one-fifth of the total land area of Holland, almost half of the country's population lives there.

At first glance, the Dutch may appear to be rather staid and formal; however, they are most friendly and welcoming. As in many other continental countries, a handshake should precede any conversation: a Dutchman will shake hands and say his name by way of introduction, and the visitor should do likewise. Many Dutch people speak English very well, although in country villages it is not so widely spoken, particularly by the older folk. Most have a great regard for the British and their allies who played such a large part in the liberation of Holland at the end of World War II. It pays to try and learn some basic phrases of the language, and your efforts will be much appreciated. In Friesland, the old Frisian language is spoken by many people, and in the south of Limburg, French and German may be used. In fact, once you get the idea of the language, it is not too difficult to work out the meaning of some of the words, for many sound very similar to the English equivalent, even though the spelling is somewhat different. For example, *huis* in Dutch sounds very similar to house in English, and means the same. Most words which are spelt with 'ui' together sound much the same as the 'ou' sound in house. *Uit* means out, or exit. *Boot* in Dutch sounds very similar to boat in English, and means the same. The Dutch 'oo' sound almost always sounds like the English 'oa'. When it is followed by an 'r' it sounds more like 'oor' as in 'door', eg *Spoorweg* (meaning railway).

Visitors should try to remember that in some of the more traditional villages — such as Staphorst, Huizen, and the former islands of Urk and Marken — the taking of photographs could cause offence. In any case, do not attempt to take photographs of local people without first asking, and never do so on a Sunday. In Staphorst, a local bye-law prohibits photography of the inhabitants.

History

The Kingdom of the Netherlands as we know it today was established in 1815 after a long history of conquest by many countries, but evidence is still visible of prehistoric and Roman occupation of the land in the huge megalithic monuments, ancient *terps* and dykes, and Roman remains.

Because of problems caused by flooding, and the natural division of the country into two halves by the great rivers, the south developed at a faster rate. Fortunes changed with the development of the wind pumping mill, which enabled the land to be drained, and with the growth of international trade.

This was the era of the East Indies Company, whose influence was a contributory factor leading to the Revolt of the Netherlands against Philip II of Spain, led by William the Silent. From this struggle the Republic of the Seven Provinces emerged as an independent nation, and the Golden Age began. During the second half of the seventeenth century, the United Provinces were at war with England, culminating in the battle of the Medway in 1667. The war ended when the English deposed James II in 1688 and offered the crown to William of Orange and his wife Mary, James' daughter.

After further wars with England and France in the eighteenth and nineteenth centuries, a constitutional monarchy gradually developed into a parliamentary democracy, since when the Dutch have emerged as a nation contributing much to both European and world civilisation. Their scholars, artists and scientists are well-known. Their Stock Exchange is the oldest in the world. Their traders to the Indies made great discoveries. In modern times the Dutch have proved their courage, having suffered terribly during World War II. Their courage also shows in their daring advances in engineering techniques, allowing the construction of huge storm barriers in areas which would have been unthinkable only a few years ago, and the reclamation of vast areas of land from the sea.

Art, Culture and Everyday Life

It is inevitable that Dutch art and culture tends to be thought of in the terms of the seventeenth century, because that is when Dutch influence spread world-wide. Much of the wealth brought back by the merchants — gold, silver, fine furniture and porcelain — is now preserved in some of over five hundred museums to be found throughout the country. The many works of Dutch painters of the Golden Age are also to be found in these museums. Modern paintings and sculptures of the nineteenth and twentieth centuries are much in evidence.

There are a surprising number of castles, country houses and estates, dating back many centuries, and modern architecture also has its place. Many old brick buildings from the Golden Age remain intact; after restoration these can look deceptively new, as the mortar has to be renewed and the surface cleaned during the process.

Music plays an important part in Dutch culture today. Most large cities have their own concert-halls, and many large churches have magnificent organs on which concerts are regularly given. Festivals of music of all kinds from 'pop' to classical, take place regularly, and on the streets music from colourful organs and student buskers can be heard.

The Dutch are a hard-working nation who make the most of their spare time. They are particularly fond of the open-air, and many families like to spend their weekends in the countryside. Cycling is a natural pastime, both for commuting to work and for pleasure.

The Dutch enjoy their food, which is usually plentiful, although there is not a great deal of variety. Breakfast normally consists of a variety of breads and rusks, and *ontbijtkoek* — spiced cake — served with sliced cheese, meat, jam, etc, and sometimes a boiled egg, accompanied by tea or coffee. Much the same is served at midday, often accompanied by soup. The evening meal, served around six o'clock, consists of meat or fish, served with fresh vegetables, and followed by fruit, yogurt or *vla*, a sort of custard.

Some Dutch specialities which the visitor is sure to encounter include *uitsmijters*, which consist of two slices of bread and butter, topped with ham or cheese and two or three fried eggs, served with pickles and a salad garnish. *Pannekoeken* — pancakes — are always large, and may be served with a great variety of toppings from bananas to bacon. All are served with thick brown syrup — *stroop* — and are delicious. Soups are thick and filling; try *erwtensoep*, a thick pea soup with sausage or bacon. Fish specialities include raw herring and smoked eels, both of which are very tasty. Indo-Chinese food is available in abundance. Try *Ba-Mie* — noodles, vegetables and pork mixed together with spices — or *Rijsttafel*, consisting of different savoury dishes served with rice and chutneys. Pastries are mouthwatering — and fattening! Try *appeltaart* and *Limburgse Vlaai* — fruit flan served with thick cream.

Customs, Costumes and Folklore

These three traditions are really inseparable from each other; they remain an everyday part of Dutch life. For example, it is customary for the women in the villages of Bunschoten/Spakenburg, Marken, Volendam and Staphorst to wear their colourful costumes every day as a matter of course. They are certainly not worn for the benefit of the tourist. Many of these costumes are works of art, for fine needle-work, knitting and crochet go into the making of all of them. Costumes may be seen in other areas, particularly on market days and Sundays. Look for the beautiful bonnets of Huizen and the strange elongated cap or *poffer* of Scheveningen. All are very different from each other. Interested visitors should look for shops specialising in genuine costume dolls, dressed in accurate copies of costumes, which are not found in general souvenir shops. The shops of Arbeid Adelt, an association of women working in their own homes, are one such source.

Many customs in Holland are linked with church festivals, and even older pagan rites, whilst others are linked to traditional sports. Easter traditions include dancing through Ootmarsum streets, and bonfires in Twente. Children hunt for painted eggs, and eat Easter men, made from bread dough, for breakfast. *Sinterklaas* (St Nicholas) arrives on 5 December, with his assistant *Zwarte Piet*, who tries to ensure all children have been good. Children may be given their initial in chocolate, or some *speculaas* — spiced biscuit — in the shape of *Sint*.

In Brabant and Limburg, Carnaval is linked with the pre-Lent festivities, and other festivals are kept with traditional ceremonies in other parts of the country.

Sporting customs include the Eleven Towns race along the frozen canals in Friesland, and jumping the dyke, which takes place in several regions. Banner-waving contests in Brabant and Limburg, and 'tilting the ring' and other medieval sports are also popular. Windmills, too, are part of Dutch folklore; the miller can set his sails in different ways to signal messages to other millers, and many secret messages were passed in this way during World War II. On festive occasions, the mills are garlanded with flowers and bunting.

Birthdays and anniversaries are always special occasions, and when children are successful in their school exams the school bag is hung from the window, together with the national flag, by way of celebration. On Queen's Day, 30 April, many towns and cities are festooned with orange balloons, coloured lights and red, white and blue bunting. Wooden shoes, or *klompen* as they are known in Holland, are often thought to be part of the traditional costumes. In reality, they are a working clog, used on farms and on fish-quays, and by families when working in their gardens. They are never worn inside the house, but are left outside the door.

Many traditional crafts, including clogmaking, glassmaking, chair-seating, pottery and cheese making can be seen at various 'folklore' markets held during the summer months, and may also be seen at some of the folk museums throughout the country.

Wherever you go in Holland, there will be opportunities to observe some of these customs, costumes, and folklore.

2 TOUR PLANNING AND GENERAL INFORMATION

Information Sources

The Netherlands Board of Tourism (NBT) has offices in a number of countries, and so may well be the first place to go when seeking information about Holland. It publishes a number of brochures and leaflets dealing with various areas of interest to visitors; tourist attractions, outdoor activities and other events which may attract visitors to the country. Copies of these are usually available free on request, and may be obtained by post or by personal callers. Addresses of these offices are given in the Further Information.

Within the country, there exists a network of local information centres in every town and many villages. They are simply identified by triangular signs with the letters VVV, and can supply a great variety of local information on places to visit, and so on. Additionally, they provide an excellent service to help visitors to obtain accommodation, and bookings for local events. They are truly mines of information on their local area, and the larger offices can supply information relating to other parts of the country on request. Many simple leaflets are free, and a very comprehensive selection of books and maps are on sale.

Usually, VVV offices will have publications in various languages, so they make a good first port of call for the visitor to any locality.

Documentation

A valid passport is necessary (or a British Visitor's passport). For stays of not more than three months, visas are not necessary. Drivers of motor vehicles must have a valid full (not provisional) driving licence and Certificate of insurance, and the vehicle registration document should also be carried. If in any doubt, check either with the NBT or with your own national motoring organisations.

Travel insurance, depending on your mode of transport and the activities you propose to follow, should be obtained to cover the period of your visit. This should include vehicle recovery in the event of accident or irreparable breakdown, although this may be difficult in the case of small capacity motor-cycles or mopeds. Special insurance for recovery of bicycles may also be expensive and its worth would depend upon the value of your machine.

Medical treatment can be expensive. However, nationals of countries within the EEC are entitled to treatment on the same basis as Dutch nationals. At least a month before your journey, apply to the local DHSS office who will supply full details.

If planning to camp, an International Camping Carnet should be obtained from an organisation which is affiliated to the FICC or AIT and of which you are a member. Such organisations include the Camping and Caravanning Club and the Cyclists Touring Club in the United Kingdom; similar organisations exist in most English-speaking countries. The Carnet will prove valuable where a camp site wishes to retain your Passport during your stay, which should never be permitted. The Carnet is usually accepted instead. It also proves that you hold Third Party Insurance cover through the membership of the issuing organisation.

Membership cards of a Youth Hostels organisation belonging to the International Youth Hostels Association should be carried if Youth Hostels are to be used.

Two further items may prove to be of use, depending on what you plan to do. One is the newly-introduced Holland Leisure Card, which may be bought from the NBT and is valid for one year. This is in effect a Credit Card which entitles the holder to discounts on a number of things including public transport, car rentals, events, and purchases in certain large stores. The other is a Museum Year Card, which entitles the holder to free admission to over 300 museums around the country during the year of its validity. The card is obtainable from any VVV office, and possession of the Holland Leisure Card will entitle the holder to a ten per cent discount.

Money
The unit of currency is the guilder (florin) written as Fl. It is subdivided into 100 cents. Bank notes are available in denominations of 1,000, 250, 100, 50, 25, 10 and 5 gulden. Coins to the values of 2.5 gulden (*rijksdaalder*), 1 guilder, 25 cents (*kwartje*), 10 cents (*dubbeltje*) and 5 cents (*stuiver*). A one cent coin no longer exists.

Currency may be exchanged at any bank, some of the larger VVV offices or at the many exchange offices of the GWK organisation which are located at main railway stations, airports, major frontier crossings and in many major tourist centres. These exchange offices stay open late during the summer. Other 'change shops' may be found in cities, but often charge a higher commission, and should be avoided.

Currency may be carried in the form of Travellers' Cheques or in currency obtained before leaving home. This should be confined to sufficient for immediate needs. Personal cheques (Eurocheques) may be cashed in banks which display the Eurocheque sign, on production of a valid Eurocheque Card. Most banks open from 9am to 4pm Monday to Friday, and some have a late opening night. Whenever exchanging money or cashing a cheque, have your passport available, as it will probably be required. Holders of National Giro accounts in the UK can draw money at Post Offices which handle Dutch Giro business. Many of the major Credit Cards, including Visa, Access and American Express, are accepted.

Postal and Telephone Services
Post Offices normally open from 8.30am to 5pm, but larger offices have an outer hall with telephone call-boxes and stamp machines, which remain

open until later in the evening, and on Saturday mornings. Pre-stamped letter cards are available from machines, in addition to stamps, although extra stamps are required for posting to other countries. The public telephone system is excellent, being fully automatic with direct dialling to most European countries even from call boxes. All call boxes have clear instructions in several languages including English. The unit of charge for call box phones is 25 cents, and in the main towns boxes which take larger denomination coins are provided. The system permits coins to be inserted before and during a call, with indication of how much remains. At the end of a call any unused money will be returned, although change cannot be given. It is, therefore, best to include one or two *kwartjes* (25 cent coins). For long-distance calls insert several coins before dialling. In case of difficulty, there should be no problems about speaking in English to the operator, but the printed instructions are quite clear.

Time
The Netherlands is in the Central European time zone, which is one hour ahead of the UK. Clocks are put forward one hour during the summer, and it is very important to check if this change occurs at the same time as it does in the UK. Ferry and air timetables quote times of departure and arrival in local time, which needs careful checking.

Getting to the Netherlands
Although international shipping lines sail into the ports of Rotterdam and Amsterdam from all over the world, most visitors travelling by sea will do so via the United Kingdom, thence by one of the ferry services. These cater for all kinds of passengers and transport, depending on the route or service used. The choice of route lies between either a direct link to the Netherlands, or a route via Belgium or France, which will involve a rail or road journey. The choice will depend, among other things, on the point of departure in the UK and what part of the Netherlands it is planned to visit first. It is also worth taking time to study the various ferry company brochures for details of such things as cheap excursion fares, whether or not bicycles or mopeds are charged for, and how car passengers are counted when calculating the fares. Cyclists may wish to carry their cycles on the car roof-rack to the ferry port, garage the car and embark with the cycles. Alternatively, take both car and cycle on the ferry, but remember to state clearly on the ferry booking form that the overall height of the car is increased by the height of the bicycles. Even so, it may be found that the cycles have to be laid flat on top of the car during the ferry crossing and it is as well to be prepared for this.

When travelling with just bicycles, these are normally stowed on the car deck, and if possible should be secured against the side of the boat to prevent them from falling over. Ropes are often available but may be greasy, and it is a good idea to carry either cord or elastic shock-cords with hooks for securing the cycles. Panniers should be safe if left on the bike, although bar bags will usually be needed during the journey.

Ferry services available are as follows:

Harwich — Hoek van Holland

Operated jointly by Sealink British Ferries and the Zeeland Steamship Company, there is one crossing each way by day and one each way by night. The crossing time varies between $6\frac{3}{4}$ hours in the daytime and 8 hours at night. Direct rail connections from Scotland, the north of England and London to Harwich, and from Hoek van Holland to all parts of Holland, and through to Belgium and Germany, make this a very convenient route.

Sheerness — Vlissingen

Operated by Olau Line, a once daily and once nightly sailing in each direction, with a crossing time of about 8 hours provides a good service from south-east England; direct coach connection with London (Victoria) is supplemented with a coach connection from the ferry terminal to Vlissingen station.

Hull — Rotterdam (Europoort)

This service by North Sea Ferries provides a nightly service of about 13 hours duration, useful for passengers from the north of England and Scotland.

Great Yarmouth — Scheveningen

This freight service by Norfolk Line offers limited accommodation for passengers and cars, with three sailings daily from Monday to Friday and two on Saturday. The crossing time is about 8 hours.

Felixstowe — Rotterdam (Europort)

A freight service operated by Townsend Thoresen with limited passenger accommodation. Two sailings daily from Monday to Friday with a crossing time of about 8 hours. Application should be made direct to the freight office in Felixstowe.

Services via Belgium are:

Dover — Zeebrugge

This Townsend Thoresen service provides six sailings daily in each direction, with a journey time of about $4\frac{1}{2}$ hours.

Dover — Oostende

A joint service by Townsend Thoresen and a Belgian shipping company, providing six or seven sailings each way daily, taking about 4 hours for the journey.

Felixstowe — Zeebrugge

Townsend Thoresen provide up to three sailings each way per day, taking about 5 to 7 hours.

Hull — Zeebrugge

A nightly service by North Sea Ferries takes about 15 hours.

Services via France, avoiding the longer sea crossings, include frequent services from Dover to Calais (journey time 75 minutes) on Townsend Thoresen ferries. Sally Line provides a number of sailings each way between Ramsgate and Dunkerque, with a sailing time of about $2\frac{1}{2}$ hours.

A 35-minute journey time is provided by the Hoverspeed service from Dover to either Calais or Boulogne, which takes cars as well as foot passengers.

Passengers without cars may also travel by the Townsend Thoresen Jetfoil service, making several journeys each way daily between Dover and Oostende, taking under 2 hours. Good rail connections are provided each end.

A number of coach services operate from the UK with direct connections to destinations in Holland, and details may be obtained from the NBT or from travel agents.

With a major international airport at Schiphol, near Amsterdam, and other airports at Rotterdam, Maastricht, and Eindhoven, there are many air services from all over the world to Holland. From the United Kingdom, services operate from no less than twenty different airports all over the country, including Scotland and Northern Ireland, together with services from Eire and the Channel Islands. Since details and timings change so quickly, it is best to enquire locally before booking. Advantage may be taken of various fare reductions, and passengers with bicycles may find they can take these as luggage, but make absolutely certain beforehand of any special conditions or requirements. Passengers landing at Schiphol will now find that there is a frequent and direct rail link into Amsterdam Central Station, taking only 20 minutes. From Rotterdam airport a bus service reaches the centre in 20 minutes.

Travellers to Holland from other European countries will find that the Netherlands Railways (NS) system is excellent, and has fast direct links into the European rail network. Good motor roads and motorways also connect with adjoining European countries. For the private tourist, frontier and customs formalities are simple, especially for nationals of other EEC countries.

Maps and Guides

For general use the series of *Toeristenkaarten* or Tourist Maps published by the ANWB (Royal Dutch Touring Club) are recommended. These maps are at a scale of 1:100,000, and cover the whole country on fourteen sheets. It should be noted that this series has recently been revised, and the sheet numbers and boundaries changed. Formerly the series comprised thirteen sheets. The maps are very detailed but clear, and show all roads; also cycle paths, with a distinction between those which are banned to mopeds and those which are not. Many other details are shown and these maps represent probably the best value in maps for general use. They can be bought in England in certain shops, but are probably cheaper to buy in Holland. Any office of the ANWB sells them, and these can be found in any major town. The explanation of the symbols used is in Dutch only, but should not present much difficulty. On the reverse side of each sheet is a gazetteer of place names and a list of addresses of ANWB offices.

Motorists may find the series of three *Wegenkaarten* or road maps published by ANWB quite useful. The sheets are designated *Noord, Midden* and *Zuid*, and show all but the smallest roads; also ANWB addresses and gazetteer of place names, together with small street plans of major towns on the area covered by the sheet. Each sheet has a good overlap with the adjoining sheet, and the set of three maps to a scale of 1:200,000 probably gives the most up-to-date information regarding new motorways and main roads. They are good value for money.

A motorist looking for cheap maps obtainable in the US and UK can probably do no better than to buy the maps published by Michelin. The familiar yellow covers contain one map, sheet 408 to a scale of 1:400,000, which covers the whole of the Netherlands. Ideal for general planning, and including a gazetteer, it has explanations in English, French, Dutch and German, and includes large-scale inserts of the Amsterdam and Rotterdam areas. Cycle-paths are not shown. More detailed motoring maps from Michelin to a scale of 1:200,000 cover the Netherlands on sheets numbered 1, 5 and 6, again with explanations in four languages, but no indication of which roads are banned to cyclists. These maps are revised frequently, so it is worth checking the date and revision number in the margin at the top left-hand corner of the sheet.

Many large-scale and specialised maps showing, for example, footpaths or cycle routes, can be obtained from local shops of the ANWB or local VVV offices. Some have English explanations, so it is worth checking this before buying.

It is worth noting that when purchasing items such as maps or guides from the ANWB, you may be asked if you are a member of a motoring organisation at home, although membership of a cycling club will also be accepted. Of course no restrictions apply to purchases made from the VVV, and many of the ANWB publications are available through this source.

TRAVELLING WITHIN THE NETHERLANDS

Public Transport
Public transport within the Netherlands includes an excellent railway network, together with bus, tram and metro services. Throughout the country, which has been divided into zones, there is a standard charge per zone on buses, trams and metro (underground) services. Generally, bus terminals in towns and cities are located within easy reach of railway stations. A national Day Ticket (*Dagkaart*) is available which is valid for use on any bus, tram or metro of the Dutch National Transport companies with the exception of KLM airline buses.

The zone system comes into its own with the use of the *Nationale Strippenkaart*. This is a ticket in the form of a long strip, each section of which represents one unit of charge. Travel within one zone, by any means, costs two strips, within two zones three strips, and so on. On trams, the metro and on some city buses there is an automatic machine for stamping the card. On suburban buses give the card to the driver. Unlimited travel within the zone or zones stamped is allowed during the time permitted, as shown on the back of the card, and changes are permitted during the journeys. If two or more people are travelling together, the required number of strips are stamped on the one card if sufficient blank spaces are available. The Strip Cards can be bought at some railway stations, transport offices, post offices, some VVV offices and often in tobacconist's shops. The cards contain fifteen strips and have unlimited validity. Six or ten-strip cards may be purchased from bus drivers but these are relatively more expensive.

For anyone likely to make use of buses, the *Nationale Buswijzer* is a guide to all the bus routes all over the country, with reference to the nearest railway stations. This small book is produced by the Netherlands Railways, and it gives tabulated information on how to reach almost every town and village in the country from the nearest station, with details of bus route numbers, zones, bus company, journey time and frequency of service. Together with a bus map of the country, the guide may be obtained from major railway information offices.

The Netherlands Railways (NS) are completely electrified and provide rapid and frequent services over most of the country, with direct links into the rest of Europe, including trains designated International Express (D-train), Trans-Europe Express (T-E-E), or International Inter-City (IC), on which supplements are usually payable. Fares are reasonable, and a variety of cheap tickets are available in addition to normal single (*enkele reis*) and return (*retour*) fares. Of special interest to the tourist might be the various Rover Tickets, ranging from the Day Rover giving one day's unlimited travel on all routes to the 7-day Rover and Multi-Rover for a family. The railways also have numerous day excursions, with combined rail and entry tickets to various events and places of interest. Information on these and all other matters relating to rail travel may be obtained at any station information or booking office, or from the VVV.

The NBT office in your own country can also help. In London, the Dutch Railways (NS) have an information counter in the same building as the NBT, and rail tickets can be purchased there in advance. Railway timetables (*Spoorboekje*) for the whole of the Netherlands may also be purchased there, valid for a whole year.

Cyclists should note that carriage of bicycles is not free in Holland. Many trains have restricted space, or no space for cycles. During the summer holiday it is possible to send cycles in advance by special cycle wagons; full details should be obtained from the NS Information Office.

Travelling by road

The road network in Holland is very good, and includes an extensive motorway system. Visitors bringing their own cars should note that the vehicle must comply with the legal requirements of its owner's country of origin, must have the headlights adjusted to prevent dazzling oncoming vehicles when on 'high beam', and must carry a nationality plate (GB,

USA, etc). A red warning triangle must be carried for use in case of breakdown. The same requirements apply to motor cycles. Trailers and caravans require no special documents, provided they are for private use.

Bicycles require no documentation, but should comply with any legal requirements of the country of origin. They should, in any case, be fitted with good lights front and rear, a large rear reflector, and reflecting pedals are advisable. Mopeds require no special documentation, but it should be noted that a moped or *bromfiets* in the Netherlands is technically a bicycle with power assistance, so it has to have a bell instead of a horn. Although this is not a legal requirement in the case of a machine brought into the country by a visitor, it is advisable to fit a bell. Wearing of a protective helmet is compulsory. The use of reflecting bandoliers for cyclists or moped riders, is to be recommended.

Road traffic regulations follow the normal ones applicable on the Continent. Vehicles keep to the right, and generally give way to vehicles approaching from the right at junctions, including bicyles. The exception to this rule is when a road is a 'priority' road, indicated by white diamond-shaped signs with orange centres. Vehicles actually on roundabouts must give way to vehicles entering the roundabout. Motorists must be on the lookout for cyclists who have priority when coming out of a side turning from the right, unless the car is on a priority road as indicated above. Pedestrians have right of way on pedestrian crossings.

Road signs in general follow the international system but there are a few signs which are used in Holland which may not be familiar elsewhere. The priority sign described above is one example, with its cancellation sign, the white-bordered orange diamond with diagonal black lines. Trunk roads, from which non-motorised vehicles are excluded, are shown by a square blue sign with the front view of a car in white. With the country generally flat, be prepared for railway level crossings, many of which will have no barriers, simply a warning bell with flashing lights. Also there are many roads which cross waterways by bridges which open for boat traffic. Warning bells and lights operate, but open bridges can often cause delays to motorists. Be prepared for this when driving to catch a ferry or train, and allow extra time. On main roads and motorways special signs on blue rectangular boards give warning of petrol stations, restaurants, cafés, parking and picnic areas, usually with an indication of the distance to go. The signs use easily recognisable pictures or symbols. In towns, increasing use is being made of a blue sign with a symbol representing a house in white. This indicates a *woonerf* or residential area, which may have restricted carriageways for cars and a strict speed limit. Watch for pedestrians and for children playing. Optional cycle paths are indicated by a small rectangular black sign with the word *Fietspad* or *Rijwielpad* in white letters. Mopeds are not allowed to use these paths. Sometimes, especially through towns or villages, a solid or interrupted white line along the side of the road, with a white bicycle painted on the ground, indicates a lane exclusively for use by bicycles and mopeds. This is obligatory. A circular blue sign with a white bicycle also indicates a mandatory cycle path, for both bicycles and mopeds. A circular blue sign with a white illustration of a man and child, or a black sign with the word *Voetpad* in white indicates a footpath, banned to cycles. Orange signs with black lettering indicate diversions. On motorways, temporary routes are allocated a number to follow, which is shown on the normal road signs above the destinations.

At junctions with traffic lights, where cycle and/or footpaths also cross, separate sets of traffic lights may be provided for cyclists and pedestrians, often operated by push buttons. Car drivers should be prepared for this. One other situation to watch for is the cycle crossing, where a cycle path along one side of a road crosses to the other side. A blue rectangular sign with a white arrow and the words *Fietsers Oversteken* (Cyclists Crossing) is accompanied by a double row of white dashes on the road surface. Cyclists and moped riders have priority over cars when on such crossings. Most other traffic signs are self-evident, as they are symbols. However, a few written signs may be encountered, such as the following:

Alle Richtingen: All directions
Doorgaand Verkeer: Through traffic
Fileforming: Queue ahead
Geen: No
Gestremd: Forbidden, Obstructed
Gevaar: Danger
Inhaalverbod: No overtaking
Langzaam Rijden: Drive slowly
Pas Op! (*Let Op*!):   Take care, Attention!
Tegenliggers: Two-way traffic
Tussen: Between (usually with parking times)
Weg Omlegging: Diversion
Werk in Uitvoering: Road Works
Zacht Berm: Soft verge
Dus NIET Brommen!   NO mopeds!
Behalve - - }
Uitgezonderd - -{   Except - -
Slecht wegdek: Rough or broken surface
Korte invoegstrook: Short entry lane (This sign appears on motorway slip-roads where the entry lane is shorter than normal. Take care!)

Speed limits in built-up areas are 50kph (30mph), and elsewhere 80kph (50mph). On motorways the limit is 100kph (62mph). These limits apply to cars and motor-cycles without trailers. Otherwise, speed limits are shown by circular white signs with a red border and the speed in kph shown in black figures. Where, on for example, a motorway or main road, there is a reduction in the permitted speed, this will be indicated in advance by a series of speed limit signs dropping in steps to the final speed.

At the approach to every town and village there is a board giving its name, followed by the name of the municipality to which the village belongs. The actual direction signposting all over the country is carried out by the ubiquitous ANWB, and follows a standard system, with the occasional exception of some country areas.

Normally, direction signs are lettered in white on blue signs, and apply to all traffic. Local signs and signs within town areas are black on white boards. Red lettering (or more recently, also green) on white boards refers to cycle routes. A bicycle symbol also appears on these signs. Note that if a symbol for a moped (a small motor-cycle without a rider) is shown with a line through it, the route is only for bicycles, and mopeds are not allowed.

Most of the above direction signs are mounted on posts painted with blue and white stripes, and each signpost carries a serial number. This is small and not always easily visible from the road, but the number is also shown, in the appropriate place, on all the ANWB Tourist and Road maps. This is a very good way to help the stranger to an area. Finally, there are the *paddestoelen* or toadstools. These are knee-high blocks, square with sloping sides on which are shown arrows pointing to various destinations, with distances. The toadstools can be found all over the country along cycling and walking routes. Here again, each toadstool carries on top a serial number, which appears on the tourist maps. Where appropriate in this book, signpost or *paddestoel* numbers have been quoted in the route descriptions. With so much road building and repairing in progress, no maps can be completely up-to-date, so occasionally a sign may not be on the map, or the number may not agree with that shown but this adds spice to one's exploring!

Signs bearing the legend "P+R" at the approaches to some towns indicate a 'Park and Ride' scheme where cycles or cars may be parked and the journey into town completed by public transport.

The ANWB has devised and signed a number of tourist routes all over the country, and sells booklets describing these, with notes on places of interest, and map extracts. The routes are signed using a hexagonal sign with the route name and direction arrow. Some routes are suitable for all types of traffic, whilst others are specifically for cyclists (*Touristische fietsroutes*). In the latter case, the bicycle symbol appears on the sign.

With so many waterways, it is to be expected that roads often make use of bridges, tunnels or ferries. Many bridges open for water traffic, but where major roads cross large busy waterways, modern bridges have been built. In the Rotterdam area, the Beneluxtunnel, Botlektunnel and Drechttunnel are banned to cyclists. It is possible for cyclists and moped riders to use the Maastunnel by means of an escalator, but it is not easy with a loaded machine.

Although Holland is not normally considered to be a country for walkers or backpackers, there are a surprising number of footpaths in the country, some of the best being through woodlands under the control of the State Forestry Service or big private estates. Many of the latter have entered a scheme whereby in return for certain tax concessions, large estates have agreed to allow *Vrije wandelingen* or free rambling, during daylight hours, along footpaths and tracks in otherwise private land. A

The 5-mile long Zeelandbrug across the Oosterschelde, between Colijnsplaat and Zierikzee

good selection of walking guides and maps are available from the ANWB or local VVV offices. Holland also has a number of Long Distance Footpaths (*Lange-Afstand-Wandelpad* or LAW) which form a network joining into the European network of long distance footpaths. Guides to these paths are available from specialist map and guide bookshops.

Hiring Transport

The alternative to taking one's own car or other means of transport is, of course, to hire. Most of the internationally-known car hire firms are well-established in Holland. As regards bicycles, the possibilities for hiring are endless. In fact, it is possible to hire a bicycle at some eighty railway stations, apart from many other sources. A list of the stations is available in a booklet *Fiets en Spoor* published by the railways (NS). At each of the stations concerned, there is a covered cycle park (*Rijwielstalling*) where not only can cycles be parked under cover, but machines can be hired. It is possible to telephone, reserving a cycle, until 11am. A deposit has to be paid in addition to the daily hire charge, the deposit being returned on return of the bike. The only problem here is that the bicycle must be returned to the same place as it was hired. If a visitor does hire a bicycle, it is as well to be prepared for the fact that Dutch cycles usually have 'back-pedal' brakes; they can be tricky if one is not used to them. The possibilities of hiring a moped are not so easy, but it is worth making enquiries.

Hotels
Lists of hotels may be obtained from the NBT offices. A voluntary star-rating system is in operation, ranging from Luxury (5-star) through First-Class, Very Comfortable, Comfortable to Plain but Comfortable (1-star), with a final class, Hotelette, with no star rating, but well-maintained very simple rooms. Hotel bookings can be made in advance through the Netherlands Reservation Centre (NRC) in Holland. Reservations can be made by post, telephone or telex, and there is no charge to the customer. Within the country itself, the local VVV offices keep lists of hotels in their area, and VVV offices which display an *i-Nederland* sign provide VVV Accommodation Service, by which a booking may be made for any other area, at a small fee. This is not available by telephone. Motels also come within this category.

Boarding Houses and Bed and Breakfast
The local VVV offices can supply information on local establishments. During holiday times advance booking is usually essential.

Holiday Chalets and Bungalows
A list of holiday bungalows is available from the NBT, although they cannot make bookings. However, their information brochure contains a booking form which should be sent to the address given for the bungalow site of your choice.

Youth Hostels
There are about fifty Youth Hostels belonging to the Netherlands Youth Hostel Association (NJHC). They are graded as simple, standard or superior, and are available to members of Youth Hostel Associations in other countries. The NBT can supply an up-to-date list.

Camping
Sites for tents or touring caravans are plentiful and range from basic quiet sites with just water and toilets to luxury sites with every facility. A list of about 450 sites is available from the NBT, all of which have been graded according to the type and standard of the facilities provided. The most comprehensive list of camp sites in the country is the book *Kampeerplaatsen Nederland*, published each year by the ANWB. After a number of pages devoted to various aspects of camping in the Netherlands, all in Dutch, there follows a page of explanation of the symbols used, in English. Details of over 800 sites are arranged by Province, with an alphabetical list of place names and a list of site names in the form of an index.

The sites listed are mainly commercial sites, with a few Forestry Service sites.

Normally, commercial camp sites become very busy during the holiday season. Those who prefer quiet, simple sites in the country will find such sites under the title of *Kampeerbewijsterreinen*. which simply means Camping Permit sites. About 100 sites are all situated in the country, many of them being on estates or on Forestry Service (SBB) land, and are only available to holders of the 'Camping Permit'. A visitor who holds an International Camping Carnet may obtain such a permit from any office of the ANWB for a small fee. The purchaser also receives a guide to the sites, which is in Dutch but the details are easy to follow. Not all the sites take caravans, and in some cases cars are not allowed to be parked beside the tent. This rule is also applied in some commercial sites.

'Wild' camping is against the law, and it is not easy to find pitches on farms. However, a relatively new idea is now becoming common in holiday areas where small sites are available with minimum facilities. Watch for signs 'Mini-camping', but take a look first before booking, and make sure of the fees to be paid.

A scheme is in existence in which a number of castles and large estates have combined to form an association *Landgoed en Kasteel Campings*, comprising sites ranging from simple to quite well-equipped, but all in pleasant country, near historic castles or country mansions and estates. Some, but not all, of the sites require the camper to hold a Camping Permit.

Another scheme designed to help cycle campers is that of the *Gastvrije Fietscampings* (GFC), run by a number of commercial sites around the country who operate a scheme by which the camper can avoid the problem of finding a site full and no other site nearby. The scheme is useful for touring cycle campers, but is rather expensive. Local VVV offices will have information about camp sites in their area.

Camping Huts

An alternative to camping is to use the *Trekkershutten*, wooden cabins fitted with bunk beds for four people, cooking stove, table and benches, lighting, and mattresses on the bunks. They are located on or nearby existing camp sites, the facilities (toilets, water, etc) of which are available to the occupants of the huts. An ideal way of travelling light. Huts must be booked in advance, and can be used for a maximum of three nights before moving on. It is reasonably cheap; no reductions are made for children, and the whole hut must be booked. The idea is spreading rapidly throughout Holland. Details and booking can be done through local VVV offices, or through the provincial VVV.

Package and Pre-planned Tours

Many such tours are available, ranging from expensive coach tours with hotel accommodation all included, to much simpler but interesting deals where pre-booked accommodation in hostels or bed and breakfast establishments is linked with cycle routes. One variation is where the cyclist rides to the pre-booked destination, and the main luggage is carried by van. Details of many such tours can be obtained from the NBT, but bookings are normally made through travel agents or directly with the tour operators. For those interested in more active holidays, there are a number of possibilities for sailing on old-type sailing vessels on the many open waters in the country.

A scheme which has become increasingly popular in recent years is the arrangement whereby a cycling tour is booked using Youth Hostels, and the total cost includes a new bicycle, with equipment. This is waiting on arrival, and after the trip the cycle may be kept and brought home. A reduction is made for those using their own machines or who do not wish to keep the bicycle.

FOOD AND SHOPPING

Generally speaking, the cost of food in Holland works out about the same as in the UK. Dairy produce and vegetables are normally cheaper, and meat tends to be dearer. Bread is available in an enormous variety, some regions having their own speciality. Spiced bread or cake, known generally as *ontbijtkoek* (breakfast cake) is available in virtually every supermarket.

Shopping from market stalls can be tricky unless you can get a Dutch friend to accompany you. There are, however, a number of supermarket chains in the country, the most well-known probably being Albert Heijn, whose quality is extremely high. Larger branches of HEMA and Vroom & Dreesmann (V&D) often have a food department. Many small towns and villages have shops belonging to the VG or Spar organisation, which provide a fairly standard range of products at reasonable prices. Many of these operate as small supermarkets, often with a surprisingly large range of foods. Butchers and bakers will be found in most villages, and all over the country the *warme-bakker* provides freshly-baked bread in various forms. Unwrapped loaves can be sliced on request.

The Queueing System
No-one seems to bother about queueing for buses or trams, possibly because tickets can be bought in advance and there is usually more than one entrance. However, in banks and many shops, including the meat, bread and delicatessen counters in supermarkets, it is usual to find a ticket machine, from which a numbered ticket is taken on arrival. An indicator above the counter shows the number of the next customer to be served, or the number may be called out, so be prepared for this.

Opening Times and Early Closing
Shops must display on the door the opening times for each day of the week, together with the early closing day and late night opening if any.

Many shops are closed on Monday morning, but normal opening times are from 8.30 or 9am to 5.30 or 6pm, often closing for lunch. Late night shopping varies but is usually on either Thursday or Friday evening, after a short break. Banks open from Monday to Friday, 9am to 4pm, sometimes 5pm. Some banks also open during late-night shopping times. Post Offices open from 8.30am to 5pm, some also on Saturday mornings from 8.30am to 12 noon. The early closing day can vary from place to place, which requires noting if one is travelling.

Eating Out
The standard of food and service in Dutch cafés and restaurants is usually high. Prices vary widely, but it is usually possible to get a good meal at a reasonable price. Owing to its history of trading overseas, Holland has a

large number of establishments specialising in Indonesian, Chinese, and other countries' food.

Over 500 restaurants participate in the 'Tourist Menu' scheme whereby, for a set price of about £5, a three-course menu created by its own chef is provided. Restaurants in the scheme display a blue 'Tourist Menu' sign.

Many of the department stores such as Vroom & Dreesmann and HEMA have cafeterias which provide good value hot and cold dishes. Good coffee is normal. Tea will be served in a glass, without milk. However, it is weaker than is common in England, and can be very refreshing. Many railway restaurants are excellent, and the sign *Pannekoekhuis* indicates a restaurant which specialises in pancakes, large, either savoury or sweet, and a meal in themselves.

A number of restaurant chains or groups exist, the members of which follow common standards. Examples are *Neerlands Dis*, with a sign of a red, white and blue soup tureen, a group of about 500 restaurants serving traditional Dutch cuisine based on home-produced ingredients. *Relais du Centre* is a group of twenty-five restaurants in the good to medium range, each one retaining its own character. *Romantische Restaurants* is a group in the good to medium range with excellent cuisine, reasonable prices and real hospitality. Many of the motorways have excellent restaurants and cafeterias, among which may be mentioned those of the 'Albert's Corner' (AC) group, offering rapid self-service at reasonable prices, and the Smits restaurants. In some towns may be found *Noord Zee Quick* cafeterias which specialise in sea food dishes, whilst in major towns one can find the usual burger-bars such as the Macdonalds chain. If all else fails, and everywhere else is closed, the *automatieks* dispense hot and cold snacks, but guilder coins are usually needed. Small cafés remain open all day and to quite late hours at night almost everywhere, and coffee and filled rolls (*broodjes*) are usually available, also *frites*, or chips with mayonnaise.

Tipping

Normally, the bill when presented is inclusive of service charge and VAT (BTW in Holland). Extra attention or service may warrant an extra tip, but this is by no means essential or expected. Taxi meter fares include service charge. However, in washrooms and toilets it is usual to give the attendant 25 or 50 cents. Sometimes there is a plate on a table inside for the contribution.

3 SOUTH WEST HOLLAND - THE OLD AND THE NEW

SOUTH WEST HOLLAND — THE OLD AND THE NEW

Originally this part of Holland, the 'Delta' area, consisted of a group of islands separated by a complex network of waterways forming the estuaries of the rivers Rhine, Maas and Schelde. Defence of expanding maritime and fishing interests, together with the need to protect the land from storms and flood, were the key factors in the development of this region in the past. Now, during the past thirty years, the separate islands have been linked by modern dams, dykes and bridges, leading to the growth of extensive recreation areas and nature reserves. The motorway system serving the rest of the country has been extended here so that easy access is possible.

However, much of the original character of the area has been preserved, and those wishing to see the islands can take minor roads at a more leisurely pace. The four routes will enable you to see much of Zeeland which is often passed by.

ROUTE 1   WALCHEREN AND NORTH AND SOUTH BEVELAND

We start our tour at **Vlissingen** (Flushing), where many visitors from Britain will arrive on the ferry. The town itself is often by-passed, but it is worth taking time to walk along the Boulevard (2km long). Near the fish harbour entrance there is a statue of Admiral de Ruyter, who sailed up the River Medway in Kent (1667) and captured several British ships including the *Royal Charles* on which Charles II had returned to England in 1660. The carved stern of this vessel is preserved in the Rijksmuseum in Amsterdam. At the other end of the Boulevard is the Gevangentoren or prison tower (1490), now a restaurant. Old frontages can be seen along Nieuwendijk (near fish harbour) and in Hendrikstraat, whilst the tall 'Oranjemolen' windmill and a monument to Commandos and civilians who died during World War II are located on the Oranjedijk.

From Vlissingen, take the direct route north to **Middelburg** (6km). Cyclists may prefer to avoid the cycle path alongside the main road by taking a very attractive path which runs beside the Walcheren Canal and brings them right into the centre of the town. (Follow 'Centrum' cycle signs). The capital of the province of Zeeland, Middelburg is one of the finest towns in Holland. Badly damaged during World War II, it has been beautifully restored using old building methods and often the original plans and materials. Parking in the centre is possible but not easy, and parking fees are payable. It is better to park on the edge of the town and walk in; there are two large free parking areas on the ramparts near the Kloveniersdoelen. When approaching the town from Vlissingen, turn right, then left after crossing the first 'moat'. Parking is near the large tower

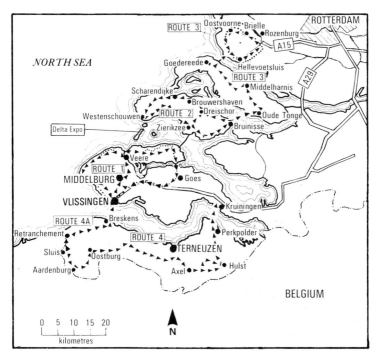

mill on the left, or a little further along, also on the left.

It is worth spending a whole day here, beginning with a town walk (2½-3 hours).

ROUTE 1A   MIDDELBURG TOWN WALK

Start from Kloveniersdoelen, a lovely Flemish renaissance-style building which once belonged to the East India Company. Cross the water to Lange Viele, continue into Pottenmarkt and the main Markt where you will find the VVV office. Note the beautiful Town Hall on the left, parts of which date from the fifteenth century. The building was extensively damaged in 1940, and the whole has been rebuilt and restored. It is open to the public, who are shown around by a guide, but days and times of opening vary, and should be checked with the VVV. The tall tower of the Abbey Church, known as 'Lange Jan', was first built in the fourteenth century, since when it has been burned down and rebuilt in different styles, most recently in 1940. Nevertheless it is a fine building, 280ft high with 207 steps! On summer weekdays it is possible to climb the tower. The whole Abbey complex surrounds a quiet courtyard. The Nieuwe Kerk and Koorkerk date from the sixteenth and fourteenth centuries respectively. Both have been rebuilt after their destruction in 1940, although this is hard to believe.

The Town Hall, Middelburg

The Abbey is now the seat of the Zeeland Provincial Government, and houses the Zeeland Museum containing a fine collection of local costumes and jewellery. Through the arched gateway between the museum and the Provincial building there is a fountain, behind which is the St Jorisdoelen, former home of the St George Company of Archers dating from 1582. Turn down St Pieterstraat to Damplein, where you will see the Corn Exchange, a lovely little colonnaded building typical of many such in old Dutch towns. At the end, pass to the right of the monument to Queen Emma, and a short distance along the Dam is a small alleyway leading to the Kuiperspoort (1586), once the headquarters of the Coopers' Guild. Return to Damplein and cross past the monument, along Molstraat, Koepoortstraat and Molenwater to the Koepoort, the only remaining town gate, dating from 1735. Opposite, entered from Molenwater, is 'Miniature Walcheren', with models of old buildings and landscapes from all over the island.

A pleasant way of rounding off the tour of Middelburg is to walk from Koepoort back to your car along the ramparts, through the gardens.

Thursday in Middelburg is market day, when traditional costumes can always be seen; you are quite likely to see them at other times, too. During the summer months a *son et lumière* spectacle is staged at the Abbey.

A pleasant diversion from Middelburg is to take a boat from the Loskade (near the station) to **Veere** at the northern end of the Walcheren

Canal. Those wishing to go by cycle should leave the town via Damplein, Dam, Rotterdamse Kaai and Nederstraat to reach the Veere road (cycle path alongside). Veere is about 7km away, and is easy to reach. It is a very small town, and busy, so parking spaces are sometimes difficult to find. Veere was once one of Holland's busiest seaports, and has some lovely old buildings. From the fifteenth to eighteenth centuries it handled the bulk of the Scottish wool trade with Europe — a privilege granted in 1444 when a Lord of Veere married a daughter of King James of Scotland. The wool merchants had their headquarters here, and their homes are still known as the 'Scots Houses', now providing a home for a museum. The great Onze Lieve Vrouwekerk dating from 1348 dominates the town, its huge tower once housing Napoleon's cavalry, including their horses. Other buildings not to be missed include the fifteenth-century Campveerse Toren, once the fortress gate to the harbour and now a hotel/restaurant, and the Town Hall (1470). The original fortifications of Veere are preserved, and a walk around the ramparts is very pleasant. The view over the Veerse Meer created by the dams of the Delta Plan is impressive, this being one of the largest lakes in Holland. Formerly a busy fishing port, and commercial centre, Veere is now a very popular sailing centre with its own municipal marina.

PLACES TO VISIT IN AND AROUND MIDDELBURG

Town Hall
Beautifully restored fifteenth-century Gothic Town Hall with later additions.

Lange Jan (Abbey Tower)
280ft high. Can be climbed for an excellent view over Walcheren.

Abbey Churches
'Sound and Light' performances take place in the summer. Cloisters open to the public.

Zeeland Museum
Historical museum for Zeeland. Exceptionally fine costumes, jewellery and furniture.

Kuiperspoort
Beautiful old alleyway with small brick houses dating back to the sixteenth century.

Miniature Walcheren
'Model Village' depicting most of the historical buildings on the island.

Veere
Scots Houses
Local museum with costumes, jewellery and folk art, fishing and other exhibits.

Campveerse Toren
Original fifteenth-century fortress gate to the harbour now a hotel/restaurant.

Goes
Tourist steam train to Oudelande. 16km, 2 hour return trip.

From Veere marina, travel north-west along the dyke road towards the Veersegatdam, where there is a choice of route. Either take the coast road through Vrouwenpolder to Domburg, thence via Westkapelle, Zoutelande and Biggekerke back to Vlissingen, or continue across the Veersegatdam to the former island of Noord Beveland. In either case it is possible to park at the beginning of the dam, near the monument marking its completion, and from this vantage point good views of the area can be obtained. To the west is a large area of dunes, parts of which are accessible to the public.

Crossing the dam, follow the Zierikzee road for about 12km, then take the turning to **Colijnsplaat**, an attractive fishing village where fresh fish can be purchased on the quayside each day. From the nearby dyke there is a magnificent view of the Zeelandbrug, which at 5km in length is the longest bridge in the Netherlands, and to the north across the Oosterschelde towards Zierikzee.

Leaving Colijnsplaat, follow the road south across the Zandkreekdam to **Goes** with its fine eighteenth-century Town Hall with Gothic tower, and the Maria Magdelena church (1427) which does not have a true tower, but a lantern-style roof containing an eighteenth-century carillon. Goes is the northern terminus of a tourist steam railway line running to Oudelande in the south of the island.

From Goes, the best way to return to Vlissingen is by the motorway (A58), but of course cyclists will have to follow the old route which, after Eindewege, runs more or less parallel to the motor road as far as Nieuw en Sint Joosland, thence via Middelburg to Vlissingen.

ROUTE 2   SCHOUWEN-DUIVELAND
The route starts at Zierikzee, and can be linked to Route 1 by crossing the Zeelandbrug instead of making the return to Vlissingen via Goes. The Zeelandbrug is a toll bridge, although cyclists are no longer charged. A separate cycle path runs alongside the roadway across the bridge.

Zierikzee is a very historic old town and port with many fine buildings and three beautifully-preserved town gates. Time spent exploring the town is well spent. The best approach from the Zeelandbrug is to follow the ring-road N256 until its junction with the N59. Turn left towards a large roundabout after which the pointed towers of the Nobelpoort appear on the left. Shortly after this, again on the left, is a sign for car parking. Follow round the town moat and parking is on the right.

ROUTE 2A   ZIERIKZEE TOWN WALK
Once on foot, cross the bridge into Weststraat and walk towards the very large square tower ahead. This is St Lievens or Monstertoren, begun in 1454 but never completed. Originally planned to be 207m tall, it only reached 58m. Keep to the right of the tower along Kerkhof, and on the right, is the Weeshuis (orphanage) with a rather attractive frontage, dating from around 1740. Continue along Poststraat and turn left — you will see the ornate tower of the Town Hall — and turn right on reaching

Meelstraat. The Town Hall, which houses a museum, is No 8, on the left. The left-hand side was built as the Vleeshal or meat market hall in the fifteenth century. Later, it was enlarged in Flemish style and the tower added, on which is a gilded statue of Neptune, reflecting the sea connections of the town. Continue to the Dam, along Appelmarkt and into Havenplein. Ahead will be seen the Noord and Zuid Havenpoorts, but to the left, in the street called Mol, is the old Gravensteen prison, with an attractive *trapgevel* or stepped gable. It is now the maritime museum. Behind is a medieval garden which is open during museum opening hours. A possible diversion, at this point, is to go down Lange Nobelstraat past the tall corn mill to Korte Nobelstraat, and see the Nobelpoort before returning to the town centre. On Havenplein is a little colonnaded building which is of interest. Built in 1651 as a market hall, it has above an additional church room for the Elisabethgasthuis church, which had become too small.

Continue along Havenpark and the old harbour towards the Havenpoorts These give the town its characteristic appearance of a seaport town from the Middle Ages. The gates date from the fifteenth century but have been restored more than once. In the open cupola of the Zuidhavenpoort hangs the old Town Hall carillon dating from 1550, the oldest in Holland. The town has close links with Britain, as shown by the nearby street, 'Engelsche Kade' or English Quay. Walking along Nieuwe Haven brings one to

The colonnade of St Elizabethgasthuiskerk, Zierikzee

PLACES TO VISIT IN AND AROUND ZIERIKZEE

Town Hall
Houses Municipal Museum as well as local offices. Costumes, silver, old plans.

Maritime Museum
In sixteenth-century Gravensteen prison. Good collection of model ships. Fishing and maritime history, also beautiful garden.

Weeshuis
Collection of paintings and ceramics, and fine gilt-leather hangings.

St Lievens Monstertoren
58m high. Can be climbed in summer.

Gasthuiskerk
Beautiful chapel of the old St Elisabethgasthuis.

Town Gates
Nobelpoort (fourteenth century), Zuid Havenpoort (fifteenth century) and Noord Havenpoort (sixteenth century).

Dreischor
Fourteenth-century church in centre of village.

Westenschouwen
Dune reserve. Footpaths and cycle paths throughout area. Pleasant picnic spots.

Oosterschelde Storm-Flood Barrier
(Delta-Expo)
Works and visitor centre, access from near Westenschouwen. Permanent exhibition concerning sea defences in this area. Films (in English) and working models. Café.

Bolwerk and the windmill 'De Haas', from which a good view over the locality can be obtained. A number of boat trips, including sailing trips, can be made from the town. Return to the car along the ramparts.

From Zierikzee, an excellent ANWB signposted route ('Schouwen-Duiveland Route') gives a good view of the island, and the hexagonal blue and white signs are easy to follow. A map and route description can be bought which, although in Dutch, lists useful restaurants along the route, as well as several picnic places.

The total length of the route is 92km (57$\frac{1}{2}$ miles) but places where this might be cut short without losing too much of interest have been suggested. From the car park in Zierikzee, the signed route follows the coast road by Ouwerkerk to **Bruinisse**, a small fishing village noted for mussel culture, situated at the southern end of the Grevelingendam linking Duiveland with Overflakkee. From the centre of this dam, where there is a good restaurant, another dam/bridge is being built to connect with St Philipsland and Tholen, at present only accessible from the islands by the ferry at Zijpe. From Bruinisse the route continues west to **Dreischor**, a picturesque 'ring village' with its church on a mound or *terp* in the centre.

The church has an interesting staircase turret built on to the main tower.

If you wish, the eastern part of the signed ANWB route can be cut, saving about 30km from the total. To do this, turn left on leaving the car park in Zierikzee and follow the road north via Schuddebeurs to Dreischor. The route then continues to **Brouwershaven**, a most attractive little town with a rich history, having had town status since 1285. The busy harbour lies right in the centre of the town, and the Market Square possesses a number of interesting old frontages, including the Town Hall with Flemish Renaissance gable (1599). The church dating from 1293 is very large for the size of the town, and can be seen from afar. Brouwershaven is the birthplace of the sixteenth-century poet Jacob Cats, whose statue is in the Market Square.

Continue west along the coast road towards the Brouwersdam linking Schouwen to Goeree. Just before reaching the dam, pause near Scharendijke and see how well the Dutch have used the essential sea defence works to create an enormous recreation area in the shape of the Grevelingenmeer, extremely popular with yachtsmen and sailboarders, many of whom travel considerable distances to make use of this unique facility. Beyond the dam the road continues through **Renesse**, a popular holiday resort, on the outskirts of which is the picturesque castle of Moermond with its elegant towers. Turning south, Haamstede and **Westenschouwen** are reached, the whole area being near to a popular dune and forestry reserve with footpaths, view-points and picnic places.

A short distance from Westenschouwen is a large car park at the approach to the new Oosterschelde Storm-Flood barrier, opened by Queen Beatrix in October 1986. If the road is open it will be possible to drive to the Visitor Centre; if not, leave the car in the car park and travel over the work bridge by the special bus service. At least two hours should be allowed for the visit.

Fine views of the estuary and the Flood Barrier are obtained from the route, which continues eastwards passing the old Plompe Toren lighthouse and the Schelphoek nature reserve. To save time, the return to Zierikzee can be made via the main road from Serooskerke, rather than following the signed route. This will save about 6km.

ROUTE 3   GOEREE-OVERFLAKKEE and VOORNE

Starting from the Grevelingendam, cross to Oude Tonge, then turn left to **Middelharnis**, which is the main town of the former island of Overflakkee, and has an attractive Town Hall dated 1639. The whole area is predominantly agricultural, and is noted for its gladioli bulbs. The route now runs via Sommelsdijk and Dirksland to Stellendam, near the beginning of the Haringvlietdam. A diversion may be made to **Goedereede**, whose huge church tower can be seen ahead. Originally built to serve as a beacon and lighthouse, it now houses a small museum, and the view from the top is worth the climb. Seaside lovers will find plenty of beaches on Goeree, also holiday houses and camp sites, the main holiday centre being Ouddorp. A number of cycle paths through the dunes and adjoining lanes make for pleasant riding. Back and across the Haringvlietdam, we pass the former site of the Delta Expo exhibition which is now on the Oosterschelde Storm Barrier. Beyond the dam is a turning to the old fortress town of **Hellevoetsluis**. The road cuts through the old ramparts, and a fire service museum is located in the same building as the VVV. It was from this old port that William III sailed for England in 1688. Every year a steam festival is held, in August, and a steam tram service is operated in conjunction with the Tram Museum. From Hellevoetsluis, take the main road beside the Voorne canal to Heenvliet, then left along Groene Kruisweg to **Brielle**. Cyclists from Hellevoetsluis may prefer to cross the canal and ride along the eastern side, which is more pleasant, thence through Zwartewaal to Brielle.

Brielle is first mentioned as early as 1257, and was created a town in 1330. It has many links with England. The ramparts of the fortified town can still be seen, and large cannons in the town centre remind us of its strategic importance in the Middle Ages and later. It was the first town to be regained from the Spanish invaders in 1572 by the so-called 'sea-beggars', after which it was placed in the care of the English until 1616. Near the Town Hall (1793) is the Tromp Museum, housed in the former town prison and weigh house. Nearby, in a small square, is a large pump dating from 1610. The Great or St Catharijnekerk is a showpiece of the town, dating from the fifteenth century. It is said that in 1688, Mary, the wife of William III, stood on the top of the tower and watched her husband sail for England from Hellevoetsluis. Certainly there is a fine view of the town and its ramparts, and the surrounding countryside. There are many fine and interesting gables on houses, notably in Voorstraat and Maarland.

At nearby Oostvoorne can be seen the excavated remains of a twelfth-century castle, and beaches and surfing are added attractions. Among the dunes are nature reserves and walking and cycle paths, also picnic areas with car parking places.

Return to Hellevoetsluis via the little village of **Rockanje**, or if you prefer, link up with Rotterdam or Den Haag by crossing the Nieuwe Waterweg by the ferry between **Rozenburg** and **Maassluis**. Cross the Brielsemeer to the east of Brielle, via the Brielsebrug, then continue over the Calandbrug, following the main road towards Rotterdam. At the T junction, four kilometres after crossing the Brielsebrug, turn left along Botlegweg. This turns sharp left at the end, by the sea dyke, along the Rozenburgse Boulevard. In $2\frac{1}{2}$ kilometres, the ferry car park/waiting area is reached. The route is signed with some of the ANWB blue and white hexagonal signs for the 'Rotterdamse Haven Route' from the Botlegweg.

A small ferry taking foot passengers and cycles only runs from the north-east side of Brielle across the Brielse Meer to a long strip of land which is an oasis amid industry, for just the other side of this landscaped area is the Hartelkanaal and the huge oil storage tanks of Europoort. It is possible to cycle along the whole length of this recreation area, as far as the Botlekbrug, a total of about 10km, whence signs may be followed to

Rotterdam. Motorists can reach the recreation island either from the Europoort road and the Suurhofbrug to the west, or over the Brielsebrug on the way towards Rozenburg. The island has plenty of parking places, picnic areas and places where one can walk and watch the shipping.

ROUTE 4 'FORGOTTEN ZEELAND'

Motorists crossing from Dover to Zeebrugge tend to drive straight on to the motorway and get away from the ferryport as quickly as possible. However, if the road through Knokke-Heist is followed on to the N58 road towards Sluis, you will arrive at the Belgian/Dutch frontier at St Anna ter Muiden. This brings you into a part of Holland which is often completely neglected by visitors, yet it offers a number of interesting places to see.

Just inside the frontier is **Sluis**, which has a long and eventful history, having received its charter in the thirteenth century. It was once the port for Bruges in Belgium before the estuary of the Zwin silted up. This, together with a succession of wars, led to the town's decline, until the emergence of the Belgian resorts on the nearby coast gave the impetus for Sluis to become a tourist centre. 80 per cent of the town was destroyed during World War II, but it has been rebuilt, with much of the characteristic atmosphere being retained. The fourteenth-century Town Hall has a unique Belfry Tower, and the Council Chamber is one of the finest in Holland. Grass-covered ramparts almost completely surround the town, and a pleasant walk can be taken along them, passing the fine corn mill which is in working condition and may be visited. Because of its position on the border, shops are allowed to open in the evenings and on Sundays, and many visitors take advantage of this.

From Sluis, the ANWB 'Westerschelde Route' signs may be followed to **Aardenburg**, known to be the site of a Roman station, preceded by a Stone

**PLACES TO VISIT IN
'FORGOTTEN ZEELAND'**

Sluis
Town Hall — Council Chamber,
paintings and tapestries. Town
ramparts.

Aardenburg
Archaeological museum. Stone Age
and Roman artefacts. French and
English medieval ceramics, tiles, etc.

IJzendijke
District Museum — farm house with
old agricultural vehicles and
implements, costumes, etc.

Axel
Farmhouse museum.

Hulst
Monument to Reynard the Fox.
Town gates and ramparts. Town
Hall — paintings and old maps.

Retranchement
Open trestle-mill. Town ramparts.

Age settlement. It is considered to be one of the oldest towns in Holland. The church dates back to the thirteenth century, being a good example of 'Schelde Gothic', while parts of the ramparts, notably the Kaaipoort (1650), can still be seen.

Passing Oostburg to the north, the route comes to **IJzendijke**, a fortified town once an important centre for the wool trade. The Market Square was used as the exercise ground for the military garrison in former times, and the first Protestant church in Zeeland was built here in 1612.

About 10km further along is **Biervliet**, where a monument in the square testifies to the fact that one Willem Beukelszoon introduced a method of curing herrings! The Town Hall weathervane has a herring as pointer. Leave the signposted route and continue along the main road N61, crossing the Gent to Terneuzen canal, then turn right via Spui to **Axel**. This is a mainly agricultural area, and local costumes can be seen at the Saturday market. The Axel farmhouse museum contains two fully furnished rooms from 1830 and 1880.

Leaving Axel, the signed route passes along tree-lined dykes via the hamlet of Luntershoek; a more direct main road also brings us to the lovely medieval fortified city of **Hulst**, completely surrounded by moats and ramparts. The fine church, founded in 1200, was used during the last century by both Catholics and Protestants, each using a different part of the building. After 1929 it reverted to the Catholics and was converted to a basilica in 1935. After war damage in 1944, the tower was rebuilt in modern style. Many other fine buildings exist, including fifteenth and sixteenth-century Abbey refuges, the Town Hall (1528-1547), and of course the ramparts and defence works which repay a walk for the extensive views over the town. One of the loveliest corn windmills in Holland is here, built in 1792, while near the Gentse Poort stands the strange monument to 'Reynard the Fox'. Hulst and the surrounding countryside is the setting for this ancient fable.

Leaving the town, follow the direct route along the N60 north to Perkpolder, whence the ferry takes you to Kruiningen in Zuid Beveland. From here it is possible to return to Goes, or go east to Bergen op Zoom (North Brabant).

ROUTE 4A SLUIS TO BRESKENS

Those who do not have time to explore this part of Holland should, if possible, take a brief look at Sluis before driving on to Breskens to catch the ferry to Vlissingen. An attractive route is to take the Cadzand road out of Sluis, then follow signs to **Retranchement**. Here are the well-preserved ramparts of a fortified border village; also a very fine open trestle windmill built in 1643. It is possible to continue along the coastal road via Cadzand-Bad and Nieuwvliet-Bad to Breskens, but the way is rather narrow and winding. It may be easier to return to the main road via Cadzand, thence to Breskens via Nieuwvliet and Groede. If making for the ferry, be sure to follow the signs for Vlissingen, and not the signs for Breskens which will take you into the small town itself. Over the past two years there has been a complete reconstruction of the ferry terminal and approaches, to ease traffic problems. Ferry tickets may be purchased either from automatic machines or from a kiosk; food is available on board the ferry.

The town mill, Hulst

39

4 ROTTERDAM, DELFT and THE HAGUE

These three cities form part of the complex of towns and cities known as the *Randstad* or Ring Town. Forty-five miles long and forty miles across at its widest point, this huge horseshoe-shaped conurbation contains the major cities and towns of Dordrecht, Rotterdam, Delft, The Hague, Leiden, Haarlem, Amsterdam, Hilversum and Utrecht. Each town is a separate entity, the country in between remaining as open space with parks and pasture, while the western side is bounded by the seacoast. It is really the idea of a 'green belt' turned inside out.

Rotterdam, a city arisen from the ashes of war, has in its Europoort the biggest harbour in the world; Delft, an ancient town, is famous for its porcelain, its artists and its University of Technology; The Hague, seat of the Dutch Government, is a busy commercial centre with a flourishing seaside resort on its outskirts. All have much of interest for the tourist.

Rotterdam is easy to reach by motorway and by public transport. Cyclists coming from the south are advised to use the Maassluis ferry to the west of the city. There is a cycle lane through the Maastunnel, but it involves using an escalator which makes it difficult with a loaded bicycle. The Beneluxtunnel is a motorway tunnel only. Bicycles may also be taken on the Metro (Underground), but only after 7pm on weekdays, and all day on Saturdays and Sundays. Carriage is free, although no special facilities are available.

As in any large city, car parking can be a problem, and although car parks are plentiful, charges can be quite high. We suggest using one of the many multi-storey car parks near Central Station or near the Lijnbaan shopping centre.

Rotterdam and Neighbourhood

One of the best ways to see the city is by tram. There is an old tourist tram which departs from the Central Station every day, taking a slow ride (with a guide) all around the city. If you prefer to find your own way, a brochure and map of all the city public transport (bus, tram and Metro) can be obtained free from the ticket office on Stationsplein. Explanations are given in English and several other languages. Tram 5 will take you to the waterside near Willemsplein, from where the 'Spido' boat tours start. A $1\frac{1}{2}$-hour tour of the harbour takes in the world's busiest waterway, and a commentary in various languages points out special features, making this an ideal way of getting the feel of the port. Longer boat trips can be taken, including one taking in the whole of the Europoort complex.

Another way of seeing Europoort is by car, following the well-signed ANWB 'Rotterdamse Havenroute'. This is designed to show the visitor as much of the area as possible, and an excellent map with full route description in English, with additional notes, is available from the local VVV office in Rotterdam. The tour is 90km in length, and ends with a drive

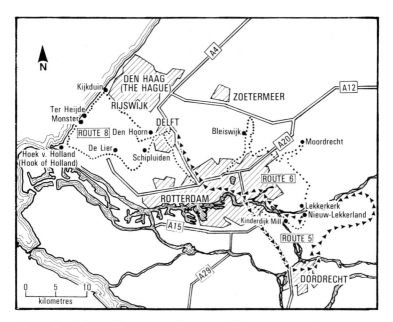

along the Brielse Maas recreation area. The return may be made by crossing the Brielsebrug south to Groene Kruisweg thence to join the motorway A15 just north of Rhoon. In this way, other interesting places may be seen including Heenvliet, once a port before Brielle became important, and the village of Rhoon which has a sixteenth-century castle.

If returning from the boat tour, walk back along Willemskade to the Veerkade, across Westplein and along Parklaan. Ahead you cannot fail to see the tall structure of the Euromast. Originally built to a height of 350ft (100m) in 1960, it towered over the city. From the 'Crow's Nest' at this height there is a wonderful view of Rotterdam in miniature. In the late 1960s, the Medical Faculty of the University opened their new building, which was higher than the Euromast. Not to be outdone, the management decided that the tower must go higher, so they added a 'Space Needle', ascended by an external rotating lift car. Opened in 1970, the extra height brought the total to 600ft (185m) enabling one to see as far as The Hague, Delft and beyond on a clear day.

Leaving Euromast, take tram 6 or 9 to Hudsonplein and walk up beside the Voorhaven to No 12, De Dubbelde Palmboom, a restored warehouse which is part of the Historical Museum. A short distance away at No 13-15 Voorstraat is the restored Zakkendragershuisje, containing a pewter workshop which may be visited. These buildings are in Delfshaven, one of the oldest parts of Rotterdam. In 1620, the Pilgrim Fathers sailed from here in the 'Speedwell'. The church in which they held their last service before setting forth is situated in Aelbrechtskolk, a continuation of Voorhaven, and every year, on the fourth Thursday in November, a traditional American Thanksgiving service is held. Having referred to the Historical Museum, reference should also be made to two other major museums, both of which have been completely renewed and enlarged before re-opening in 1986. These are the Ethnological Museum on Willemskade, and the Maritime Museum on Leuvehaven, near Churchillplein.

Further to the west is **Schiedam**, famous for its distilleries which produce Genever. Two windmills belonging to the distilleries are still in operation.

To the west of Rotterdam, best reached via the motorway, is the town of **Vlaardingen**, first given town status by Floris V in 1273. Principally a fishing town, it has an excellent Fishery Museum and colonnaded fish market, restored in 1950 and now housing the VVV offices, and a Town

Dordrecht

Hall dating from 1650. Its position has made Vlaardingen an ideal place to develop a marina, on the place where once Crusaders sailed for the Holy Land and fishermen landed their herring catch.

ROUTE 5   DORDRECHT and KINDERDIJK MILLS

To the south-east of Rotterdam lies **Dordrecht**, the first known town of Holland (as distinct from the Netherlands) whose charter dates back to 1220. Until the sixteenth-century it was the most important and powerful town in Holland.

There are some marvellous buildings here, both in the town centre and around the harbours.

ROUTE 5A   DORDRECHT TOWN WALK

Starting at the Railway Station, where there is carparking, walk down Johan de Wittstraat into Bagijnhof and Visstraat. Just before the Visbrug turn right into Voorstraat. Just after passing Scheffersplein on the left, at the bend in the road, is an archway (on the right) leading to the Hof or Court. It was here, in the Statenzaal (States Hall) that, in 1572, the foundations of the independence of The Netherlands were laid. The hall is now used for weddings, concerts and similar functions.

Continue along Voorstraat, leading to Boomstraat and across Boombrug into Wijnstraat, thence to the Groothoofd. From the quayside a fascinating view of the confluence of two major rivers is obtained, made more interesting by the continual flow of traffic on the Oude Maas and the Merwede.

The magnificent Groothoofdspoort has a number of elaborate carvings, including pictures of the patron saint and the coat of arms of the town. Walking along Wolwevershaven, past some superb old warehouses, brings you to Nieuwe Haven and the Museum Simon van Gijn at No 29. Housed in a beautiful 'patrician's house', the interiors are reminiscent of paintings by Vermeer, while the top floor contains a fine collection of antique toys. Continue down the quay to Engelenburgerbrug, pausing on the way to glance down Korte Engelenburgerkade to the Catharijnepoort. Beyond the bridge is the Grote Kerk, dedicated to Our Lady, on the site of a chapel possibly dating from 1064. The tower, like many of the houses in the town, leans noticeably due to the marshy ground beneath its foundations. The church is one of the largest in Holland, and possesses a lovely pulpit (1756) and a fine organ built in 1671, on which concerts are given during the summer.

Return via Grootekerksbuurt and Groen Markt to the Visbrug, thence back to the Station.

The return to Rotterdam is by a very pleasant route passing the windmills of **Kinderdijk**. These fine mills, nineteen in all, were built in 1740 to drain the surrounding polder. The mills are in operation on Saturday afternoons during the summer, and one mill is open for the public to visit. Cars must be left in the carpark near a café, and visitors walk along the Molenkade past the mills, although cycling is permitted.

From Dordrecht, the route follows the main road towards Papendrecht, then crosses the motorway A15 on to a main road beyond. After about 2km the road takes a right-hand bend, and at this point take the secondary road on the left towards a group of windmills. At the crossroads, do not cross the bridge but turn right along the river Alblas, past Bleskensgraaf to Vuilendam, where the road turns left towards **Groot-Ammers**. The whole area is pleasant farmland with roads running along the dykes, often dotted with windmills. Groot-Ammers has a stork colony under the control of the Netherlands Association for the Protection of Birds. From this village, turn left and follow the dyke road west along the River Lek past Streefkerk and Nieuw-Lekkerland, following signs to the mill area at Kinderdijk, as described above.

From Kinderdijk, a ferry crosses the River Lek to **Krimpen a/d Lek**, from whence signs for Rotterdam should be followed via **Krimpen a/d IJssel**.

ROUTE 6   A CYCLE RIDE FROM ROTTERDAM

Starting from Rotterdam, leave via the Van Brienenoordbrug in the direction of Dordrecht. Once across the Nieuwe Maas, take the dyke road eastwards to the ferry at **Slikkerveer**. (Note: this carries cyclists and pedestrians only). Cross to the Kinderdijk mills and follow the path

alongside the mills as far as Paddestoel 20712. Turn left and ride through
Nieuw-Lekkerland to the road along the dyke (Signpost 3431). Turn right
and ride to the passenger ferry landing-stage (pedestrians and cycles only).
Cross on the ferry to **Lekkerkerk**, and ride north, through the village and
straight on until the main road is reached at signpost 4509. Cross over and
turn right at the next junction (Paddestoel 21340). This road soon becomes
a cycle path, and at Paddestoel 22363 bear left. Continue along the cycle
path until it joins the dyke road just past Paddestoel 22432. Turn right and
follow this road to **Gouderak**, where a ferry crosses to **Moordrecht**. Return
along the opposite bank of the river, the Hollandse IJssel, to **Nieuwerkerk
a/d IJssel**. Turn into the town under the railway bridge by the station, and
continue through the town towards the motorway, where the route crosses
the motorway and continues in a northerly direction to signpost 8442. At
this point turn left towards Oud Verlaat. Keep to the road skirting the
Zevenhuizer Plas along its west side, past signpost 7245, and continue
northwards alongside the Rotte Meren. At the northern end of this stretch
of water the route passes a group of three windmills which are very
attractive. When the railway is reached, turn left across the water and
return south along the other side of the Meren and the west bank of the river
Rotte, finally following the shore of the Bergse Plassen to Rotterdam
Noord railway station.

Delft
It is just 11km along the A13 (E19) Motorway from the Rotterdam junction
(Knooppunt Kleinpolderplein) to the exit for Delft. From this junction
follow the signs marked 'P-route' and 'P-route West'. Free parking is
allowed under the railway viaducts near the tall windmill on Phoenix

Straat, parallel with the railway. There is parking in the town, but it is on meters, and the railway viaduct parking place is most convenient for the town centre. A good route for cyclists coming from the direction of Rotterdam is first to follow signs for **Overschie**, then follow the cycle path alongside the river Schie, coming into Delft past the porcelain factory on Rotterdamseweg. The safest place for parking cycles is in the Rijwielstalling at the station.

ROUTE 7   A WALK AROUND DELFT

Delft is a town of narrow tree-lined canals, picturesque bridges, narrow alleyways and courts, dominated by the tower of the Nieuwe Kerk in the Markt. This is the best place to start a walk. At one end is the Stadhuis or Town Hall, the main part of which dates from 1620, whilst the Nieuwe Kerk stands at the opposite end. Now dedicated to St Ursula, building commenced in 1381, and contains the family vault of the House of Orange. The 100m high tower contains a fine seventeenth-century carillon which is played regularly every Tuesday, Thursday and Saturday morning. The walk now continues along Oude Langendijk (once a canal) and around the back of the church to Kerkstraat, thence along Volders Gracht to Hippolytusbuurt, site of the Thursday Flower Market. Turning right brings us to the Oude Kerk or St Hippolytuskerk, founded even before the Nieuwe Kerk, in 1240; the present building dates from around 1500. In the tower, which visibly leans, hangs an enormous bell, cast in 1570, which weighs 9000kg, and has a circumference of 7m. It is now only rung on special occasions, notably in 1962 on the occasion of Princess Wilhelmina's funeral.

Nearby, in St Agathaplein, is the Prinsenhof; built as a convent in the fifteenth century, it was later to become the residence of the Princes of Orange. In this building, William I was murdered in 1584; it now houses part of the Municipal Museum.

Walk back along Oude Delft, cross over the Boterbrug and turn right along Wijn Haven and back to the Markt. Continue along Oude Langendijk as far as Oost Einde, and follow this to reach the Oostpoort, resting on its own little island among the canals. It is the only remaining one of Delft's original eight fourteenth-century town gates.

While in Delft, the opportunity should be taken to visit one of the potteries making the world-renowned Delft ware. Three establishments still carry on the old trade, namely De Porceleyne Fles in Rotterdamseweg, De Delftse Pauw on Delftweg, and Atelier de Candelaer in Kerkstraat. All these are open to the public. As in many tourist areas, you will find souvenir shops selling what appears to be Delft ware, but always look for the trademarks, and avoid cheap imports from Germany and the Far East.

ROUTE 8   A CYCLE RIDE FROM DELFT

From the railway station, follow Westsingel Gracht north, then turn left along Buitenwatersloot and Hoornseweg, heading in a westerly direction. At a fork (signpost 704) keep straight on along Woudse Weg for about 2km, then at signpost 5768 turn right along a side road leading into a cycle path which circles the little church of 't Woudt before gaining a small road alongside the Zweth canal. Turn right and at the first bridge turn left, heading towards the tall white windmill at **Wateringen**. On reaching the major road, turn right, away from the mill, and then left (signpost 427) into Kerklaan, past the Town Hall. Cross the junction of Poeldijk-seweg/Noordweg and continue to Erasmus weg. Turn left, then take the next major road to the right at signpost 8770. This takes you along Lozerlaan, a wide road which leads to Loosduinen, from here follow signs to **Kijkduin**. Ride up on to the promenade, looking out over the North Sea, turn left and follow the cycle path along the dunes to **Ter Heijde**, thence continue towards **Hoek van Holland**. At Paddestoel 23695, the junction with the beach road, turn left and cross the main road as if going into the town centre, then at Paddestoel 23098 pick up the cycle path towards **Maasdijk** and continue for about 4km until the path runs into a road. Turn left at Paddestoel 20556 along a road closed to cars, to the main road N20 at Paddestoel 23100. Cross over and continue in the direction of Delft, keeping on the cycle path on the right side of the road. After 2km, at signpost 6389, a cycle path leaves the road on the right, leading towards **Gaag**. Here, cross over the Maasland road and continue left along the cycle path to **Schipluiden**, a rather attractive polder village. Follow the cycle signs 'Doorgaand Verkeer' through the village on to the path at signpost 6384, which will bring you back to Delft at the junction of Hoornseweg and Woudse weg.

The whole route will give a good impression of the market garden area of South Holland, and a chance to ride along some of the fine cycle paths through the dunes.

The Hague

The Hague and Scheveningen

First of all, we should perhaps clear up any possible confusion by explaining that the city which is known to English-speaking visitors as The Hague has *two* names in Dutch, being called either Den Haag or 's Gravenhage. The original place was called Den Haag or 'The Hedge', and later it became the 'Count's Hedge' or 's Gravenhage. Today the more common name is Den Haag, and this is the name used in this book.

Den Haag is the seat of the Government of the Netherlands, and is also a busy commercial centre. However, the main influences are diplomatic and political, and much of the city displays a dignity and elegance from the eighteenth and nineteenth centuries, with a number of broad streets and avenues lined by fine residences.

As in so many cities, parking is rather difficult and free parking is only possible outside the city. Look for the signs P+R, which indicate parking areas from which public transport into the city may be used. Coming from Delft along the A13, the most useful is just past the Ypenburg motorway junction as you approach the suburb of Rijswijk. From this point the city can be reached by tram, even as far as Scheveningen on the coast. If parking in the centre is essential, parking places are well signed and there is a large open-air park on the Malieveld near Central Station. Parking meters are also plentiful.

ROUTE 9   A WALK AROUND DEN HAAG

From Central Station, turn left along Herengracht and just after passing the post office on your left, cross the road and walk along Korte Poten. In the centre of the square at the end of this street is a statue of William the Silent. Turn right into the square and at the far side is Korte Vijverberg leading to the famous Mauritshuis, at present being restored and due to re-open in 1987. Once the residence of the Duke of Marlborough, ancestor of Sir Winston Churchill, it houses a wonderful collection of paintings by Rembrandt, Rubens, Vermeer, Holbein and Frans Hals.

Further along the street, a left turn brings us into Lange Vijverberg. On the left is the Hof Vijver, an attractive lake with fountains, whilst ahead is the Gevangenpoort or prison gate, originally an entrance to the count's castle (fourteenth century) and later used for political prisoners.

Turn left at the end of the Hof Vijver past the statue of William II to reach the entrance to the Binnenhof, for centuries the centre of political life in the Netherlands. Its history extends back to the thirteenth century, and the original building of the Ridderzaal (Hall of Knights) dates from this period. This has now been restored to much of its original form, and it is now used for state occasions, such as the opening of Parliament. Other buildings around the Binnenhof house the First and Second Chambers of the States General, the Parliament of the Netherlands.

Return past the statue of William II to the Buitenhof, the old outer court of the castle, and walk through to the main shopping area, which includes many pedestrian precincts. Beyond is the Oude Stadhuis or old Town Hall dating from 1565, and the Grote Kerk or St Jacobskerk, which dates mainly from the mid-fifteenth century.

Returning towards Gravenstraat, turn left, and follow Hoogstraat and Noordeinde to cross Hogewal and Mauritskade, where the canal is part of the original city moat. Across the canal is Zeestraat, in which is located the world-famous Panorama Mesdag, which depicts in a very realistic fashion a 360° panoramic view of the old fishing village of Scheveningen and the surrounding dunes, sea and landscape. With a circumference of 394ft and a height of 46ft, the painting by H.W. Mesdag, his wife and other artists covers 18,000sq ft of canvas. Further along Zeestraat is the Postmuseum, covering many aspects of communications, including postage stamps, telegraphs and radio.

Still following Zeestraat, cross the junction of Laan van Meerdervoort and Javastraat into Scheveningseweg and Carnegieplein, site of the Vredespaleis or Peace Palace, home of the International Court of Justice. Most of the countries of the world contributed towards the building, which was initially financed by Andrew Carnegie as an International Court of Arbitration intended to reduce or prevent future wars.

Tram 7 runs past this point, and can be taken either back to Central Station or on to Scheveningen. From Central Station, trams 1 or 9 will provide an easy way to get to Madurodam, the world-famous miniature town situated near the junction of Prof B.M. Teldersweg and Haringkade. Described as 'Holland in a Nutshell', this is a complete miniature Dutch town built to a scale of 1:25, with buildings modelled on actual examples, beautifully landscaped with miniature trees and flowers. It is true to say that if you cannot spare the time to visit some of the places in the country which you would like to see, it is probable that many of the buildings are at Madurodam, in miniature. Quite apart from the interesting way in which the whole project has been carried out, and is still being added to, many visitors are surprised to learn that Madurodam is, in fact, a war memorial. The original financing was by the parents of George Maduro, a student who distinguished himself and subsequently lost his life during World War II. Together with many donations from firms and other interests, the scheme has grown, and all the profits are donated to charity, mostly for the benefit of young people.

Visitors wishing to travel by car should follow the local route signs, black lettering on white ground; there are full facilities for disabled visitors.

Scheveningen

This is a thriving holiday centre and port on the coast to the north-west of Den Haag. Again, local route signs guide the driver, who will find adequate parking at the northern end, near the tram terminus.

Famous for its Casino, luxury hotels and fresh fish landed in the harbour, the town presents quite a variety of faces for those who walk through. From the tram terminus and car park, walk southwards along the Boulevard. The Kurhaus has a nineteenth-century exterior but has been completely modernised inside to make it into a major leisure complex, with casino, hotel, restaurants and up-to-date conference centre. The pier is modern, replacing one which was destroyed during World War II. At the far end of the Boulevard lies Scheveningen Haven, site of the old fishing village and the harbour which served as the port for Den Haag from the sixteenth to the nineteenth century. The fishing industry still flourishes together with herring and eel curing, and there is a modern roll on-roll off ferry terminal.

In spite of modern developments there is still some trace of the old town to be seen, including the tower of the church in Keizerstraat which dates from the fifteenth century. One notable event in the history of Scheveningen was the embarkation in May 1660 of Charles II for his return to England at the Restoration.

For those wishing to explore a little farther afield, or who do not wish to use cars or trams, the area is ideal for cyclists. Anyone without a bicycle can hire one without difficulty from the VVV office in Zwolsestraat, next to the Europa Hotel near the northern tram terminus in Scheveningen.

Groningse Straat (which runs behind the carpark by the VVV office) leads to a network of cycle and footpaths among the dunes, through which cyclists can ride to Katwijk and beyond to Zandvoort. A shorter ride of about 5-6km will take you to Meijendel, where there is a café and Pannekoekhuis. From here, a return can be made towards the city, and if your visit is during the month of May, the opportunity can be taken to visit the Japanese Garden at Clingendael, adjacent to the head office of the

ANWB on Wassenaarseweg. (Follow signs for ANWB Kantoor).

Alternatively, from Scheveningen go south along the Boulevard, around the harbour by Westduinweg to Duindorp, and rejoin the cycle path through the dunes from Duivelandsestraat. The cycle path may then be followed all the way through Kijkduin and Ter Heijde to Hoek van Holland.

For those wanting seaside resorts, the stretch of coast north and south of Den Haag is well provided. In addition to Scheveningen itself, with its pier, beaches and other attractions, there is Kijkduin, as small attractive resort to the south, with the largest camp site on the Dutch coast at Ockenburg; there is also a Youth Hostel. To the north is Wassenaar, a select residential suburb where the beach is partly reserved for residents. However, there is also the Duinrell estate, which is a country park with facilities and attractions for the whole family, including a modern fully-equipped campsite. It is possible within the area to find resorts to suit every taste from the most sophisticated, with casino, through family holiday beaches for the children, to quiet restful places where the only sounds are from the waves and the birds in the dunes.

5 GOUDA, UTRECHT AND THE CENTRAL LAKES

Gouda, famous for its cheese, is only 33km by motorway from Utrecht, former Roman fortress town at the eastern end of the Randstad. The area between these towns contains many pleasant surprises for the tourist who leaves the beaten track.

Gouda is a pleasant town which was granted its first charter in 1272. During the fourteenth and fifteenth centuries it was a centre for the cloth trade, later turning to a variety of industries including the making of smokers' pipes, pottery, bricks, candles and, of course, cheese. The Market Square is the largest in Holland, and in its centre stands what is possibly the oldest Gothic Town Hall, dating from 1450.

Much of the town centre is pedestrianised, and car parking is easier in the free parks on the outer edge of the town, near the station, at the northern end of Raam, and near Klein Amerika.

ROUTE 10   A WALK IN GOUDA

Begin the walk in the Market Square. If you can time it to begin on the hour, you can watch the little figures on the east wall of the Stadhuis move when the carillon plays; they depict Count Floris V bestowing civic rights on the town in 1272. Notice too the beautiful Renaissance staircase on the south side of the building. Behind the Stadhuis, on the northern side of the Markt, is the Waag or Weigh House. Built in 1668, and formerly used for weighing the cheeses at the weekly market, it is now only open on Thursday mornings during July and August, when an old crafts market is held. There are demonstrations of clog-making, pottery, pipe-making, candle-dipping and *stroopwafel* baking. Stroopwafels, or syrup waffles, are a speciality of the district.

From the south end of the Markt, through Kerkstraat, the great St Janskerk is reached, whose 123m long nave is the longest in Holland. Dating from the fourteenth century, the church is renowned for its 70 stained glass windows, mostly sixteenth century, and illustrate scenes from the Bible and Dutch history. They are fully described in a detailed guide which is available in English.

On leaving the church, on the south side, the Lazarus Gate (1609) leads from Achter de Kerk into the Catharina Gasthuis, a building from 1665 which, with older buildings on the same site, served as a hospital from 1306 to 1910. It is now the Municipal Museum with period rooms, collections of old and modern art, an old dispensary and surgeons' instruments.

Leave the building by the exit into Oosthaven, cross the bridge and turn left along Westhaven. On the right is a seventeenth-century merchant's house named 'De Moriaan' (The Blackamoor) which now accommodates a museum devoted to tiles, earthenware and clay and other pipes. The

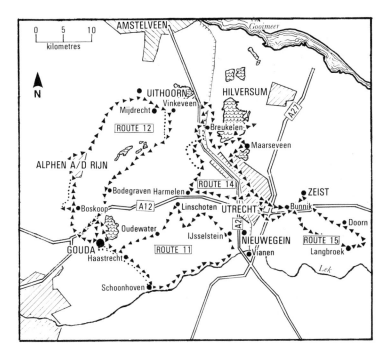

history of pipe-making in Gouda goes back to the early seventeenth century, when Puritan refugees included several pipe-makers from Boston and other ports on the east coast of England. One of these, named William Baernelts, first started making clay pipes in Gouda in 1617, branding his work with a Tudor Rose symbol. Until 1637 the English pipe-makers had a monopoly of the industry in Gouda, after which their Dutch competitors took over.

Continue along Westhaven to the next bridge and turn left into Lange Noordooststraat, then left again into Spieringstraat. A short walk brings you to the old Weeshuis (orphanage) which now houses the fine collection of old and rare books and other documents belonging to the Municipal Archives, known as the Goutse Librij. On the other side of the street is the Willem Vroesenhuis (1614), a former almshouse for old men. At the west end of the St Janskerk is Torenstraat, leading to Lage Gouwe, with the canal on your left. On both sides of the water is a picturesque colonnaded building, one being the cornmarket and the other the fish market. The latter is now used for pottery and art demonstrations. From the fish market, turn right up the narrow Visstraat and right again into Achter de Vismarkt, following this street until Lange Groenendaal opens on the left. Here are two shops selling Gouda specialities; one is an excellent cheese

*The Waag, or cheese weigh
house, Gouda*

shop, and the other is a baker specialising in the local Stroopwafels.

The walk ends by returning along Korte Groenendaal to the Markt and the Stadhuis.

ROUTE 11   A CIRCULAR TOUR OF THE LOPIKERWAARD

Lopikerwaard is the name given to the country lying between the rivers Lek on the south, the Vlist to the west and the Hollandse IJssel to the north. The name Lopik is derived from a natural stream in the peaty soil called the Lobeke. The embankments of earth built to enclose and retain the water, the dykes, became natural routes for roads. The landscape is pleasantly broken up by clumps of trees, small picturesque houses built behind the dykes, and reed-thatched farmhouses.

From Gouda, a very pleasant tour of the area can be made. Leave the town via the bridge to the south, across the river, and take the road leading to **Haastrecht**. This road follows along the south bank of the river, but cyclists will find that a more pleasant way is to take the dyke road along the north side. At Haastrecht, take the minor road leading south to **Vlist** and **Schoonhoven**. Just outside the town, ignore the turning to the right to Stolwijk, and continue alongside the river Vlist to the centre of the village of Vlist. Just past here, cross the bridge over the river on the left, signed to Bonrepas. Cyclists can cross at another bridge before reaching the village; by crossing the river, a much prettier road is followed, and in springtime the whole route is extremely attractive. A short distance before reaching the outskirts of Schoonhoven the road passes quite close to a fine example of a *wipmolen* pumping windmill.

Schoonhoven, an old fortress town on the banks of the River Lek, is noted

PLACES TO VISIT IN AND AROUND GOUDA

Town Hall
Oldest Gothic Town Hall in the Netherlands, with fine double outside staircase and attractive carillon.

Weigh-House
Seventeeth-century cheese-weighing house. Open only on Thursdays in summer.

St Janskerk
Magnificent stained glass windows and a beautiful roof. Accessible for disabled visitors.

Catharina Gasthuis
Municipal museum. Period rooms, old medical instruments.

De Moriaan
Pipe museum, tiles and other clay objects.

Goutse Librij
Municipal archives in old orphanage.

Vlist
Picturesque 'ribbon' village along river. Fine *wipmolen* pumping windmill.

Schoonhoven
Weigh-house, now pancake restaurant. 't Silverhuys with Netherlands Gold and Silver museum, also with clocks.

IJsselstein
Interesting old town centre and seventeeth-century fire engine house. Museum in Town Hall.

Montfoort
Town Hall and Waterpoort.

Oudewater
Weigh-house with collection of old books, coins and paintings. Picturesque town centre.

Reeuwijkse Plassen
Lakes and nature reserves. Ideal for exploring by cycle.

Alphen a/d Rijn
Avifauna bird park.

Vinkeveen
Small fen museum.

chiefly for the manufacture of silver articles, especially the ornaments worn with traditional costume. In the centre of the town is the former Weigh-house, now a recommended pancake restaurant. The building itself dates from 1617, but the Stadhuis is even older, built in 1452. The St Bartholomaeuskerk is a Gothic structure, with an interesting sixteenth-century official pew. Perhaps of more interest to the visitor is the Nederlands Goud-Zilver-en Klokkenmuseum. Housed in a restored building, called 't Silverhuys, beside the harbour, it contains unique collections of gold and silver work, also an original silversmith's workshop.

Following the harbour down through the town to the river brings us to the Veerpoort (1601), the only remaining gate of the original five. There is a ferry here across the Lek to Nieuwpoort, but turn left and follow the dyke road along the north bank of the river almost as far as the Lekbrug near Vianen. All along here there are interesting views across the landscape, and of the shipping using the waterway. At signpost 7409, turn left away from the river and take the road towards **Lopikerkapel**. This is a village typical of the Lopikerwaard, and has a Dutch Reformed church built about 1450, with a beautiful interior. Dominating the view in this area are two modern structures, namely a 400m high television mast and the tall observation mast of the Meteorological Institute.

Passing these, we cross the main road into **IJsselstein**, a town with a long history. Inhabited since Roman times, the medieval street plan can still be traced. The remains of the thirteenth-century castle tower with a beautiful arched staircase houses a permanent photographic exhibition dealing with its history. The municipal museum is located in the restored Stadhuis or Town Hall, originally built in 1560. Holland's first Renaissance tower dating from 1535 forms part of the Dutch Reformed Church; the original building was constructed in 1310. There was only one road leading to Utrecht, and access to it was by the IJsselpoort. Near this gate is a little building, the Brandspuithuisje, originally built in 1622 to house a small fire pump, but now containing a collection of historic fire-fighting equipment.

Leave the town by a minor road running north, parallel to the river Hollandse IJssel, towards Achtersloot thence left to **Montfoort**. The name means 'castle on a ford', and the town grew up as a settlement around a castle in 1163, receiving a charter in 1329. The gatehouse of the castle still stands and is being restored. The seventeeth-century IJsselpoort (town gate) stands adjacent to the eighteenth-century Town Hall; the layout of the town centre still recalls the Middle Ages.

From Montfoort, take the road out of town to the south-west, then turn right along road N212 to **Linschoten**, a beautiful rural village in a loop of the river Linschoten. Many houses are in their original seventeeth and eighteenth-century condition. Settlements existed in the polders of the area in AD900, and between 1290 and 1490 there were four castles, although only traces remain. The fine Grote or St Janskerk possesses a fifteenth-century tower, and the village is situated in the centre of a large nature reserve along the Hollandse IJssel and the Lange Linschoten.

The road south along the Lange Linschoten is particularly beautiful, lined by pollarded willows on the bank of the winding river, and particularly pleasant for cycling. The road finally leads to **Oudewater**, which was granted a city charter in 1295, and was beseiged during the Eighty Years' War. Here is the famous Weighhouse, with stepped gable dating from 1595, which, because of its reputation for honesty and accuracy, became used for weighing people accused of witchcraft. Apparently a person was deemed to be a witch if their weight was not compatible with their size, height and so on! Today visitors can still be weighed, and receive a certificate stating that their weight is 'in accordance with the natural proportion of the body'. On the upper floor of the

Heksenwaag is a collection of books, old coins and paintings. The town itself has many attractive seventeeth-century façades and backwaters, a Town Hall with a Renaissance façade of 1588. The Gothic St Michael's Church with a thirteenth-century tower and vestry stands on the site of a church from 1100. You may even see storks nesting on the roof tops. The Market Square is built over the river, and parking, even for cycles, is forbidden. It is necessary to park in one of the side streets on the edge of the town.

Leave Oudewater by the road to **Hekendorp**, which runs along the northern side of the Hollandse IJssel, with old farm houses below the dyke on the right and fields leading to the river on the left. Many fruit farms are to be found in the area. Beyond the junction for Haastrecht, on the left, the road continues back towards Gouda. In about $1\frac{1}{2}$km, at Paddestoel 21509, a steep road leaves the dyke on the right, leading to the Reeuwijkse Plassen. This is an area of water which is the result of peat cutting over hundreds of years. Popular with sailors and fishermen, it is an ideal place for viewing water birds. It is possible to drive along the narrow lanes across the lake, although there is restricted access at weekends and holidays. The roads are very narrow, so care is needed. It goes without saying that a bicycle is the best form of transport for exploring such an area.

The return to Gouda is made via Reeuwijk-Brug.

ROUTE 12   BUSHES, BIRDS AND BOG

Leave Gouda in the direction of **Alphen a/d Rijn**, along the road which follows the river Gouwe in a northerly direction. At **Boskoop** turn left towards the prominent water tower. In this immediate area are many nurseries specialising in trees and shrubs of all descriptions. This industry has grown up here because in former times it was so remote that peat cutting did not take place, so the sandy soil has been enriched to provide ideal growing conditions. An arboretum and tree research station may be visited, and boat trips around the nurseries are available.

Return to the main road for Alphen a/d Rijn. Cyclists can follow the lanes and cycle paths between the nurseries to avoid re-crossing the river.

Alphen aan den Rijn is noted for the bird and recreation park, 'Avifauna', where, visitors may wander through a sub-tropical house with free-flying birds from all parts of the world. In addition there are tropical plants and even banana trees with fruit on them.

From Alphen, take the road along the west side of the Aar Kanaal to Nieuwveen. Immediately after crossing the canal turn left (signpost 2415) following the Amstel-Drecht canal to Uithoorn. From here take the main road (N201) to **Vinkeveen**. As its name suggests, it is a fen village situated in an area of extensive water-filled depressions formed in past years by peat cutting. The area north of the village is known as the Vinkeveense Plassen, whose artificial islands and excavations have been overgrown by reed beds. Here also is the Fen Museum, where the history of the peat cutters is told by means of exhibits, photos and pictures, together with old documents. A restored peat cutting machine is to be seen, which was in service from 1895 to 1977.

Leaving Vinkeveen, take the road south (N212) through Wilnis and after 4km, turn right at signpost 8117 towards Woerdense Verlaat. Cyclists must use the parallel road from Wilnis. The road then takes a pleasant winding course along the south side of the Nieuwkoopse Plassen, following the river Meije through the village of the same name until it reaches the larger river Oude Rijn. Turn left (signpost 370) to Bodegraven, cross the river, and return south to Gouda.

Although **Utrecht** may be reached quickly from Gouda by the A12 motorway, it is more pleasant to take the old road via Bodegraven, Woerden and Harmelen, following the Oude Rijn.

Utrecht is the fourth largest city in Holland, and the capital of Utrecht Province, often called the heart of Holland.

There is plenty of car parking space (for which one must pay) in the Hoog-Catharijne, the largest covered shopping centre in Europe. Because of its size, it can be extremely confusing, although well signed. Since there are seven car parks within the complex, it is essential for the visitor to take careful note of where the car is parked, and it is recommended that a copy of the illustrated guide (*wegwijzer*) is obtained from the centre Information Office.

There is so much to see in and around Utrecht that it really requires several days to enjoy the city fully.

Utrecht was built on the site of a Roman settlement, its name meaning the downstream ford. A Roman fort built in AD48 stood on the spot where the Dom Square is now located. Utrecht was granted city rights in 1122, and during the prosperous years of the twelfth to fourteenth centuries a network of canals was dug within the city walls, with merchants' houses, cellars and quays. The huge Dom (Cathedral) tower, separate from the adjacent church building, dates back to the fourteenth century, and is topped by a weathervane depicting St Martin (to whom the Cathedral is dedicated) cutting off part of his coat to give to a beggar. The tower rises to a height of 112m, the tallest of Holland's tall church towers and is open to visitors.

ROUTE 13   A WALK AROUND UTRECHT

An excellent map with a good explanation in English of a 2-hour walk around the city is available from the local VVV offices, but, this shorter walk covers many of the interesting sights.

Starting at the Hoog-Catharijne centre, location of the bus and railway stations and central car parks, make your way to the Vredenburgkwartier and along Lange Viestraat. Cross the Viebrug and turn right along Oudegracht. On the left, at the corner of Drakenburgstraat, is the medieval house Drakenborch, while across the canal may be seen Huis Oudaen. Built in the fourteenth century, it was the residence of the French Ambassador at the time of the Treaty of Utrecht (1713). Cross over to the

Jansbrug and look below, where the old cellars are visible along the quayside. Many small cafés are built into these cellars. Walk along the quay past the next two bridges, Bakkerbrug and Bezembrug. At the Stadhuisbrug, almost a square built over the water, cross to the Stadhuis, parts of which date from the thirteenth century. Continue along the Vismarkt to the Maartensbrug and turn left, where you will be confronted by the great tower of the Dom. The large arch in the base of the tower is big enough for a city bus to pass through. Here also are the Dom church, the University buildings and a copy of a Danish Rune Stone from Jutland, presented to Utrecht to commemorate the fact that St Willibrord, the English founder of the cathedral, introduced Christianity to Denmark.

Just by this memorial is an archway leading to a peaceful fourteenth-century cloister. Go through and turn right into Achter de Dom and Pausdam. Here you will find the Paushuize (Pope's House) built for Pope Adrian VI, the only Dutch Pope, who in fact never lived here. Turn into Achter St Pieter and St Pieterskerk will be seen on the right. Continue to Korte Janstraat, where at the end of the street can be seen the Janskerk. These two churches were built as collegiate churches linked to the Cathedral, forming part of a cross around the Dom. The other two churches are St Catharijnekerk and the Buurkerk or parish church. Walk down Oudkerkhof, cross the bridge and turn left into Choorstraat, then right into Zadelstraat. The Buurkerk is on the right, but continue to Mariaplaats where, behind the University Arts and Sciences building (Gebouw voor Kunsten and Wetenschappen) can be found the twelfth-century cloisters of the Mariakloostergang. From here, return to the start in Hoog-Catherijne.

Another method of viewing the city is to take a boat trip on the canals, starting from the Oude Gracht near the Viebrug. This trip lasts about an hour and many of the most interesting sights of the city can be seen in this way.

To the south of Utrecht, in the vast new town of Nieuwegein, lies the protected village of Vreeswijk, where, in 1373, a new canal was connected to the river Lek by two wooden locks, the Oude Sluis, which still exist.

The motorway system around Utrecht is extremely complicated, with many multiple junctions. The network is being extended even further, so it is very important to watch for signs to your destination well in advance of the expected junction.

A boat trip can also be made to Loenen, one of the prettiest villages on the river Vecht, noted for country estates and castles. A drive or trip by cycle through this area is also well worth while.

ROUTE 14   THE CASTLES AND LAKES OF THE VECHT AREA

Leave Utrecht by the road to **De Meern** and **Harmelen**, which follows the Leidse Rijn. At Harmelen, turn right at signpost 3112 towards the Vijverbos nature reserve, continue across the railway, and at signpost 937

Kasteel de Haar, near Utrecht

---

look for the entrance to 'Kasteel de Haar'. This beautiful castle was rebuilt last century on the ruins of a fifteenth-century castle, in the Romantic style — a real fairy tale castle. Inside is a fine collection of sixteenth and seventeenth century Gobelin tapestries, furniture, carpets, Chinese vases and many paintings, and the castle is surrounded by a splendid park and gardens.

The route passes along the road fronting the castle moat and grounds, turning left at signpost 6639, passing the large wrought-iron gateway to the park on the left. Continue straight ahead to Laagnieuwkoop (signpost 935) and on to **Portengensebrug**, turning right towards **Breukelen**.

Motorists can join the motorway A2 north for 6km to **Loenersloot**, then take the N201, turning right (signpost 2125) into **Loenen**, one of the prettiest Vecht villages. Cross over the river and follow the road south beside the river towards Breukelen. This is an area noted for its castles and manor houses, and it is interesting to note that although many of the buildings constructed during its long existence have disappeared over the centuries, its name was taken by Dutch emigrants and became the present-day name of Brooklyn, New York. The town of Breukelen is now the centre for an outstanding water sport area based on the Loosdrecht lakes.

About 1km further south, on the right, is the rather impressive Nijenrode Castle, based on an original thirteenth-century foundation and considerably altered and enlarged from 1632 on. It is not open to the public, and is now used as a college for Business Management Studies.

In about 500m the route turns left (signpost 240) and follows alongside the lake before turning right through Tienhoven and Oud Maarsseveen, along the edge of the Maarsseveense Plassen to Maarsseveen and **Oud-Zuilen**, where is to be found the castle known as Slot Zuylen. The first references to a castle here date from 838, and the present building was commenced in 1300. The park around the castle is open to visitors to the museum within the building, and has a unique garden sheltered by a so-called 'snake-wall' which traps the warmth of the sun, making it possible to grow sub-tropical fruit.

From a point just before reaching Tienhoven, at signpost 2620, a diversion can be made along the road to Nieuw-Loosdrecht across the lakes. This road passes yet another castle, the Kasteel Sypestein. The original castle was built in 1288, but the present building was completed at the beginning of this century, carefully reconstructed using the original foundations, and using old materials from other castles of the same period. The result is quite impressive, and the castle houses a fine museum collection of old masters, furniture, porcelain, silver and glassware. The gardens and park have been laid out in the style of the late sixteenth and early seventeeth centuries, and are open to visitors to the museum.

From the original route at Maarsseveen and Oud-Zuilen, we return to Utrecht.

ROUTE 15   ZEIST, DOORN and the LANGBROEK CASTLES
To the south-east of Utrecht, between the Utrecht hills and the rivers Rijn and Lek, lies an area particularly rich in castles. The explanation for this is two-fold: good hunting was available and sufficient land for tenant farmers could be found, and much of the area was protected against attack from the east and south by natural barriers.

Along the Kromme Rijn and the Langbroeker-wetering, a small canal running parallel with the river, lies a string of castles, and although most of them are not open to the public, a tour of the area or a walk around those which are open will give a good insight into the countryside and the sixteenth and seventeenth-century castles and mansions, many of which have been built on the sites of older structures.

Leave Utrecht along the A12 motorway, in the direction of Arnhem. After about 5km, leave at the turn-off for **Bunnik**, and go south following signs for **Odijk** and **Wijk-bij-Duurstede**, past the actual village of Odijk, then take a minor road at signpost 9329. This leads to Beverweerd castle, dating from the thirteenth century but rebuilt in neo-Gothic style in 1751. It is not open to view, being occupied since 1958 by an international Quaker school. The grounds, apart from the immediate vicinity of the castle, are open for walking.

Continue past the castle for about $1\frac{1}{2}$km, turning left, then right alongside the Langbroeker-wetering, where castle Sterkenburg can be seen on the right. Other castles can be seen on both sides of the road, including Kasteel Hinderstein, originally built in 1320, and completely rebuilt in 1847, but retaining the original tower. As before, free access to the grounds is possible, but not to the castle.

PLACES TO VISIT IN AND AROUND UTRECHT

Dom Tower
Highest in Holland, with magnificent views from top.

Catharijne-Convent (State museum)
History of Christianity in Netherlands, situated in the sixteenth-century Hospital of Knights of St John.

Central Museum
Paintings by Utrecht masters from the fifteenth century. Period rooms. Seventeenth-century doll's house, pottery, porcelain, silver and costumes.

National Railway Museum
History of Dutch railways and transport systems.

National Museum van Speelklok tot Pierement
Early music boxes, fairground and street organs, pianolas, etc.

Mariakloostergang
Twelfth-century cloisters.
Boat tours depart from Viebrug and last approximately one hour.

Kasteel de Haar
Magnificent fairy-tale castle with sixteenth and seventeenth-century tapestries, furniture, etc. Park open to public.

Slot Zuylen
Castle and grounds open to public. Museum contains Gobelin tapestries, manuscripts, porcelain and furniture.

Kasteel Sypestein (Nieuwe Loosdrecht)
Collection of sixteenth to eighteenth-century art and applied arts.

Doorn
Huis Doorn, home of exiled Kaiser Wilhelm after World War I. Museum contains much of his personal collections.

Zeist
Slot Zeist, conference and exhibition centre, parkland and open-air theatre.

Bunnik
Rhijnauwen Estate country park, with Youth Hostel, etc.

Cross the main road in the village of Langbroek, and in 1km the two castles of Sandenburg (left) and Walenburg (right) will be seen. Sandenburg is an ornate turreted nineteenth-century edifice, white-plastered in neo-Gothic style, but built on the site of a medieval castle. It is not open to view, and stands in an estate which is the largest in the district, including about twenty-one farms. The estate includes Kasteel Walenburg, purchased by the owners of Sandenburg in 1865, and completely restored in 1967. Neither castle is open to the public, but free access for walkers is permitted on the estates.

In approximately 1km, turn left at the crossroads, right at the next T-junction, then second left (following local signs) and Kasteel Broekhuizen will be seen on the right. This is a massive building with a portico supported by Ionic pillars. In the fourteenth century, a castle stood here surrounded by moats, but it was demolished in 1794 and a larger structure built, being further enlarged in 1810. After a fire in 1906 it was rebuilt once again. Now the buildings are occupied by the national institute for landscape management (RIN), so are not open to view. Part of the surrounding park is used for zoological and botanical research, but the remainder, which is open to the public, is landscaped in the English style, with hedges and copses and a fine nineteenth-century beech avenue.

Although the main N225 road is very pleasant, it is better to take the country lane from Broekhuizen to **Doorn**. In the centre of the small town is St Maartenskerk, with a stone-built twelfth-century nave and a brick tower in Gothic style. There is a Norman doorway and leper-squints in the church wall.

The main interest in Doorn is the Huis Doorn, since the fourteenth century the summer residence of the Diocese of Utrecht. From 1920 it was the residence of the exiled Kaiser Wilhelm II of Germany, who died here in 1941. The house, which during extensive reconstruction and enlargement in 1780 incorporated parts of the original medieval castle, now belongs to the Dutch Government who maintain it as a museum with fine collections

Kasteel Nijenrode, on the River Vecht

of paintings, tapestry and silverware, also many items belonging to the ex-Kaiser. The interior is kept precisely in the state in which it was when he lived there. The surrounding park is most attractive, with centuries old trees, a pinetum and deer park. The orangery is now a tea room.

From Doorn, follow the main road to **Zeist**, a small town surrounded by beautiful wooded countryside. Its early origins are recalled by the terp or mound upon which the church stands, and the town has some stately houses and delightful villas built in the last century by wealthy merchants.

On the edge of the town lies the Slot Zeist, a very large seventeenth-century mansion built on the site of a medieval castle. Inspired by the French baroque style, the interior and gardens were designed by the refugee French Huguenot Daniel Marot, who introduced painted walls and ceilings, and laid out the gardens in the fashion of Le Nôtre, similar to those at Versailles. The mansion has a chequered history, starting with its commissioning in 1686 by Willem Adriaan, Count of Nassau, grandson of Prince Maurits. Due to various sales and bequests it changed hands many times, until in 1924 the local authority bought the mansion to save it from falling into disrepair.

It was eventually restored to its original state, and is now used as a conference and exhibition centre, with a music school and restaurant. Little of the original gardens remain; in the eighteenth century the grounds were landscaped in English style, and only a small part is still as planned on the Versailles model. The main area contains lawns, paths and canals, with trees, and an open-air theatre which is used on summer afternoons.

From Slot Zeist, take the road south-west at signpost 6697 towards **Bunnik**, then follow the Utrecht road through Bunnik, keeping north of the railway. Watch for a signpost for **Rhijnauwen**, on the right after about 1 km (signpost 7300). From this point there is a one-way system which must be followed to the car parks within this large estate, which was purchased by the city of Utrecht in 1919. The eighteenth-century mansion is now used as a Youth Hostel, while the grounds, together with two adjoining estates, are open to the public. Within the park, the 'Theehuis Rhijnauwen' is famous for its wide selection of pancakes.

From Rhijnauwen, it is a short journey back to Utrecht. It is possible to visit this estate by boat from the city, the journey taking about 90 minutes.

Madurodan Model Village, The Hague

Kasteel de Haar, near Utrecht

The Waag and bridge over the River Spaarne, Haarlem

6 LEIDEN, HAARLEM AND AMSTERDAM

These three cities form the north-west and north edges of the Randstad. All three have long and varied histories, and are full of interesting places to see. Between Leiden and Haarlem lies the centre of the bulb-growing industry, and along the coast the resorts of Katwijk, Noordwijk and Zandvoort attract many holidaymakers. Extensive dune areas include the Amsterdam water purification scheme and the Kennemer Dune Reserve, while further inland is the Haarlemmermeer polder, once a huge inland lake and now containing Schiphol International airport. Amsterdam itself is continually expanding, both south and north of the busy North Sea canal, but within its boundaries some of the old villages still retain some of their former charm.

Leiden

A sixteenth-century poet described Leiden as a labyrinth of canals, streets, bridges and ramparts, and this 'renowned city of Leiden' bears a name which probably means 'situated on waterways'. The castle or Burcht was built in the middle of the twelfth century, on an artificial mound of either Saxon or Roman origin. Leiden has always offered asylum to refugees from religious persecution; these include the Pilgrim Fathers, and the Flemish weavers, which explains the growth of the cloth industry between the fourteenth and eighteenth centuries. The wars with Spain during the sixteenth and seventeeth centuries had their effect on Leiden, which was beseiged during 1573-4. After the lifting of the seige, the courage and loyalty of the citizens was recognised by Prince William the Silent in 1575 when he endowed the city with a University, a foundation which has enjoyed international renown ever since.

1606 saw the birth of the painter Rembrandt, just one of many great Dutch painters who lived and worked here during the 'Golden Age'. The spirit of liberty shown by the resistance to the Spanish invaders was further demonstrated in 1609 when the Pilgrim Fathers found refuge here, and their pastor, John Robinson, attended the University. He remained behind after the Pilgrims sailed for America, and died in the city in 1625.

Around 1670, Leiden was the second largest city in Holland, and with such a history it is not surprising that there is much of interest to see. The difficult choice is made easier by a series of four waymarked walks arranged by the local VVV office. Each is signed by coloured arrows set into the pavements, and free leaflets are available detailing the routes and pointing out interesting places along the way. The four routes are named 'A true Dutch Heritage' (red arrows), 'A town full of monuments' (blue), 'The road of freedom' (green) and 'Following in Rembrandt's footsteps' (yellow). The walk below takes in some of the more interesting places from all four routes.

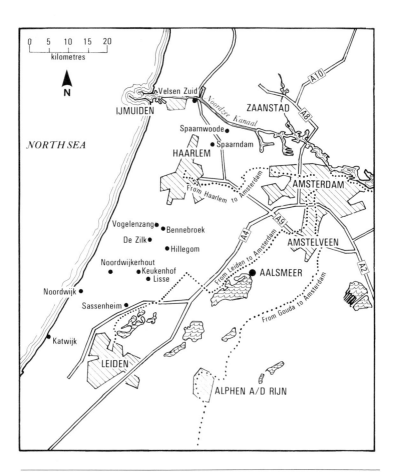

ROUTE 16   A WALK AROUND LEIDEN

Starting at the railway station (plenty of parking nearby), walk down Stationsweg and cross the outer moat into Steenstraat. At the Blauwpoortsbrug, turn right into Morsstraat, at the end of which is the seventeenth-century Morspoort, one of the two remaining town gates. Turn left through the grounds of the old Morspoort Barracks, and cross the Rembrandt bridge. Look back and you will see the old City Carpenters Yard, an attractive seventeeth-century building. Rembrandt was born in the Weddelsteeg, through which you pass before turning left into Noordeinde. Turn right into Oude Varkenmarkt and pass the Loridanshofje, a 1657 almshouse now used as a University students' residence. Cross the bridge, turn left along Groenhazengracht then right into

Rapenburg, and continue to the University building at the end of the street, where, on 20 May 1620, Rembrandt registered as a student. Here also is the entrance to the oldest botanical gardens in Europe, belonging to the University. These may be visited on payment of a small fee, and they make a pleasant diversion. Crossing the Nonnenbrug into the Kloksteeg brings you to the Jean Pesijnshofje, built on the site of the Groene Poort house. This is where John Robinson, spiritual leader of the Pilgrim Fathers, lived from 1611 to his death in 1625. A plaque on the wall of the fifteenth-century Pieterskerk commemorates the voyage of the 'Mayflower' to America in 1620.

Turning left at the church brings you to Het Gravensteen, once the County jail and now used by the University Faculty of Law. Rembrandt's studio was in the nearby Muskadelsteeg. Almost opposite Het Gravensteen, on the corner of Lokhorststraat and Schoolsteeg, is the fine gabled building of the Latin School, in use as a Grammar School until 1864.

Continue the walk up Lokhorststraat and Diefsteeg into Breestraat, where on the left a short way along the street is the restored sixteenth-century Rijnlandshuis. Returning along Breestraat, at the crossing with Maarsmansteeg and Pieterskerkchoorsteeg near the Stadhuis, can be seen the 'Blue Stone', marking the former place of executions and the spot where faulty cloth was burned before it could be marketed.

The sixteenth-century Renaissance façade of the Stadhuis was the only part of the building which could be restored following a disastrous fire in 1929. Notice the rings where visitors tethered their horses, the Town Crier's stand and, behind this, the *Rijnlandse Roede*, the standard measure of twelve Rijnlandse feet or 3.7674m. The remainder of the building is modern.

Beyond the Stadhuis, turn left towards the beautiful Koornbeursbrug or Corn Exchange bridge which was built in 1440, with twin colonnaded buildings added in 1825. Cross over and walk up Burgsteeg. On the left is the gated entrance to De Burcht, Leiden's twelfth-century citadel built on an artificial mound. Climb the steps to the top for a magnificent view over the town. From the battlements the view is even better. To the south-east is the St Pancras or Hooglandsekerk (sixteenth century), behind which, in the Hooglandse Kerkgracht, is the entrance to the former Holy Ghost orphanage, now the National Museum of Geology and Mineralogy. Continue across the drawbridge and into Hooglandse Kerksteeg, left into Haarlemmerstraat, then in a short distance left again through Donkersteeg into Hoogstraat. To the left, across the water, is the seventeeth-century Waag or Weigh-house.

Return to Haarlemmerstraat again and turn left, then right into Vrouwenkerkkoorstraat. Ahead is the dome of the seventeenth-century Marekerk, and to the left are the remains of the fourteenth-century Vrouwenkerk, the original outline of which may still be seen.

Turn left into Vrouwenkerkhof and continue into Lange Sint Agnietenstraat, where, on the right, is the sixteenth-century Boerhaave

PLACES TO VISIT IN AND AROUND LEIDEN

Burcht
Twelfth-century castle on mound in centre of town. The battlements may be climbed for view over the town.

Municipal Museum 'De Lakenhal'
Housed in old cloth-hall. Paintings by Lucas van Leyden, Rembrandt, Jan Steen and Gerard Dou; silverware and period rooms.

Windmill Museum 'De Valk'
Tall corn mill on town ramparts with original machinery, workshop and living quarters.

Pilgrim Fathers Documentation Centre
Copies of records relating to the Pilgrim Fathers.

University Botanical Gardens
Amongst oldest gardens in the world. Collections of all kinds of plants, including hot-house plants.

Rijksmuseum Boerhaave
Instruments used in mathematics, medicine and physics.

National Museum of Geology and Mineralogy
All kinds of minerals, meteorites and gemstones. Housed in an old orphanage.

Museum of Clay Tobacco Pipes
Fine collection from more than 40 countries.

'Het Plantsoen'
A park on the ramparts along the most beautiful moat in Leiden, with an aviary.

North Sea Resorts
Katwijk and Noordwijk, ideal for families. Peaceful rides and walks in the dunes.

Amsterdamse Waterleiding Duinen
Miles of wild dune-land, open to walkers only.

Keukenhof
70 acres of parkland, site of the world-famous flower show.

Cruquius Museum
Unique steam pumping station, used to drain Haarlemmermeer and now a museum showing how the polders were drained, and the effect of steam power on the struggle against the water.

Zalen, in need of restoration, where the world-famous Professor of Medicine Herman Boerhaave and his successors taught. It can be considered as the world's first teaching hospital.

Continue across Klooster, then turn right into Lange Lijsbethsteeg, passing on the left the beautifully restored Sint Elisabethgasthuis, dating from 1428 and still in use as a hospice. Across the bridge can be seen the Municipal Museum De Lakenhal, originally the Guild Hall of the Cloth-Makers, and now housing a fine collection of paintings. Past here is the

Lammermarkt, at the end of which can be seen the huge corn-mill 'De Valk', now a museum of milling.

Return to the station by crossing the bridge beyond the mill into Schuttersveld, thence left into Stationsplein.

To the north-west of Leiden is a stretch of the North Sea coast with fine sandy beaches backed by large areas of dunes. Because of the risk of erosion, access for cars and cycles is restricted.

Behind the dunes, between Leiden and Haarlem, are the bulb-fields and the famous Keukenhof gardens. The fishing village of **Katwijk** lies about 9km north-west of Leiden, and is now the centre of a popular beach resort, ideal for families with children. Permits to visit the dunes to the north of the village are obtainable from the local VVV. Among these dunes is the European Space Centre ESTEC. The dunes to the south are freely accessible but visitors must keep to the waymarked paths. Car parking is available at both ends of the esplanade. A trip worth making from Katwijk is by boat to the Kager Plassen or lakes, and the windmills, or to the Avifauna bird garden at Alphen a/d Rijn.

Just 3km north of Katwijk is **Noordwijk**, another very popular resort with an extensive beach. Both horses and cycles can be hired here, and the dunes form a natural setting for an 18-hole golf course.

To the north of the village these dunes stretch for miles, and have been planted with trees by the Staatsbosbeheer; many trails and cycle paths have been established. At the northern end of the woods is Langevelderslag, a popular holiday area with campsites, holiday houses and a youth hostel. Not far from here is a small gliding field, and at De Zilk is the entrance to the dune area known as the Amsterdamse Waterleiding Duinen. Tickets permitting entry for walkers only are obtainable at the nearby café. Once inside the gates, visitors are free to walk anywhere on the vast network of paths within this area of natural dune-land, which is the site of the water purification system for Amsterdam, and a nature reserve. The water is allowed to flow through concrete channels or leats, during which it is aerated and also allowed to filter through the sand of the dunes. The footpaths are well signed, and maps are available if required.

The area inland from the dunes, running north from Leiden, includes the villages of **Sassenheim**, **Lisse**, **Hillegom** and **Bennebroek**, which are the heart of the Dutch bulb-growing industry. From Lisse, signs direct visitors to the **Keukenhof**, site of perhaps the most famous flower show in the world. In its 70 acres of parkland are magnificent displays of flowering bulbs, shrubs and old trees, all landscaped among lakes and fountains, forming a show-case of the Dutch bulb growers and nurseries. There are also 5,000sq m of greenhouses full of all kinds of flowers, and exhibitions are mounted in the pavilions. The gardens are only open in the spring, when the bulbs are at their best, but it really is a superb way to spend a day out, wandering along the paths between the lawns, lakes and flower beds. Climb to the stage on the windmill for a breathtaking view of the surrounding bulb

De Cruquius steam pumping engine

fields, the scent of which is almost overpowering at times.

About 4km north-east of Bennebroek, alongside the N201 main road, is a distinctive round castle-like building known as 'De Cruquius'. This is one of three steam pumping stations used to drain the Haarlemmermeer between 1849 and 1852, thus creating what was at that time the largest polder in Holland. The stations continued to keep the polder drained up to 1933, when the other two stations were modernised. This caused the Cruquius to become redundant, but the whole building with its unique Cornish steam beam engine and pumping installation, has been preserved. The 144in diameter engine is the largest steam engine ever built. It operated many different pumps at once, all situated around the building. Together with scale models of the country, of wind and steam pumps, old machines and a collection of maps and drawings the whole building has been turned into a museum to show the story of the struggle against the water, and to demonstrate the effect of the age of steam on this work. In addition, the museum houses some superb examples of cast iron work.

Between De Cruquius and the village of Bennebroek is the Linnaeushof Recreation Park, with many attractions for children, whilst a short distance to the west is the village of **Vogelenzang** (bird song), site of the well-known Frans Roozen nurseries.

Haarlem
Lying a few kilometres to the north of the bulb-growing area, the city of

Haarlem is an attractive place with many old and interesting buildings. The name is from the old German word *harulahem*, meaning a settlement on a sand-hill. The city lies on the river Spaarne, and like so many old Dutch towns, it was built on a ring of canals, with ramparts on the north side of the town. These were landscaped as a park during the nineteenth century. The city is noted for its beautiful *Hofjes* or almshouses, many of which are still in use for their original purposes. The best way to see the city is by following a walking route which is described below.

ROUTE 17   A WALK AROUND HAARLEM

The walk starts at the railway station, where there is a well-signed multistorey car park, also the local VVV office.

On leaving the main entrance of the station, turn right then left along Kruis Weg, crossing Parklaan to the bridge over Nieuwe Gracht. From the bridge, looking east, may be seen some attractive old houses alongside the canal. Continuing along Kruis Weg, there is a particularly fine carved façade of an old apothecary's house on the right, followed a little later by the lovely 'Hofje van Oorschot', dating from 1770, with a wrought iron gate and garden in front of the elegant buildings. Turn right along Krocht into Ursulastraat, passing the Remonstrants Hofje (1744), and cross the wide Nassau Laan into Magdalena Straat. Half-way along, turn left into Witte Heren Straat, where can be seen the Lutheran Church and Hofje, the courtyard of which has an open-air pulpit. Nearby is the seventeenth-century Frans Loenen Hofje with an attractive little gate. At the end of the street, turn left into Zijl Straat, thence back to the Grote Markt in the centre of the town. Across the square will be seen the great church of St Bavo, built between the fourteenth and sixteenth centuries, with its tower standing high above the surroundings. Frans Hals, the artist who lived and worked in Haarlem, is buried here, and the interior is probably best known for the magnificent organ built in 1738, played upon by Mozart and still in use for recitals. In the centre of the Markt is a statue commemorating Lourens Janszoon Coster who, in the fifteenth century, founded the printing industry in Haarlem which still exists.

Other fine buildings surrounding the Markt include the old Hoofdwacht or Guard House dating from around 1650, the Vleeshal, a lovely gabled building in Dutch Renaissance style (1603), and the Vishal. Once used as markets, these are now used as museum and exhibition centres. On the opposite side of the Markt from the church is the Stadhuis. Once a thirteenth-century hunting lodge belonging to the Count of Holland, it has been in use as a town hall since the fourteenth century. Behind the building, leading off Zijl Straat, is a small alley called 't Pand leading to the Prinsenhof, once a monastic garden, and later a herb garden (1721-1865). Walk through Prinsenhof to Jacobijne Straat, then turn right to Gedempte Oude Gracht, a wide street whose name reveals that it was once an old canal, now filled in. A left and right turn brings us into Zuider Straat, followed by a left turn into Gasthuis Straat; about half way along is the former Kloveniersdoelen, on the right at No 32. This sixteenth-century building was once the headquarters of the local militia. The inner courtyard, through the arched gateway may be visited during weekdays. In Barrevoete Straat, a short distance along on the right, is the 'Hofje van Loo', dating back to the fifteenth century. The typical courtyard appearance has been lost because one row of houses was demolished when the street was widened in the nineteenth century.

Return to Gasthuis Straat, turn right into what now becomes Tuchthuisstraat. Continue past the Brouwershofje, along Lange Anna Straat to the Hofje van Guurtje de Waal then turn left along Doel Straat to the junction with Gier Straat and Grote Hout Straat. On the right is the Proveniershuis, built in 1591. The almshouses around the courtyard date from 1700, and make up the largest of the *Hofjes* in Haarlem.

Walk down Grote Hout Straat to the bank of the canal called Raamsingel, turn left along Gasthuis Vest then left into Groot Heiligland. On the right are some fifteenth-century *huisjes* (cottages) which belonged to the St Elisabeth Gasthuis or hospital, which was formerly situated nearby. Opposite them, in an old almshouse dated 1608, is housed the world-renowned Frans Hals Museum, containing a selection of works by the Haarlem masters including paintings by Frans Hals himself, all displayed in period settings.

By cutting through into the parallel street known as Klein Heiligland, and turning right, across into Franke Straat, right along Anegang then left again into Warmoesstraat, the walk passes another *hofje*, 'In den groenen tuijn', originally built in 1614. At the end of the street, turn right into Oude Groenmarkt and continue along Dam Straat to the river, where stands De Waag or Weigh-house. Built in 1598, goods were weighed here after being brought by boat along the River Spaarne. Nearby, fronting on to the river bank, is Teylers Museum, the oldest museum in the Netherlands, built as the result of a bequest by Pieter Teyler van der Hulst, a cloth and silk merchant and manufacturer who died in 1778. Devoted to both the Arts and Sciences, it has exceptionally fine collections of paintings and old scientific instruments.

Spanning the river nearby is the picturesque Gravenstenenbrug, a lifting bridge which leads across to Wijdesteeg, and thence to Spaarnwouderstraat. Turn left, and in about 500m the only surviving city gate, the Amsterdamse Poort, can be seen, standing on an island between busy roads. Returning to the museum, continue past the river bridge to Bakenesser Gracht, then turn left along the canal bank past the fourteenth-century Hofje van Bakenes, continuing along to Groene Buurt on the left and into the Begijnhof. The Walloon Church, originally a fourteenth-century nunnery, is here, and nearby in the Goudsmidspleintje is the seventeenth-century Goudsmidskamer or Guildhall of the Haarlem gold and silver-smiths.

The walk continues back along Jansstraat and Jansweg, passing the elegant Hofje van Staats (1730), and ends back at the station, which is itself a listed building dating from 1908.

To the west of the city are the 'garden suburbs' of Bloemendaal and Aerdenhout, with fine country houses, parks and gardens, while beyond them, towards the sea coast, is the National Park 'De Kennemer Duinen', an area of surprisingly hilly dunes in which a whole day can easily be spent walking and cycling. Within the park is a campsite, and a number of car parks are provided at the entrances along the road from Haarlem to the coast. Where this road reaches the beach approaches, it turns south past the famous Zandvoort motor racing circuit to the popular holiday resort of **Zandvoort**. The main beach area along the promenade is constantly patrolled, and quieter beaches can be found further away.

To the north of the Dune Reserve are the great sea locks at **IJmuiden**, at the entrance to the North Sea Canal which links the sea with the port of Amsterdam. Originally opened on 1 November 1876, it was soon realised that the locks were too small, so the size of the canal and of the locks was increased in 1896 and again in 1930, when the great lock, more than 1,300ft long, 160ft wide and 50ft deep, was opened. It is quite an experience to see the lock complex at night, with all the lights of the waterway installations, backed by the lurid flames from the steel works at Hoogovens, across the water.

The fishing harbour at IJmuiden serves as a base for trawlers from many other ports, and from the nearby beaches visitors can watch the constant flow of shipping negotiating the lock entrance.

Nearby **Velsen**, with numerous pleasant walks, and estates open to the public, is also the location of the Velsen road tunnel under the North Sea Canal. (Note: tunnel forbidden to cyclists.)

To the east of the motorway leading to the tunnel is the recreation area of Spaarnwoude, with a number of car parks, a cycle track, canoe courses and a 27-hole golf course. There is also a camp site.

It is possible to drive alongside the River Spaarne from Haarlem to the village of **Spaarndam**, a typical North Holland village of green and white painted houses with old wooden gables, built along the dyke. Here too is the little statue of Hans Brinker, the boy of whom legend says, quite untruthfully, put his thumb in a hole in the dyke to prevent a flood. The river opens into a lovely lake, the 'Mooie Nel', with an excellent marina and water sports facilities.

Haarlem makes a good base for visiting Amsterdam. It is not recommended to take a cycle into Amsterdam; lock it securely in a guarded *Rijwielstalling* somewhere outside the city, and go in by train. Never leave a cycle unattended, even if locked.

Amsterdam

The city with the greatest number of listed buildings in Europe, Amsterdam is the capital of the Netherlands. There are over 7,000 houses and other buildings under the care of the Dutch equivalent to the English National Trust. The city was built around the famous network of canals, dug in the early seventeeth century and encircling the old medieval town whose name means the 'Dam on the Amstel', the river upon which it was built.

The city has a unique atmosphere, with Dam square as the focal point. The Royal Palace is situated on one side, and the city spreads out over a spider's web pattern of canals, roads and bridges. From the Dam radiate some of the famous narrow shopping streets, many of which are now pedestrianised. There are many opportunities for the visitor to buy souvenirs of the city, and at several points it is possible to board a boat for a tour of the canals. It is even possible to rent a 'Canal-Bike' and pedal yourself around the city's waterways.

Undoubtedly the best way to see many of the sights of the city is to take one of the guided tours by canal boat. Details of these may be obtained from the VVV office in Stationsplein, in front of Centraal Station. After that, other sightseeing suggestions include a walk through the city to the Rijksmuseum, thence either a further walk or return to Stationsplein by tram, bus or Metro. Details of the public transport system are available from the Information Office opposite Centraal Station.

ROUTE 18   A WALK IN AMSTERDAM

Starting from Centraal Station, cross from the tram and bus station

The Begijnhof, Amsterdam

outside and walk down the wide street across the harbour basin towards the city. This leads down Damrak, which takes you to Dam square. Any of the narrow streets to the right from Damrak lead into Nieuwendijk, one of the pedestrian shopping streets. Facing on to the Dam is the Royal Palace, originally built in the seventeenth century as the Town Hall. In the centre of the square is the National Monument to victims of World War II. Nearby is the Nieuwe Kerk dating from 1400, used for Royal coronations since 1815. The pear-drop shaped towers of the Main Post Office may also be seen. Continue beyond the Dam along Kalverstraat, another pedestrianised shopping street, and look on the right about two-thirds of the way down for an alley leading to a magnificent gateway (sixteenth century) decorated with the City Coat of Arms. This is the entrance to 92 Kalverstraat, formerly an orphanage. Pass through the arch into what is now the Amsterdam Historical Museum, where there is also a good restaurant. Almost opposite is a small alley now roofed over with glass. This is the Schuttersgalerij, the walls of which are lined with enormous paintings of seventeenth-century marksmen. Through here, and another narrow passage, leads to what must be one of the surprises of the city — a peaceful and secluded close with trees and flower beds, surrounded by beautiful houses dating originally from the fourteenth and fifteenth centuries. This was the Begijnhof, for centuries a home for Lay Sisters, where can now be found the 'English Church', a Presbyterian church granted to the English community in the seventeenth century. Opposite this building is a very small Roman Catholic church dating back to 1671, and used as a clandestine church until 1795. Tucked into a corner is Amsterdam's oldest surviving house, of wood, built in 1475.

From the Begijnhof, there is an exit directly into the street called Spui, opposite the Maagdenhuis, the main building of the University of Amsterdam. Walk past here to Singel, once the outer defence line of the city. Turn left then right via Koningsplein to cross Herengracht, a lovely canal lined with exceptionally fine houses. Walk alongside the Herengracht to Nieuwe Spiegelstraat, the 'antiques street' of Amsterdam, at the far end of which will be seen the large building housing the Rijksmuseum. Although especially noted for the world-famous painting by Rembrandt, the 'Night Watch', there is much, much more of interest than that to be seen, and to do justice to all the collections one should obtain a guide book in English from the museum bookshop.

A wide central archway runs through the centre of the building, leading into Museumplein, where the Van Gogh Museum, and the Stedelijk or Municipal Museum are situated, whilst at the far end is the renowned Concertgebouw or Concert Hall.

From the neighbourhood of the Rijksmuseum, either a boat trip, or a return to Centraal Station by bus or tram can be made. Alternatively, the walk may be continued by returning to the waterside of Singel Gracht, turning left along Stadhouders Kade, thence across the bridge to Leidseplein. Follow Leidsestraat crossing three more of the main canals,

A 'canal-bike' in Amsterdam

PLACES TO VISIT IN AND AROUND AMSTERDAM

Royal Palace
In the centre of the city, from where the new monarch is proclaimed.

Historical Museum
In former City Orphanage. Contains paintings, prints, and objects relating to the city's history. Magnificent 'Schutters Gallery' leading from the museum, with wall paintings.

Begijnhof
Beautiful peaceful garden surrounded by old houses, behind Historical Museum. English Church and tiny Roman Catholic church (formerly clandestine), also Amsterdam's oldest house.

Rijksmuseum
World famous, particularly for Rembrandt paintings, notably the 'Night Watch'. Also many galleries devoted to applied arts, etc.

Rembrandthuis
Superb collection of etchings and drawings by the master, who lived here.

Joods Historisch Museum
Paintings and objects illustrating the history of the Jews in Amsterdam.

Rijksmuseum Vincent van Gogh
A fine collection of paintings and drawings by the artist and his contemporaries.

Anne Frank House
The hiding place of Anne Frank and her family 1942-4. Changing exhibitions concerning World War II.

Stedelijk Museum
Municipal museum of modern art, from 1850 to the present day. The main accent is on art since 1950.

Canal Tours
Various tours along the city canals and waterways, including the harbour, all with commentaries in various languages.

Diamond Cutting
A number of diamond cutting and polishing factories arrange guided tours. One such is the Amsterdam Diamond Centre, at 1 Rokin.

Schiphol
'Aviodome' National Aeronautical Museum has exhibits of air and space travel, past, present and future.

Aalsmeer
Flower auction and historical gardens.

Amsterdamse Bos
Pleasant area for walking and cycling, and other recreation facilities. Electric Tram museum with working tram line.

eventually coming back to Koningsplein. Turn right past the flower market to Muntplein and the Munt Toren. Walk along Nieuwe Doelenstraat on the other side of the water, then along Kloveniersburgwal to the Nieuwmarkt, where you will see the Waag or Weigh-house. Built in 1448 as a city gate, it was converted into a weigh-house in 1617 to weigh cannons made nearby. The upper room was used by various guilds, and Rembrandt painted the famous 'Anatomy Lesson' here. The building now houses the Jewish Historical Museum.

The red light district, between Nieuwmarkt and Warmoesstraat to the west is not recommended to those who may be offended, and especially at night this area and the surroundings of Centraal Station should be avoided. The best way to return to Centraal Station from Nieuwmarkt is by Metro.

There are, of course, many other aspects of the city of immense interest, such as Anne Frank's house at No 263 Prinsengracht. This is the house with a 'back house' behind it, which was the home of the Frank family from 1942-4, when they were betrayed and deported; only Anne's father survived. The house is maintained by the Anne Frank foundation, who have mounted an exhibition to record German persecution as a warning to others that this must never be allowed to happen again. We recommend a visit to the local VVV, who publish a series of leaflets describing walks relating to various aspects of the city, as well as much other information to help the visitor. Almost hidden from the main city by the Centraal Station building is the busy harbour complex located on the River IJ, which separates the south of the city from the northern suburbs. Two vehicle tunnels cross the IJ, the Coentunnel to the west and the IJ tunnel to the east of the station, in addition to which there are free ferries for foot passengers and cyclists running from behind the station buildings.

To the south-west of the city lies the Amsterdamse Bos, claimed to be the largest landscaped park in the Netherlands. Laid out in the 1930s to give work to the unemployed, the area includes attractive walks and cycle rides through the woods, a children's farm, varied sporting facilities, and a municipal campsite. An old 'museum tram-line', operated by a voluntary society, runs along the eastern side of the Amsterdamse Bos.

Separated from the Bos by a road and drainage canal is the great international airport of **Schiphol**, one of the earliest such airports and now developed into one of the most modern. Situated in the Haarlemmermeer polder, the name Schiphol recalls the days when this was an inland sea, and westerly gales blew ships on to the northern shore to be wrecked in the 'ship hole'. Near the main entrance to the airport, is a hemispherical aluminium building, the 'Aviodome', where exhibits portraying the history of aviation, together with many models and actual historical aircraft and spacecraft, can be seen.

Not far to the south of Schiphol airport is, by way of contrast, the town of **Aalsmeer**, in the centre of the Dutch flower-growing industry. With about 70 acres of greenhouses, more than 3,000 growers send their flowers and plants to be auctioned daily, before being sent all over the world. Visitors can, between 7.30-11am, sit in on the unique flower auctions (they are best visited as early as possible), and also visit the Historical Garden in the nearby town.

7 NORTH OF THE NORTH SEA CANAL

The North Sea Canal, stretching from IJmuiden to Amsterdam, cuts the Province of North Holland in two, and can be crossed by tunnel (for cars and trains) or by ferry. The only road bridge is that at Schellingwoude, across the eastern end of Amsterdam harbour.

North of the canal, the city of Amsterdam extends its boundaries virtually without a break until it meets the boundaries of Zaanstad, an industrial complex along the river Zaan which includes the towns and villages of Zaandam, Koog a/d Zaan and Zaandijk. To the east is the polder area of Waterland, and the picturesque villages of Monnickendam, Edam, Volendam and Marken, together with the expanding old town of Purmerend. The western part contains the extensive North Holland Dune Reserve and the well-known old town of Alkmaar, east of which lie the polders of Schermer and Beemster, first drained in the early seventeenth century. Further north are more bulbfields, dunes and holiday resorts extending to the naval base at Den Helder. The eastern boundary of the area is the former Zuiderzee coast, along which are to be found the old West Frisian towns of Medemblik, Enkhuizen and Hoorn. From the former island of Wieringen, in the north east corner of the province, at Den Oever, the great Afsluitdijk or 'enclosing dyke' runs 32km across the water to the other side of the IJsselmeer.

Alkmaar

This busy town originally owed its importance to its proximity to Egmond, seat of the Counts of Holland. The town received its first charter in 1254, and with the reclamation of the surrounding polders in the late seventeenth century its importance increased. The cheese market for which Alkmaar is famous is more than 350 years old. The exceptionally fine Weigh House, originally built as a chapel in the fourteenth century, was converted to its present use in the sixteenth century, and is still used during the traditional Friday Market; it also houses the local VVV and an interesting Cheese Museum. The tower of the building dates from 1595 and contains an interesting clock with jousting horsemen and a trumpeter. The town, which has much of interest, is well worth exploring.

ROUTE 19   A WALK ROUND ALKMAAR

Starting from the VVV office in De Waag, cross over the Bathbrug, a bridge named after the English town of Bath with which Alkmaar is twinned, and walk to the next bridge on the left. From the bridge turn and look to the right, where there is a sixteenth-century house with a cannonball embedded in the front wall, and overhanging upper floors. The cannonball dates from the Spanish siege of 1573. Return towards the Bathbrug but before crossing the bridge turn left along the Mient past some houses with fine gables. At No 23 the gable is decorated with the arms of

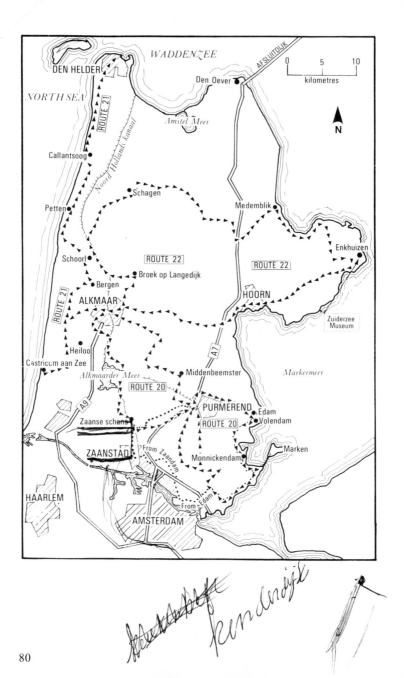

Waag
Cheese museum in the old weigh-house contains antique cheese-making implements. Cheese market on Fridays.

Grote Kerk (St Lawrence)
Beautifully preserved fifteenth-century church with impressive interior. Two fine organs on which recitals are given in summer.

Town Hall
Fine Council Chamber and Mayoral rooms containing antique furniture.

Alkmaar, but with a difference! The owner was in dispute with the City Council, so deliberately reversed the lions in the coat of arms. The walk is continued past the Fish Market (1591) to the square by St Janskerk founded in the fifteenth century. Look down the Verdronkenoord canal, and at the far end may be seen the Accijnstoren or Excise Tower. Built in 1622, and moved to its present position in 1924, it now houses the Harbourmaster's office, and serves as a reminder that although Alkmaar, like so many Dutch towns, is situated away from the sea, it still handles much waterborne trade through the canals and other waterways.

Turn back to the church, originally built by the Knights of Malta. It was rebuilt after a fire in 1760, and contains a fine Müller organ. Pass the church, cross over the street named Laat and walk down the road to the Oude Gracht, cross the bridge and turn left to look at the attractively-restored Wildemanshofje, built in 1714 for elderly ladies of both Catholic and Protestant faiths.

Return across the bridge and turn left. Walk along Oude Gracht, admiring the old buildings with their gables. The style of the gable indicates the age of the building, triangular from the sixteenth century, stepped from seventeenth century and bell-shaped from the eighteenth century. At the end of Oude Gracht is the junction with Koorstraat to the right and Ritsevoort to the left. Along Ritsevoort, immediately on the right is another hofje, the Hofje van Splinter, whilst at the end of the road is Molen van Piet, a windmill built on the ramparts in 1769 and still in use as a flour mill.

Back along Koorstraat, on the left, is the Grote Kerk or Church of St Lawrence, a most beautiful building from between 1470 and 1516. It contains two organs, a large one from the seventeenth century, and a small one dating from the early sixteenth century, one of the oldest still in regular use. From the east front of the church, turn down Langestraat to the Town Hall or Stadhuis, parts of which date back to the late fifteenth and early sixteenth centuries, and whose entrance has a fine double stairway. Just past the Town Hall, turn left and walk through to Nieuwesloot, where opposite, on the corner, is the Huis van Achten, a home since 1656 for eight old men, both Catholic and Protestant. Next to this is the Hof van Sonoy, named after Diedrick Sonoy, Lieutenant-Governor under the Prince of Orange, who lived here for a number of years. Later, it came into the possession of the Dutch Reformed Church, who still own the property. There is now a restaurant in the house. Straight ahead can be seen the Waag, and Cheese Market, the starting and finishing point of the walk.

The polder landscape to the south and east of Alkmaar provides a very pleasant area for exploring, either by car or, if you have the time, by bicycle.

ROUTE 20   THE SEVENTEENTH-CENTURY POLDERS AND WATERLAND

The Beemster, Purmer, Wormer and Schermer lakes were drained by the use of windmills between 1612 and 1635, and the polder landscape thus created is typically what visitors imagine to be representative of Holland. However, despite the flat landscape, the distant views and the quality of light above the large areas of water present a great attraction.

The route leaves Alkmaar by the road to the south towards Heiloo and Castricum. In about 3km (signpost 299) turn left towards the hamlet of **Boekel** which lies on the far side of the motorway A9. On reaching the Noord Hollands Kanaal, turn right and in about 2km cross the canal by ferry, continuing alongside the Alkmaardermeer for 3km before turning right on the road to **Markenbinnen** and **Zaanstad**. At this junction (signpost 560) is a car park and a very pleasant picnic area by the lake. Continue past Markenbinnen, following signs to **Zaandijk** and **Zaanse Schans**. Cyclists can turn left 1km after leaving Markenbinnen, cross on the ferry to Oost Knollendam, then follow the river Zaan through Wormer to Zaanse Schans.

The Zaanse Schans is a village museum of buildings from the Zaan area dating from around 1700, re-erected together on an attractive site on the river. Many of the old houses are actually lived in, and some are open to the public. In addition there are several different types of windmill typical of the area, including a sawmill, a paint-mill, a mustard mill, and an oil-seed mill. There are also old shops, including the original shop opened in Zaandam by Albert Heijn, forerunner of a country-wide chain of food supermarkets bearing the same name. In the neighbourhood, other places of interest include the windmill museum at Koog aan de Zaan and the Tsaar Peterhuisje in Zaandam.

On leaving Zaanse Schans, take the road leading east to the A7 main road to **Purmerend**. Cyclists may take the parallel road to the north, turning left at signpost 10726. The town of Purmerend is a busy and expanding community with an old centre. The Koepelkerk church is now used as a cultural centre, and the Renaissance Town Hall is the location of the Historical Museum. This is open when the Cheese Market is being held, on Thursdays; it is no longer held in nearby Edam. There is plenty of car parking in the town.

The Town Hall, Edam

From Purmerend, take the road eastwards to **Edam**. Parking discs are required in the town, so park just outside. When approaching from Purmerend, turn left along the N247 road (direction of Hoorn) and the carpark is in the first road on the left. Edam was formerly a settlement of farmers and fishermen, receiving city rights in 1357. It became an important shipbuilding centre, and when the polders began to be created in the sixteenth century, the foundations for a flourishing cheese trade were laid. From 1573 to 1922 a cheese market was held weekly, and much of the cheese produced in the area today is stored and matured in the warehouses in the town. There are some lovely old houses, some with surprisingly large gardens with elegant 'summer-houses' by the water's edge. The town hall dates from the eighteenth century, and the square in front of the building is actually a stone-covered bridge built across the locks. In Edam's oldest house (1530), now a museum, is a 'floating cellar', and the story goes that the retired sea-captain who built the house wanted to spend the rest of his life at sea! Walk along Spui and look at the Speeltoren, all that is left of the fifteenth-century Onze Lieve Vrouwe church. It now houses the local VVV office and also one of the oldest carillons in North Holland, dating back to 1561. Return to Spui and walk past the eighteenth-century Waag and cheese market. Opposite here is a shop specialising in beautiful costume dolls, whose owner is happy for visitors to look around. In addition to dolls, the shop sells craft objects such as pottery and silverware. Continue alongside the water along Matthijs Tinxgracht to the Grote Kerk or St

Nicholas Church, with its 30 early seventeenth-century stained glass windows. On the other side of the water, on J.C. Brouwersgracht, is the Proveniershuis, built for a nursing order founded in 1555, and now used as an almshouse for both young and old.

From Edam, a diversion may be made to the old fishing port of **Volendam**, home of the well-known (and incorrectly-named) 'Dutch National Costume'. It is now very commercialised and always over-crowded, and many other places merit more time.

Continue south along the road N247 from Edam to the small 600-year-old town of **Monnickendam**; car parking is possible near the VVV office near the edge of the town. The original method of smoking eels is still carried out, this being one of the most important of the town's industries, now supplemented by watersports. Once again, many old buildings exist, some with new uses. The Speeltoren houses an archaeological museum, and the seventeenth-century Waag or Weigh House, is now a restaurant. Also worth a visit is the Grote or St Nicolaaskerk, built in the fifteenth century. A number of traditional ships are moored in the Inner Harbour, which is surrounded by Eel Smoke Houses. Middendam is the spot where Frisian monks founded the town in the twelfth century, and the nearby locks were restored in 1968.

To the south is the area known as Waterland, a typical polder landscape stretching to the outskirts of Amsterdam. From Monnickendam, the coast road may be taken south along the dyke towards Uitdam, diverting to visit **Marken**. Once an island, it was only connected to the mainland in 1957 by a dyke and road, and for this reason, it still retains much of its old character. The islanders are strictly Protestant and tend to intermarry. It is possible to see many of them wearing traditional dress, which is much more attractive than that of Volendam, but visitors with cameras are not always welcome, particularly on Sundays. Since the opening of the road, a museum has been created in a traditional Marken house where the old way of life can be seen, together with exhibits showing the history of the former island from the thirteenth century to the present day.

On returning from Marken to the mainland, turn south again passing through typical country landscape of the Waterland district. The road is narrow and winding, with a few parking places alongside, from which the dyke may be climbed to look out over the former Zuiderzee, now Lake IJssel. As the road continues towards Durgerdam, a number of little lakes on the right show where the sea broke through in former times. Many of these lakes are now nature reserves, and the whole of the Waterland is a conservation area. At about 2km beyond the parking place on the Kinselmeer, turn right towards the village of **Ransdorp** with Waterland houses, often made of wood and painted green and white. Continue along narrow roads to **Zunderdorp**, another very small protected village, then right to **Broek in Waterland**. Here is a cheese dairy which may be visited by appointment, a clog-maker, and again many picturesque old houses.

From Broek, follow the main road N247 in the direction of Amsterdam, until the junction with the road alongside the Noord Hollands Kanaal is reached. From here a diversion may be made to visit 'Het Twiske', a country park with footpaths, cycle paths and plenty of opportunities for watersports of all kinds. From the road junction, cross the canal by ferry and follow signs for Het Twiske via Landsmeer and Den Ilp.

The return to Alkmaar may be made by taking either the main road alongside the canal, or the road through Den Ilp and Purmerland to the outskirts of Purmerend, then along the northern side of the Noord Hollands Kanaal for about 3km, and turn right towards **Middenbeemster**. In the village turn left towards **De Rijp**. Here, follow signs 'Doorgaand Verkeer' and Graft, until signs for the car park are seen.

Walk into the pleasant little village with its interesting Town Hall, and Weigh House. The old house, "'t Wapen van Munster', is now a pancake restaurant and coffee house, and the whole place is an attractive polder village.

Continue to **Graft**, and turn right, following the winding road to **Grootschermer**, where, unexpectedly for such a small place, you will see a fine old Town Hall dated 1652. The road carries on to Schermerhorn, but on reaching the small canal before the main road, turn immediately left along the minor road on the south side of the water. Park by the three windmills, the centre one of which is a museum showing how the polder was drained and kept dry. The mills were built in 1634 and have been beautifully restored and maintained.

The road is followed back to Alkmaar, with views across the polders with windmills to be seen in the distance in many directions.

ROUTE 21   THE COASTAL ROAD TO DEN HELDER

The town of Alkmaar makes an excellent base for exploring the whole of this area. Leave the town by the road to Egmond, joining the coast road at Egmond a/d Hoef. Turn south, and at Bakkum take the road towards **Castricum aan Zee**. About 1km along this road is a parking area and Visitor's Centre, where maps and admission tickets to the Dune Reserve may be obtained. From this point many paths may be followed through the high dunes and woodland which stretch for 19km from Wijk aan Zee in the south to Bergen aan Zee in the north. Cycles may be hired in Castricum, and all paths are waymarked.

The dunes are Holland's natural defence against the sea, and at only one point in the whole of this coastline is there a man-made dyke. Beyond the dunes are family holiday resorts with miles of sandy beaches, most of which have been developed from farming and fishing villages.

After visiting the Dune Reserve, return via the coast road north to the village of **Bergen**, inland from Bergen aan Zee. It is particularly popular with artists, who regularly hold open-air exhibitions at which their work is offered for sale. Here also is an old seventeenth-century step-gabled house converted into a folk-lore museum with period rooms and old costumes, and the remains of a medieval church. Follow the winding road north from Bergen towards **Schoorl**, passing country houses with attractive gardens. On the outskirts of Schoorl is a Visitor's Centre explaining the work of the Staatsbosbeheer or Forestry Commission who control the dunes in this area. These contain particularly fine walks, giving spectacular views inland from the highest points, especially in the bulb season.

The road bears towards the coast, and at the north end of the dunes, at **Camperduin**, begins a long sea dyke known as the 'Hondsbosse Zeewering'. In 1421 the villages of Camperduin and Petten were washed away, and the local population began building a dyke. In 1780 the sea broke through again, so a new dyke was made. **Petten**, at the north end of the Hondsbosse Zeewering, now a holiday resort, has been rebuilt four times, the latest occasion being in 1947, having been completely destroyed by the Germans during World War II. The dyke has also been raised several times, and although it held during the flood disaster in 1953, it was decided to commence increasing the height again in 1977 to bring the total height above mean sea level to 11.5m, in order to reduce the risk of such a disaster happening again. The history of the dyke and the neighbourhood can be seen during the summer months in a free exhibition entitled *De Dijk te Kijk* ('The dyke on show').

To the north of Petten, in the dunes, is the Dutch Alternative Energy

PLACES TO VISIT ALONG THE
COASTAL ROAD AND DEN
HELDER

Noordhollands Dune Reserve

The whole area from Wijk aan Zee to Schoorl Forestry district is a protected area for breeding and migratory birds. The dunes are freely accessible but tickets are necessary.

Petten

Exhibition 'de Dijk te Kijk' of the history of the sea defences in this area. Good beaches at Petten, also sea angling.

Den Helder

Marine museum shows the history of the Royal Dutch Navy from 1813 to the present day. Many ship and plane models, weapons, uniforms, nautical instruments, etc.

Dorus Rijkers museum depicts all aspects of life-saving equipment and documents, news cuttings, etc.

Centre, where research on nuclear, wind and sun energy is carried out, and the nearby nature reserve of Zwanenwater has one of the largest breeding colonies of spoonbills in Europe, together with a rich abundance of flora and fauna.

The road from Petten runs through Callantsoog, thence close under the dunes past access roads to a number of beaches, eventually coming to **Den Helder**. This is the main Dutch naval base, called by Napoleon the 'Gibraltar of the North'. It is also the departure point for the ferries to Texel, largest of the Wadden Islands. Several holiday parks and camp sites are to be found in the area, with numerous hotels. Foot and cycle paths wind through the Donkere Duinen nature reserve on the edge of the town, which itself has two interesting museums, namely the Marine museum on the Hoofdgracht near the Texel Ferry landing stage, housed in a former dockyard store, and the Dorus Rijkers Lifesaving Institution museum, named after a famous local lifeboatman.

ROUTE 22   THE OLD NORTH - AROUND THE WESTFRIESDIJK

Before the long dyke at Petten, on the coast, was built in the fifteenth century, West Friesland was separated from the dunes by the waters of the Zijpe, and bordered on the south by the Schermer and Beemster lakes. To the east was the Zuiderzee, so in 1300 West Friesland was quite isolated. To protect the area from the sea, a dyke had to be built, and almost the whole length of it may be followed. Some roads follow the line of other, secondary dykes which can be seen on old maps. In some cases, these are very narrow single-track roads, so care is needed. The route takes in the old towns of Schagen, Medemblik, Enkhuizen and Hoorn.

Leave Alkmaar along the minor road through Sint Pancras towards **Broek op Langedijk**, where there is a unique museum combined with the world's oldest vegetable auction, established in 1887. Called the Broekerveiling it includes waymarked walks around the museum area, and a guidebook is available in excellent English.

From Broekerveiling, travel west to **Koedijk**, then turn north alongside the Noord Hollands Kanaal to **Schoorldam**. Here, take the dyke road north to **Krabbendam**, then along a narrow winding road to **Sint Maarten**. Away to the left may be seen the mills used to drain the Zijpe and Haze polders, while to the right are small ponds made when the sea broke through hundreds of years ago. Leave the dyke road at Sint Maarten and drive east to **Schagen**, famous for its summer folklore market and festivals.

From here, the road along the Kanaal Schagen-Kolhorn runs parallel to the old sea dyke. **Kolhorn** is an old whaling port, now completely surrounded by polder. Follow the road to where it crosses the Groet Kanaal, then turn right along the top of the dyke to the main road at signpost 511. Here, cross over the main road and turn right, still along the dyke, then left at the next junction (signpost 3489). Continue for about 5km, then turn right again to **Abbekerk**, through the village, and continue to cross the motorway by a bridge on the left, thence left and right following signs to **Twisk**, a picturesque village with a fourteenth-century church and fine East India merchants' houses.

Continue through Opperdoes to **Medemblik**, the smallest and oldest town in West Friesland. Although small, the town is most attractive. Note the little cottages along Heere-steeg, the orphanage gateway in Torenstraat, and old buildings in Nieuwstraat, including the Weigh House at one end and the Town Hall at the other. Look at the East Harbour, beyond which is Kasteel Radboud, first recorded in the thirteenth century, and now open to visitors.

Medemblik is one terminus of the Hoorn-Medemblik Steam Train, operated as a museum train.

The dyke enclosing the Wieringermeer Polder, first of the IJsselmeer Polders, stretches away in the distance to the north of the town.

From Medemblik, take the coast road south towards Wervershoof. After about 1km the old steam pumping station, 'De Vier Noorder Koggen', now a fascinating museum devoted to steam engines and machinery, is passed on the right.

From Wervershoof, keep to the dyke road along the coast towards the hamlets of Geuzenbuurt and Broekoord. After passing another small pumping station (now a museum) on the left, the site of the experimental Andijk Polder, constructed to test the feasibility of the schemes for closing the Zuiderzee is reached. The dyke road may be followed all the way to **Enkhuizen**, but the main road through Andijk is more convenient.

Enkhuizen was once a very prosperous sea port, evidenced by houses built by East India Company merchants. Here, too, is the award-winning Zuiderzee museum. More than one day is needed to see Enkhuizen properly, as the museum alone can take a whole day. The Open-air Museum should, perhaps, be visited first. On approaching the town, follow

Broek op Langedijk

Broekerveiling vegetable auction exhibition. An unusual insight into nineteenth-century marketing in this area.

Schagen

Folklore market in summer.

Medemblik

Kasteel Radboud, a thirteenth-century castle.
The northern terminus of the Hoorn-Medemblik steam railway.
Steam Museum in old pumping station, 'de Vier Noorder Koggen'.

Enkhuizen

Zuiderzee Museum, an outstanding museum with indoor and outdoor sections. Wapen Museum (weapons) in the old town prison, and Waag-Museum (municipal museum). Sprookjeswonderland — Fairyland — park for children.

Hoorn

Westfriesmuseum in the Staten College. De Waag, now a good restaurant. Terminus and workshops of the Steam Train museum.

signs for **Zuiderzee Museum** and **Lelystad**. These lead you to a free car park where tickets can be bought for the museum. A ferry then takes visitors direct to the *Buiten-Museum*, giving an excellent view of the town en route. The tickets cover the return ferry journey and admission to the *Binnen-Museum*, or indoor part, located in the town. After touring the outdoor section, walk through the old town to the station, where the ferry can be picked up. However, take care to note the time of the last ferry. If a longer time is to be spent in the town, it may be better to park by the railway station, and take the ferry from there to the museum.

The Zuiderzee Museum really is a must for visitors, and if there is only time either for the museum or the town, then the museum takes precedence. Opened in 1950, and expanded ever since, it was established to study and show the everyday life and work of the inhabitants of the Zuiderzee region as it was before the Afsluitdijk was built. Fishing, shipping and many associated trades were badly affected when the dyke was closed, so it was felt that as much as possible should be preserved. To do this, a complete Zuiderzee town has been recreated in great detail, using actual buildings and materials brought here from their original locations and re-erected. Interiors have been furnished or equipped as workshops and other such premises, providing a mirror of life as it was from 1880 to 1932. First thought of in 1942, the indoor section was opened in 1950, and in 1983, just fifty years after the closing of the Afsluitdijk, the Outdoor Museum opened to the public. The vision and effort involved were rewarded by the gaining of the European Museum of the Year Award in 1984.

The open air section of the Zuiderzee Museum, Enkhuizen

ROUTE 22A   A WALK IN ENKHUIZEN

Starting at the railway station in the town, the quay immediately to the south is the point of departure for ferries to Stavoren, Urk and Medemblik in the summer. Walk around the Old Harbour, on the town side past the Visafslag (fish auction), from where the old locks may be seen. The grassed area was originally used for drying nets. Nearby is the large Drommedaris tower, or fortified water-gate.

Cross the bridge by the tower, and follow the canal towards the Zuiderkerk, whose tall and elegant tower forms a distinctive landmark. With the church on the left, cross the end of the canal towards the Stadhuis, and the Wapenmuseum (museum of weapons), formerly the old prison from 1686. Beyond these buildings, across the bridge, is the little Staverse Poortje, and to the right along Wierdijk, which dates from 1567, is the entrance to the Zuider-Zee Binnenmuseum. The building, known as the Peperhuis (1625) was formerly the head office in Enkhuizen of the East India Company. The museum includes ship models, interiors from old houses, collections of costumes, fully-equipped workshops from former Zuiderzee villages and towns, and a collection of boats of various types, which are now under cover to preserve them.

Walk back to the Zuiderkerk, turn right and you reach the Waag, now the Municipal Museum. A left turn leads to the pedestrian precinct, where, on the right, is the Westerkerk or Gomarus Church, commenced in 1472, which has a wooden belfry. Continue along Westerstraat to the Koepoort, once a land-gate. Turn right and walk along the ramparts to the other gates, the Boerenboom and the Oudegouwsboom, then return along the canals through the town to Westerstraat, after which a left and right turn leads back to the Old Harbour and the railway station. The yacht harbours are very busy, and old traditional sailing vessels can be hired for sailing holidays.

On leaving Enkhuizen, take the road west to **Bovenkarspel**, then left through Broekerhaven to the main Enkhuizen-Hoorn road. If time allows, take the narrow dyke road through **Oosterleek** and **Schellinkhout** to Hoorn, passing old dyke houses built below the embankment. Otherwise, follow the main road into Hoorn. There are plenty of car parks around the edge of the town, in which there is much to see.

Hoorn is another town which in former times was of world-wide importance through its connections with the East India Company, yet has lost much of its influence through the enclosing of the Zuiderzee. However, the town is enhanced by magnificent buildings beautifully restored, particularly those dwellings and warehouses along Veermanskade, near the inner harbour. Here you will also see the Hoofdtoren or Gunpowder Tower, probably the most familiar landmark for visitors. Until the end of the seventeenth century, Hoorn was noted as a port for herring fishery, and records exist of net-making here in the fifteenth century. Cape Horn was so-named by the navigator Willem Schouten, a native of Hoorn. In the town centre is the fine Staten-College or Council House, built in 1632 as the meeting place of delegates from the seven member towns of North Holland north of the river IJ, namely Alkmaar, Hoorn, Enkhuizen, Medemblik, Edam, Monnickendam and Purmerend. The building now houses the Westfries Museum. Opposite is the Waag, a typical North Holland building with veranda built in 1609, and now used as a restaurant. Nearby, in Kerkplein, is the Boterhal, formerly St Jans Gasthuis (1563) and now part of the Westfries Museum complex.

There are many other attractive old buildings in the town and on the ramparts. The terminus of the Hoorn — Medemblik Steam Train, and the Museum workshops of the railway are located here.

From Hoorn, the old Westfriesdijk is followed south to **Scharwoude**, turning right across the main road and under the motorway to Avenhorn and on to Ursem and **Rustenburg**, where three windmills are to be seen, the middle one of which is a small museum. The return to Alkmaar is via Oterleek.

8 THE IJSSELMEER POLDERS

In Roman times, there was a great lake, with a narrow outlet into the North Sea — the Flevomeer. Owing to floods in the Middle Ages, this lake, now known as Lake Almere, grew in size to become the Zuiderzee. To protect the towns on its shores, it became necessary to control the waters, and in the seventeenth century a bold plan for closing and partially reclaiming the land was proposed by Hendrik Stevin. Due to the lack of technology at that time, the plan was dropped, but by the nineteenth century, the idea was thought to be possible, and more plans were put forward to reduce the size of the Zuiderzee to that of the original Flevomeer. After much thought, the plan of Cornelis Lely, presented in 1891, was accepted, although it was not until 1918 that the Dutch Government passed the Zuiderzee Act to allow the enclosing dam to be constructed. Work began in 1920, with the dyke linking North Holland to the island of Wieringen, closing off the Amstelmeer. Many engineering problems had to be overcome, and the changing tidal heights in the Waddenzee had also to be considered. An experimental polder was reclaimed near Andijk to investigate these problems and the possible solutions. Unlike the huge inland lakes already drained, the water in the Zuiderzee was salt, so the problems of producing land fertile enough to grow crops had to be solved.

In 1932, the last gap in the Afsluitdijk (enclosing dyke) was closed and the Zuiderzee became the IJsselmeer. The precise spot, 8km from Den Oever, is now marked by an observation tower from which visitors may look out over the Waddenzee to the north, and the IJsselmeer to the south. A footbridge across the motorway at this point enables the visitor to climb to the top of the sea-dyke, also to look around a small exhibition about the whole project. The 30km long dyke was built wide enough to take a road, a railway and a cycle path, but the railway was never built. Instead, the original single carriageway was enlarged to a motorway in 1976, and the cycle path was improved. At each end of the dyke there are large locks to permit the passage of shipping and to regulate the water level in the IJsselmeer. A statue of Dr Lely stands at the western end, near Den Oever. It was unveiled in September 1954 to mark the centenary of his birth.

The Wieringermeer Polder

This was the first of the Zuiderzee polders to be drained, and it stretches 21km south from the former island of Wieringen to Medemblik. Work began in 1927, and the polder was drained by 1930. The old island itself has four main settlements, including Westerland, with a fifteenth-century church tower, and Hippolytushoef, even older, with many attractive houses and farms. In Oosterland the old Norman church has been extensively altered, whilst Den Oever, the fishing port of the island, is noted mainly for shrimping.

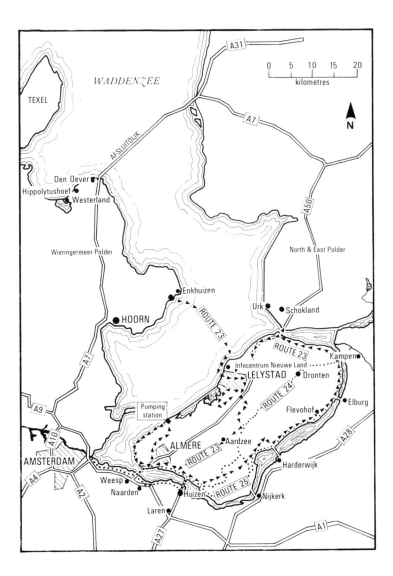

Just 8km south of the island, is the spot where, fifteen years after the draining, the ring dyke was blown up by the retreating German forces in 1945, flooding the polder and destroying 80 per cent of the land and property. A small lake has been designated a Nature Reserve, and the nearby woods have been named the 'Dijkgat Bos' or dyke-opening woods. These are part of the recreation area created here by the Dutch Forestry Service. Fortunately, by the time the dyke was breached, the IJsselmeer had become fresh water, so there was little problem with salt, and wheat was growing again in the Wieringermeer Polder by 1946. This is the most sparsely populated area in the Netherlands, with only sixty people per sq km, compared with 2,400 in the Randstad. Most of the land is agricultural, with more than 10 per cent devoted to bulb-growing.

The North-East Polder

Work began in 1937 on the draining of the north-east Polder, which incorporated the former islands of Urk and Schokland. Drainage was completed during World War II, and the land was then left untouched until the end of the war, and became known as the 'Nederlands Onderduikers Paradijs'. The letters 'NOP' stand also for 'Noord-Oost Polder'. This was a 'safe' retreat for resistance fighters (Onderduikers) and other refugees. Work began on the task of bringing it into cultivation in 1945. The focal point of this area is the town of Emmeloord, which is continually expanding. The whole polder is primarily agricultural, although Urk retains its character and charm as a fishing village. In summer, a ferry service for pedestrians and cyclists operates from here to Enkhuizen on the opposite side of the IJsselmeer. The former island of Schokland, which was very small, has been used as the basis for a country park, and the old island church is now an interesting archaeological and geological museum, with artefacts dating from Roman times. There are exhibits showing the history of Schokland, which in former times was joined to Urk. However, in the face of continued threats from the sea, it was decided in 1859 to evacuate the whole population, and the church is the only building which survived the onslaught of the waves. The old coastline of the island can still be followed on foot or by cycle.

A great advantage resulting from these first two polders, apart from the obviously increased potential for food production, is the reduction in travelling time to other more remote areas of the country brought about by the building of motorways across former stretches of water.

In 1950 work began on the huge 'Flevo-polders', starting with the south-east polder, now named Eastern Flevoland. Because problems had arisen with sinking of the land as it dried, a new idea was introduced whereby each polder was created as an 'island surrounded by a belt of water, the polder being linked to the mainland by long bridges. It was recognised at an early date that new towns would be required to house the population which would settle here, both to relieve congestion in the Randstad and to man the new industries which would be attracted to the area. In addition, large recreation areas, with woods, lakes and country parks, would cater for the leisure-time of the residents of the new towns. In 1965, in the middle of a swampy area of reclaimed land, the foundations were laid for the new city of Lelystad, named after the man whose plans made these polders possible. The first residents arrived in 1967, and today there are more than 60,000 people living here, with extensive shopping and other facilities. The railway line from Amsterdam is due for completion in 1988.

The last major new town, Almere, named after the former lake, is now well established. Because of excellent motorway links, many of its residents commute to Amsterdam, although new local industry is developing rapidly. Almere is situated at the western end of the south-west polder, now named Southern Flevoland, work on which began in 1968. Most of this south-west polder has been devoted to agriculture, particularly to the growing of rape seed, used for production of oil for use in industrial and food products. This in itself has provided a tourist attraction as there is a special Rape-Seed Route to follow when the bright yellow flowers are in full bloom.

The final stage of the IJsselmeer Polders Plan is the creation of the Markerwaard, on the western side. Currently there is much debate as to whether or not this last stage should be carried out. There are many reasons both in favour of and against the plan. The Houtribdijk, between Lelystad and Enkhuizen, forms one of the enclosing dykes for the projected polder, and provides a major route from North to Central Holland, avoiding Amsterdam. During the work on the whole IJsselmeer project, many problems have been encountered and many lessons learned. Not all were foreseen, and it seems likely that the Markerwaard polder will eventually be created.

The development of these polders has meant that the Dutch now have room for the growing population, and for recreation and leisure. The large waterways and lakes surrounding the Flevoland have been used as a basis for many of these leisure facilities, and new beaches, marinas and holiday

Informatiecentrum Nieuwe Land
Exhibition and displays explaining
the history of land-reclamation and
the development of the IJsselmeer
Polders.

Natuurpark Lelystad
A small zoo containing a collection
of rare breeds, such as Przewalski's
horses and Père David's deer.

Nationaal Gietencentrum
Modern goat farm of 75 acres, 500
goats. Cheese and yogurt
production.

Pleisterplaats 'De Aardzee'
Sculptured Landscape representing
the shape of the bottom of the
Zuiderzee.

Ketelhaven
Museum of Marine Archaeology.
Mainly devoted to vessels and
aircraft recovered when the
Zuiderzee was drained.

Biddinghuizen
Flevohof Recreational Park.
Children's Farm. Gardens and
agricultural displays.

resorts are attracting visitors from all over Europe.

There are numerous Nature Reserves, the most important being the Oostvaardersplassen in the north, between Lelystad and Almere. Unique in Europe, it provides an important wintering ground for many rare birds.

The woods in Eastern Flevoland were primarily intended for commercial exploitation, but it was decided that recreational facilities should be incorporated, and the whole area is now well provided with signed cycle and walking routes, camp sites, picnic places and other such features. Woodland being developed in other parts of Flevoland will follow the same pattern, and with the accent on landscaping it is difficult to believe that these lovely afforested areas were, within living memory, at the bottom of the sea.

ROUTE 23   A TOUR OF FLEVOLAND (Approx 200km)

Perhaps the ideal way to start this tour is by crossing the Houtribdijk from Enkhuizen to Lelystad, a distance of 28km. There are parking places alongside the road, so it is possible to stop and look around at the water birds, fishing boats and sailing craft on the water. On reaching **Lelystad**, follow the signs for Informatiecentrum Nieuwe Land, which is situated close by. Here the visitor may see the progress from water to mud to dry land in a series of different 'theme' displays, using modern audio-visual techniques. Commentaries in several languages, including English, explain the presentations, and the whole is excellently portrayed. Some of the artefacts discovered during the drainage of the polders are on display. Currently the whole exhibition is indoors, but plans are in hand for an outdoor demonstration showing the cultivation and development of a polder in

Sightseeing by boat in Amsterdam

Het Hulsbeek, Oldenzaal

Open-air museum, Arnhem

miniature.

On leaving the centre, turn left and follow the minor dyke road to **Lelystadhaven**. This was the first part of the city to be built, and the hotel/restaurant is aptly named De Eerste Aanleg (the First Structure). The city of Lelystad is very confusing, both for the motorist and for the cyclist. Traffic and pedestrians are separated throughout the city, which together with continuing building works, makes it difficult to give general directions. The signposting is not always easy to follow. If you *must* go into the city, follow the Centrum, then Parking signs. The Agora centre is the most useful, as the VVV office is situated there, as well as plenty of shops.

There are many parks in the city, and in the Gelderse Hout on the eastern outskirts is the National Gietencentrum, a Goat Farm where 500 goats are kept to provide milk for yogurt and cheese, and which is open to the public. A municipal camp site is located in the city, and to the south, near the main A6 motorway, is the Natuurpark Lelystad. This is a small zoo with collections of rare species, including Père David's deer and Przewalski horses.

From the Natuurpark, take the ring road around the south-west of the city, then turn left on to Buizerd Weg. This leads to Knardijk, from where the various birds on the Oostvaardersplassen may be viewed. Knardijk may also be reached from the sea dyke at Lelystadhaven. There is a public observation hide, approached from Buizerd Weg (access on foot). Return to the ring road and turn south, taking the Harderwijk road (Larserweg). Take the second turning on the right after the motorway junction, signed for the airfield, which is passed (there is a good restaurant here), and continue to the T-junction with Knarweg. Turn left, then right into Vogelweg. In about 4km there is a sign on the right, 'De Aardzee', (the Earth-Sea). This is a sculptured landscape intended to represent the shape of the bottom of the IJsselmeer as it was found to be when drained. Unusual, and somewhat perplexing, but interesting, nevertheless. Continue further for 8km to the cross roads junction with Wulpweg and Gruttoweg, where during May, an exhibition dealing with the cultivation of rape-seed, can be seen.

By following Vogelweg to the end, the main N27 road will be reached, and turning right will lead to **Almere-Haven**, the first part of the new city of **Almere** to be developed. It is made up of small residential estates with different types of buildings, to give a varied environment. Most of the residential units are houses with gardens, and much more thought seems to have been put into the planning of this city than that of Lelystad. Traffic is still segregated, and until the town is completed, there will still be problems in finding the way around.

Those with time and an interest in such things might like to see the huge Blocq van Kuffeler pumping station to the north-west of the city, on the Oostvaardersdijk. This contains the largest pumping installation in the Netherlands, and may be visited by appointment. Returning along the dyke road, which leads all along the water's edge into IJmeerdijk and

Pampuspad, the approach to the Hollandse Brug is reached, carrying the main A6 road to Amsterdam. Remain on the A6 in the direction of Almere, with Kromsloot Park, an area where the natural polder vegetation has been preserved, on the right. Turn off on to Waterlandseweg at signpost 6574 towards **Zeewolde**, and continue past the Almeerder Hout, on the left. De Kemphaan, an 'environmental' garden information centre, with a 'bee'-garden, herb-garden, and other 'natural' gardens may be visited. The road leads past the junction to the Stichtse Brug and runs into the Gooise Weg, coming eventually to a turning on the left to De Trekker industrial estate, where there is a snack-bar. Zeewolde, a new holiday resort with camping and boating facilities, is reached along Spiekweg opposite the turning to De Trekker. Wooded areas such as the Hulkesteinsebos and Horsterwold, with picnic and parking areas, lie along this part of the shore. Continue on the main road signed **Harderwijk**, the N302 Ganzenweg, but just before crossing the bridge, take the road along the Harderdijk, towards **Flevohof**. Cyclists will have to make use of minor roads, but once past the Harderbrug they can follow the coastline all the way, signed Veluwemeer.

Flevohof is described as a 'look, play and do' park, and is a combined agricultural, horticultural and recreation centre, particularly suited to families. Numerous different attractions include a miniature train to carry visitors around the park, and a children's farm. Visitors can see cows being milked, and there are attractive floral gardens and agricultural displays. On the site there are some holiday bungalows.

After leaving Flevohof, continue in the direction of Elburgerbrug, over the cross-roads, and along the dyke road following signs to **Kampen**. This is a very attractive area, with in the surrounding woods a number of cycle paths, walks, camp sites and picnic areas, with plenty of parking places. At the junction at Roggebotsluis, the road to Kampen goes to the right, but continue straight ahead, along Vossemeerdijk to **Ketelhaven**. For cyclists, the cycle tracks through the Roggebotzand woods are much more pleasant.

At **Ketelhaven** is the Museum of Marine Archaeology, containing the remains of many historic vessels which were wrecked centuries ago in the Zuiderzee, and have been recovered since the polders were drained. Their

The fishing harbour, Urk

cargoes and other salvaged items are also displayed, including some eggs from 1620. Much research into ways of preserving such remains has been carried out here, and one section of the museum is devoted to wartime remains of 'ditched' aircraft found under the water. In the nearby town of **Dronten** is a touching memorial in the Town Square to those who died in regaining Dutch freedom. It takes the form of the twisted propellor from an RAF bomber, mounted on a suitable base.

From Ketelhaven, continue along the Ketelmeerdijk road to Ketelbrug. At this point it is possible to make a diversion over the bridge to visit the north-east Polder, including **Urk** and **Schokland**. Both are signed from the A6 motorway which crosses the bridge. It should be remembered that the residents of Urk value their privacy, and do not take kindly to visitors taking photographs of them in their local dress. Both Urk and Schokland, with its museum and old island coast path, are easily accessible from the motorway.

The return to Lelystad can be made directly along the motorway, and camp sites and hotels are to be found there.

A word of warning. With the roads being so straight, with few trees and a very flat polder landscape, it is essential to keep one's wits about one when driving. It is very easy to fall asleep. This has been a cause of some concern to those planning the development of these areas.

Cycling in the Flevopolders

Because of the fast motorway network and continual development in the towns, cycle path direction signs tend to lead one in very roundabout ways. The winds also make cycling difficult on the polders. If it is necessary to cross the Flevopolder, for example to go from Kampen to Amsterdam, the officially-signposted route for cyclists leads via Lelystad and becomes very confusing at that point. Two routes which follow as much shelter as possible are given which avoid too many long diversions, and each is about 60km long, from the Roggebotsluis to the Stichtsebrug.

ROUTE 24 A CYCLE ROUTE FROM KAMPEN TO AMSTERDAM

From Kampen, cross the Vossemeer at Roggebotsluis, and take the Hanzeweg towards **Dronten**. Disregard the Biddinghuizen signs, and take the next road towards the town centre. Turn right through the recreation area, across the main road, and on to Rietweg. There is a cycle path alongside this road, slightly below road level for part of the way. On reaching the Larserbos there are several cycle paths through the woods, and it makes a good place to stop for a rest, although there are no facilities. Continue to the cross-roads, over Larserweg (along which cycles are banned), and continue to Meeuwenweg. At the end of the road a diversion may be made along a cycle path through woods on the right, coming out on to Vogelweg. The cycle path continues on the other side of this road, westward until the Knardijk is reached. Cross over again and ride south down Knardijk for a short way, and another cycle path runs down the steep side of the dyke to the right, crosses over a small bridge, then runs through a wooded area with open clearings to join Lepelaarpad. Turn right here, and left at the end of the road, along Lepelaarweg to the first turning on the right. This is Appelvinkweg. It may be noticed that parts of this route are waymarked with the Long Distance Footpath signs for the 'Schokkerpad'. At the end of Appelvinkweg, a cycle path leads through to Sterappellaan. Turn left and follow down the next cycle path to Schollevaarweg. Turn right, then first left, to De Trekker Light Industrial Estate, where there is a small café, the only one in this area. Return to the cross-roads, turn west along Bosruiterweg to the end, turn left across Gooiseweg and follow signs for **Nijkerk** until the next cross-roads. Turn right along Winkelweg. Where this road turns off towards the left, take the right turn along Priempad. This road makes several sharp turns before coming out at the main road, where a left turn brings the cycle path on to the Stichtse Brug.

From the bridge it makes a pleasant ride to go through **Huizen** to **Naarden**, following cycle signs, thence alongside the Naarder Trekvaart canal to **Muiden**. Continue along the cycle paths beside the motorway, cross the Amsterdam-Rijnkanaal, then turn right along a small cycle path which follows the canal, taking you to the Schellingwoude bridge on the outskirts of Amsterdam. Care should be taken at **Diemen** as extensive motorway works are in progress, which may require diversions. The alternative to this path is to follow the cycle path beside the main road into the city.

ROUTE 25 A CYCLE ROUTE FROM KAMPEN ALONG THE SOUTH OF THE POLDER

From Kampen, cross the Roggebotsluis and take the road left along the Drontermeer Dijk. This cycle path should be followed as far as the Harderbrug. There are four restaurants along the way, which is much more sheltered than the northern route already described. It runs through pleasantly landscaped recreation areas, and passes a number of beaches. At the turning to the Harderbrug, keep along the dyke road towards **Zeewolde**, then right along Horsterweg, turning left on to Spiekweg, which leads through the wooded Horsterwold to the junction with Nijkerkerweg. Cross over this road on to the cycle path which leads into Slingerweg and on to Eemmeerdijk. This runs for about 6km to the Stichtse Brug, and the route across the bridge has already been described.

An alternative route is to remain on the Flevo-polder and continue past the bridge, along the Gooimeerdijk past **Almere-Haven** to the Hollandse Brug. This is crossed and the previous route picked up along the Naarder Trekvaart near **Muiden**.

Of the two routes described, the second is the more interesting and much more sheltered, but in any event, a cyclist must be prepared for some hard riding, especially with a south-westerly wind.

9 FRIESLAND AND THE WADDEN ISLANDS

When you enter Friesland you enter a different country. Here signposts and name boards are in both Dutch and Fries, for the people here, like the Welsh are fiercely proud of their language and customs which they understandably wish to preserve as living entities. It may be a little disconcerting to find shop assistants who insist on speaking Fries, but once they know you are a visitor your welcome is assured.

The Province offers a wide choice for the holidaymaker, and it is rather surprising to find how few tourists find their way here. True, it is in the north of the country, yet distances are not exceptionally great and road and rail communications are improving all the time. Friesland contains a unique lakeland paradise for water-sport and sailing enthusiasts. There are large farms, for this is the dairy centre of the Netherlands. Here you will find centuries-old churches built on mounds (*terps*) for protection against floods. There are many miles of dykes, both along the edge of the sea and inland and old wooden belfries in village churchyards. Called *Klokkenstoelen,* these were built in the days when the villagers could not afford to build church towers. Variety is provided by wooded areas in the south-east, interspersed with dunes, heathland and fen areas, whilst in the south-west is Gaasterland where sand-martins still nest in the sand-cliffs along the edge of the IJsselmeer.

The eleven towns of Friesland form the basis of a route which has traditionally been followed by skaters taking part in the well-known 'Eleven Towns Tour', a fiercely-contested race which requires a severe winter to make it possible. In later years others have taken up the theme with bicycle, walking and running tours around the eleven towns of the Province.

The towns and terp villages of the north form an interesting tour in themselves, as does the lake area in the south-west, whilst the south-east is less well-known than it deserves. The Wadden Islands form a separate but nonetheless interesting area to visit.

ROUTE 26   HARLINGEN and FRANEKER
Coming to Friesland from the west, across the Afsluitdijk, keep on the E10 main road which bears north to **Harlingen**, the historic port from which ferries now leave for the Wadden Islands of Terschelling and Vlieland. The town is notable for its very fine old dwellings and warehouses, virtually the whole of the town centre being a conservation area.

ROUTE 26A   A WALK IN HARLINGEN
Park on the southern approach road, Westerzeedijk near the football fields, and walk towards the town. Turn right and cross the railway by the locks into Werfpad and continue along Schoolstraat, turning right at the

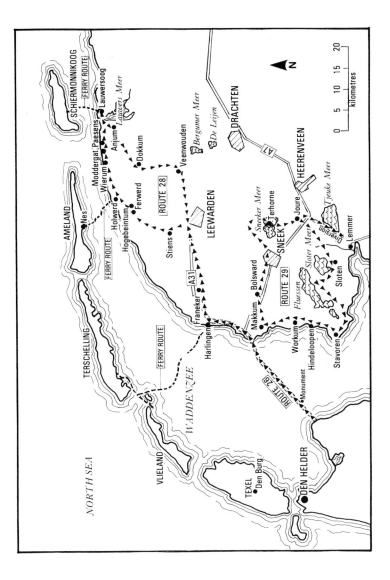

end into Zuiderhaven and on to Zuider Plein. Cross to the north side of Rozengracht where a little brick building originally used to house a fire engine bears the legend 'Brand Spuit No. 1. 1767'. Across the canal are many old East India Company warehouses. Continue across Zuider Plein and along Brouwersstraat, which has some lovely bell-shaped gables on the fronts of houses. Turn left into Schritsen, and shortly after passing Raamstraat a typically Dutch alley or *steeg*, Woudemansteeg, leads between two old houses with stepped gables on the right. Walk through to Lanen, turn left, and after a short distance, right again into Kleine Bredeplaats, a street full of beautiful old buildings. Pay special attention to No 12, richly decorated in Renaissance style with a façade which has the arms of Harlingen on it. At the end of the road turn left into Grote Bredeplaats. On the right is an old fruit and wine warehouse, beautifully restored and, like so many other of the town's buildings, put to another use: it is now a restaurant. Continue to the end of the road, turn right into Prinsenstraat, then right again along Noorderhaven with more lovely buildings on both sides of the water. Part way along stands the Town Hall (1730), very similar in style to an English Georgian building and behind it, in Raadhuisstraat, stands the octagonal Raadhuistoren. At the bottom of the street at the junction with Voorstraat is an old tobacco factory, now used for the VVV offices. The interior is preserved with the original shop fittings. If time permits, it is worth paying a visit to the Municipal museum in the Hannemahuis, at No 56, Voorstraat, then return to the Noorderhaven and follow the waterside to the end. Cross the Leeuwenbrug and walk down Rommelhaven, along Scheerstraat and into Lombardstraat, to the English Gardens, laid out and planted in nineteenth-century style on the remains of the city walls. Walk through this peaceful part of the town, cross the bridge to the south side of Franekereind, and return to Zuider Plein along Heiligeweg, and Brouwersstraat, thence back to the car park.

Leave Harlingen via the dyke road, along Havenweg and Havenplein, Oude Ringmuur and Harlingerstraatweg on the north of the town, cross the motorway and follow the old road via Herbayum to **Franeker**, another old town.

Smaller than Harlingen, it was once famed for its University. Unfortunately Napoleon took a dislike to this seat of learning and it was closed down.

ROUTE 26B   A WALK IN FRANEKER

In the main street, Voorstraat, is the old Waag, which houses the VVV offices, next door to two Professors' houses dating from the seventeenth and eighteenth centuries. They now accommodate the Town Museum. Further on the right, is a beautifully-restored building, the Martenahuis, dating from 1498, with a beautiful garden. This building is now the office of the Rural District Council. At the end of Voorstraat turn left into Raadhuisplein, to the Town Hall, one of the earliest Frisian Town Halls,

Harlingen
Hannemahuis
Municipal museum of Harlingen. Collection of silver, china, tiles, old maps, model ships, etc. in fine old house dating back to the eighteenth century.

Stadhuis
Eighteenth-century Town Hall beside the Noorderhaven.

Old Warehouses
In town centre, relics of East India Company.

Old houses
With elaborately carved gables and doorways.

English Gardens
Gardens on the town ramparts, planted in nineteenth-century style.

Franeker
Eise Eisinga Planetarium
An eighteenth-century amateur astronomer's self-built Planetarium, which still works.

Renaissance-style Town Hall
(1591) One of the loveliest town halls in Friesland.

Coopmanshuis
(1746) and next door building (1662) Town museum. Collections of china and silver, period rooms, etc. Objects connected with the years when Franeker was a University town.

Waag
Seventeenth-century weigh house.

Camminghastins
Old fortified house, now containing a collection of coins and associated objects.

Martenahuis
Another old fortified medieval house, with a beautiful garden.

built in 1591 in Renaissance style. At the end of Raadhuisplein, is Eise Eisingastraat, where during the years 1774 to 1781 the wool merchant and amateur astronomer, Eise Eisinga built a Planetarium. The operating mechanism is located in the attic of the house where he lived. At the end of this street is an attractive little building known as the Korendragershuisje, (grain-porters house) now used by a local potter as a workshop, which visitors are welcome to view. Apparently grain was brought in along the canals by boat, and was weighed here for tax purposes before being allowed into the town. Return along Groenmarkt, on the opposite side of the canal to the Planetarium, to the Camminghastins, a fortified dwelling recently restored and now the site of the Friese Munt and Penningkabinet, an annexe of the Frisian Museum. Just beyond is the Martinikerk, built in 1421. A stroll around the rest of the town shows that it was originally built within an encircling canal or moat with ramparts, the latter having been mostly levelled to provide a promenade.

From Franeker it is just 15km to **Leeuwarden**, the provincial capital. On

*Entrance to the
Boshuizen-Gasthuis,
eighteenth-century
almshouses, Leeuwarden*

approaching from the A31 motorway, follow signs for VVV or Station opposite which, in Oude Veemarkt, is a very large 'Pay and Display' car park. There is a second one not far away, in Klanderijstraat.

Leeuwarden is another old fortified town, originating from the amalgamation of settlements on three *terps* at the confluence of the rivers Ee and Vlie. Its centre is completely surrounded by a ring canal, with further intersecting waterways.

The town makes a good touring base and has excellent shops. A map showing a detailed walk is available from the VVV. A shorter walk taking in some of the most interesting places is described here.

ROUTE 27   A WALK AROUND LEEUWARDEN

Leaving Oude Veemarkt, walk up Prins Henrikstraat, opposite the station, which leads into Doelsteeg. At the end, turn left along Nieuwestad and continue to the landscaped ramparts. Turn right, and walk through the gardens, past the Resistance Monument on the second bastion, then cross over to the huge sixteenth-century leaning tower of the Oldehove. This is part of a Gothic tower, built between 1529 and 1532, intended as part of a cathedral, but because of ground subsidence, never completed. The outline plan of the building is laid out behind the tower in the Olde Hoofsterkerkhof, on one of the original mounds.

In nearby Grote Kerkstraat is the Princessehof, which, with the adjoining house, is one of the finest museums in the world specialising in ceramics. Walk along Grote Kerkstraat as far as Pijlsteeg, turn left, then right into Perkstraat where there are some lovely old almshouses with arched gates leading into quiet private gardens. Return to Grote Kerkstraat and cross into Beijerstraat, on the corner of which is Mata Hari's house, now the Frisian Literary Museum. Notice that the road goes down-hill, as the top of this street is the highest part of the town. At the bottom, turn right into Hofplein, and continue into Raadhuisplein, down Weerd and on to Waagplein, where there is the old Weigh-house (1598). Continue along Peperstraat into Groentemarkt, bear left then right along the street called 'Over de Kelders'. This runs along one of the town's canals, with an upper quay over a lower quay from which cellars open, similar to those in Utrecht. Along Over de Kelders, on the right, is Koningsstraat, down which is Turfmarkt. A left turn reaches the Frisian Museum, with very good regional collections of art, history, costume, archaeological finds, etc. On the opposite side of Turfmarkt is one of the loveliest buildings in the town. Dating from 1566 and known as the 'Kanselarij', it was once the Frisian Court.

Walk back to Groentemarkt, along Peperstraat and turn left along Wirdumerdijk, a long street leading to Zuiderplein, with a huge sculpture of a Frisian Cow, known as 'Us Mem' (Our Mother). Return to the car park in Oude Veemarkt along Stationsweg.

ROUTE 28   FRISIAN TERPS and TOWNS

An interesting tour can be made of the area to the north of Leeuwarden, particularly noted for the *terps* or mounds on which small villages were built.

Leave Leeuwarden by the road which turns off the ring road at signpost 4819, leading north to **Stiens**. A short distance away on the right may be seen the *terp* villages of Jelsum, Cornjum and Britsum, all on low mounds rising above the surrounding countryside. Continue past Stiens towards **Hallum** and **Marrum**, passing more *terp* villages on the left beyond which the sea dyke can be seen. At **Ferwerd**, turn right at signpost 7510, and keeping right, take the road to **Hogebeintum** the highest of the existing *terp* villages. Park on the road and walk back into the village. A board can be found near the approach to the church, explaining the purpose of the *terp* which translates to read: 'Terps were lived on in 600BC. People first lived on the (normal) highest ground, then, because of the sea, the level of the high ground was raised by degrees. Houses and farms, and later the Church itself, were built on the mound. There are about 1,000 known terps in Friesland, of varying ages and heights. Hogebeintum is the highest, 8.8m above sea level. By the year 1,000AD, building of sea dykes had commenced, which did away with the function of the terps. Around the year 1800 excavations had begun on several terps, and valuable information was discovered about the terp dwellers. Much of this is now in the Fries Museum in Leeuwarden.' The central part of many of the *terps* has been left intact, as old churches stand on them.

The road from Hogebeintum running north to **Blija** is very narrow as it runs across the fields, so motorists may prefer to return to the main road at Ferwerd, then turn right. On the left may be seen farmhouses built on *terps*. The road continues through **Holwerd** and **Ternaard** to signpost 10206, where a minor road leads off to the left to **Wierum**. On the sea dyke is a memorial made of anchors, commemorating an occasion when local fishermen were lost in a great storm. The twelfth-century church, opposite the memorial has a typical saddle-roof tower, and is one of the most photographed churches in Friesland. At Wierum is the 'Wadloopcentrum Friesland', from where it is possible to go on a guided but strenuous walk across the mud flats at certain times of the year. Such walks vary in length, and must only be undertaken in company with local guides who know the tides, weather and the varying pattern of the mudflats. (The word *wad* means mudflat.)

Leave Wierum by the road below the sea-dyke leading to **Nes**, another *terp* village, then back towards the dyke and the villages of **Moddergat** and **Paesens**, where there is a small fishermen's museum. From Paesens take the minor road past the windmill, across at signpost 2265 and so to **Anjum**, where the tall windmill houses the VVV office and a small shell museum. The church, built on a *terp*, dates back to the eleventh century. At nearby **Oostmahorn**, from where the ferry once left for the island of Schiermonnikoog, there is evidence of Napoleonic forts built into the sea-dyke. The stretch of

PLACES TO VISIT IN NORTH FRIESLAND

Hogebeintum
Thirteenth-century church on the highest *terp* in Holland.

Wierum
Twelfth-century church on small *terp* behind the dyke. Fishermen's monument, made of anchors, on the dyke. Wadloopcentrum Friesland — guided walks across the mudflats to Ameland.

Moddergat-Paesens
't Fiskershuske — a fisherman's cottage converted to a museum about fishing in the area.

Anjum
Attractive tall windmill, housing the local VVV office and a museum of shells. Eleventh-century church.

Lauwersoog
'Expo-Zee' exhibition about the Wadden Shallows and control of the sea in this area.

Dokkum
Seventeenth-century Admiralty House, now the municipal museum. Seventeenth-century Town Hall. Old moats and ramparts, with two high mills actually built on the ramparts. Eighteenth-century Waag building. Old pump (Fetzefontein) near the market.

Veenwouden
Schierstins (fourteenth-century fortified tower).

water beyond is now the Lauwersmeer, having been closed off from the Waddenzee by a long dyke with sluices, so the ferries now leave from Lauwersoog. Once again, the need to protect and drain land has been turned to good advantage by creating an extensive recreation area for sailing, sailboarding and other sports. It is worth making a diversion to **Lauwersoog**, actually in Groningen Province, to visit the permanent exhibition, 'Expo Zee', which deals with the sea in general and with the Wadden Shallows in particular. Proposals for linking the chain of Wadden Islands by barrier dams, so enclosing the Waddenzee, caused great debate over the years, and the controversial 'Wadden Plan' has now been rejected, as its effect on the whole environment is considered to be unacceptable.

From Anjum, the main road is followed south-west to **Dokkum**, an interesting old town built on a series of connected *terps*. Once a sea port, and headquarters of the Frisian Admiralty, its importance diminished when the sea inlet silted up, and the Admiralty was moved to Harlingen. The best car park is in the Harddraversdijk near the camp site and sports centre.

ROUTE 28A   A WALK IN DOKKUM

From the car park walk across the bridge and along the side of the

The seventeenth-century Town Hall, Dokkum

Grootdiep, the former inner harbour. This is called Diepswal, and on the right is the seventeenth-century Admiralty House, now the municipal museum. Further along Diepswal is De Zijl, a bridge where the sea locks were located. The Town Hall is situated by this bridge, from which may be seen a number of seventeenth-century houses. Nearby are two fine tower windmills standing on the ramparts, and many attractive small canals. From De Zijl, walk up Hoogstraat to the Markt, the site of the old Abbey of St Boniface, an English missionary who brought Christianity to this part of the Netherlands, and was murdered here. The Grote or St Martinus Kerk, dating from the fifteenth century is also here. On leaving the Markt, along Boterstraat will be seen, on the left, a rather fine pump, the Fetzefontein; it is a typical example of an eighteenth-century town pump, with the date 1712. Continue to Grote Breedstraat and turn right. Look down the wide street to the Waag (1752) which now houses the VVV office. Note the ornate carving on the gable. From here, walk along Kleine Oosterstraat and De Dam to the Oosterbolwerk, and so back to the car park.

If returning to Leeuwarden, take the road south through Damwoude to **Veenwouden**. Visit this little town to see the old square fortified tower known as Schierstins, built in the fourteenth century and the only surviving example of its type in Friesland. It now houses a small museum. From Veenwouden it is about 2km to the main E10 motorway which leads back to Leeuwarden.

ROUTE 29   THE FRISIAN LAKES and IJSSELMEER TOWNS

This route starts at **Sneek**, some 20km south west of Leeuwarden. It is a beautiful old town, second largest in the province and a well-known yachting centre. The lovely old watergate dating from 1613 is the only remnant of the town defence works, with a guardroom built over the water. It is possible to park near here, in Veemarkt on the Geeuwkade. After looking at the Waterpoort, walk down Waterpoortgracht to Martiniplein, where the sixteenth-century Martinikerk, stands on foundations from the twelfth century. The unusual wooden belfry standing beside the church dates back to 1489, and has recently been restored. Beyond the church, in Marktstraat, is the beautiful fifteenth-century Town Hall with later additions including a fine double staircase to the entrance. Although the town is about 20km away from the sea, the network of waterways means that one is never far from sight of yachts and other craft.

From Sneek it is possible to follow the signposted ANWB 'Friese Meren' route, but the shorter tour described takes in some additional places.

Leave Sneek by the road signed for **Grouw**, following the blue hexagonal signs for the 'Friese Meren' route. After passing through Offingawier, keep straight on instead of turning left, following the road running north-east towards **Irnsum**, where at the cross-roads beyond the village (signpost 3098) turn right, and cross the Prinses Margriet Kanaal. Cyclists can turn off along the north side of the Sneekermeer, cross the Terzoolstersluis and follow the road alongside the canal. After crossing the canal, in about 1km turn right at signpost 357 towards **Terhorne**, back on the signed route. Through the village are two good viewpoints with parking, from which it is possible to watch the sailing and wildlife on the Sneekermeer and Terkaplesterpoelen and at the next village, **Goingarijp**, is a *klokkenstoel*. Continue south to **Broek-Noord**, where the road turns right at a T-junction (signpost 4896) passing another *klokkenstoel* at Snikzwaag before reaching **Joure** which has two important industries. One is the manufacture of Fries clocks, and the other is the main factory of Douwe Egberts, the well-known Dutch suppliers of tea and coffee. The latter is well represented in the local museum, Johann Hesselhuis. A diversion may be made along the motorway A50 to **Lemmer**, another town devoted to sailing and boating of all kinds, where locks provide access from the IJsselmeer to the Frisian lakes.

Otherwise, leave Joure along the signed route through Sint Nicolaasga to **Sloten**, the smallest of the eleven Frisian towns. Park outside the town near the Slotermeer, and walk along the street beside the central canal. Old locks stand at either end of the central waterway, and a fine windmill overlooks the whole town from the ramparts.

On leaving Sloten, continue to Wijckel, then turn right to **Balk**, with its rather nice seventeenth-century Town Hall with belfry and small central steeple. A short diversion may be made at this point to look at the Slotermeer; there is a car park at the edge of the lake. Back in the village, follow the signed route to the main road, at signpost 1728, cross over to

PLACES TO VISIT AROUND THE FRISIAN LAKES

Sneek
Seventeenth-century Watergate, with twin steeples and double 'gallery'. Sixteenth-century Martinikerk, with fifteenth-century wooden belfry alongside. Magnificent fifteenth-century Town Hall. Frisian shipping museum, illustrating activity on the sea and on inland waters.

Terhorne
Views over the lakes. Sailing centre.

Joure
Johann Hesselhuis Museum. Section dealing with tea and coffee.

Sloten
Attractive small fortified town, windmill at one end of the main street, and old locks at either end.

Balk
Small seventeenth-century town hall.

Rijs
Sybrandy's Vogelpark — Birds and small animals, children's farm and amusements for the whole family.

Rode Klif
Monument to Frisian fight for independence.

Hindeloopen
Old Zuiderzee port, now a busy sailing centre. Hidde Nijland Museum of local antiquities and costumes in old Weigh House. Lockkeeper's house by harbour, now harbour-master's office. Lifeboat Museum in old lifeboat house on quay.

Workum
Old town centre. Seventeenth-century Waag and eighteenth-century Town Hall.

'Aldfaers Erf' Route
Four villages linked to give a historical trail of Frisian heritage. (Ferwoude, Piaam, Allingawier, Exmorra).

Makkum
Tichelaar's Royal Makkum Pottery and Tile Factory. Seventeenth-century Waag, with small museum.

Bolsward
Elaborate seventeenth-century town hall.

Harich, turn right in the village and follow the minor road, which runs near the main road for about 1km. Where it bends sharply to the left, take the right turn, bearing right in about 2km to a T-junction (signpost 2410), turn left and continue to where the road turns left again alongside the Fluessen lake to **Elahuizen** and **Aldegea**. Here it is possible to turn left along the signed route which passes through Gaasterland, the most heavily wooded part of Friesland. There are plenty of walks and cycle paths, and a number of bird sanctuaries including Sybrandy's Bird Park and Recreation Centre at **Rijs**.

Our route is shorter, and at Aldegea we continue straight ahead to **Nieuw**

Buren. After crossing the main road at signpost 594, take the next turning on the left, then after 1km turn right, back on the signed route. The road is now followed to the shore of the IJsselmeer, turning right along the sea cliffs. Although very low by English standards, these are real cliffs, not dykes or sand dunes. After following the shoreline for about 5km, to the monument at Rode Klif, a huge boulder bearing an inscription which translates 'On 26 September 1345, the Frisians, in defence of their independence, stood as one man against an overseas attack by the Dutch, and repelled the enemy'. There is car parking nearby, and from this point a fine view is obtainable out across the water of the IJsselmeer. Along this stretch of coast there are many opportunities for observing waterbirds.

The road along the coast continues to **Stavoren**, a prosperous port in the Middle Ages which is now mainly noted for the locks which give access to the yachting areas of the Frisian lakes, and for the summer ferry service across the IJsselmeer to Enkhuizen, available to pedestrians and cyclists only.

On leaving Stavoren, instead of following the signed route, turn left at the T-junction 2km out of the town (signpost 2405) and follow the road to Molkwar, then on to the dyke road to **Hindeloopen**, where parking is only permitted outside the town. This little place was raised to the status of a town in 1255, and became a member of the Hanseatic League in the fourteenth century. Once a very busy sea-port, it is now an equally busy centre for yachting. Behind the sealocks are many houses with old façades, linked by characteristic wooden bridges across the drainage canals. Many of the houses were the homes of sea captains, and the place is known for its beautiful painted furniture and unusual costumes, which may be seen in the Hidde Nijland museum in the former Town Hall and Weighhouse. Behind the sealocks is the old lock-keeper's house with a wooden belfry, dating from 1619 and now used as the harbourmaster's office. Near the sea dyke is the church (1658) with a leaning tower dating from 1593, the weather vane on top being a model of a sailing ship. In the old lifeboathouse on the quay is a small museum. During World War II, the local lifeboat was 'stolen', to take over 40 refugees to safety in England. Today there are about eight large modern motor lifeboats stationed around the IJsselmeer, which seems excessive until one realises just how quickly the sea can get up and how rough it can become in a strong wind, with the shallow waters of the inland sea.

From Hindeloopen, take the road inland towards the main road, where the signed route is rejoined along the parallel minor road to **Workum**, noted for its local pottery. The Waag (1650) stands in the Market square, and houses the VVV office. The main part of the Town Hall dates from the Middle Ages, and was enlarged in about 1725. In the town are many fine gabled houses. The Grote or St Gertrudiskerk, commenced in the sixteenth century, and whose tower stands separately was like that in Leeuwarden, never completed. The organ, built in 1697, is one of the oldest in the Province. Near the lock is the old shipbuilding yard 'De Hoop', where boats are being built and restored using old-fashioned tools and methods.

The signed route is followed from Workum north to **Makkum**, passing on the way two villages, **Ferwoude** and **Piaam**, which lie on what is called the 'Aldfaers Erf Route'. The name is best translated from the Fries as 'Forefathers' Heritage', and it could be seen as a historical trail where various shops, old farms, workshops, dwelling houses, etc have been carefully restored and furnished to show visitors how people lived and worked during the period at the end of the last century. The villages belonging to this project are located within a triangle bounded by the towns of Workum, Makkum and Bolsward, and the whole route is signed, descriptive literature being available locally.

Makkum is well-known for pottery. The Waag (1698) is the site of the VVV, together with a museum devoted to Frisian pottery and earthenware. The church dates from 1660. The most interesting feature of the town is undoubtedly Tichelaar's Royal Makkum Pottery and Tile Factory. The industry has existed here since the seventeeth century, and the present factory has been owned by one family for over 300 years. It is the only surviving factory in the world still using the original white tin glazing process introduced into the Netherlands in the sixteenth century. It is claimed that the products of Makkum rival those of Delft; certainly each piece, which bears the Royal Makkum mark together with the signature of the individual painter, is a real collector's item. Tours around the factory provide a fascinating insight into this old but thriving craft.

Turning again along the signed route from Makkum, turn right at signpost 7661, then left at 7665 to **Allingawier**, another 'Aldfaers Erf' hamlet with just twelve houses and two churches, and including an old restored farmhouse which may be visited. Before reaching the hamlet, the road passes the lovely Frisian mansion-house or *state* called Allingastate. About 1km beyond Allingawier is **Exmorra**, where there is an antique grocer's shop and school, furnished and stocked with genuine old items.

Beyond Exmorra the road continues, passing under the A7 motorway to enter the town of **Bolsward**. Built on a *terp*, this old Hanseatic port first received its charter in 1455, and was at the height of its prosperity in the sixteenth century. The red brick Town Hall with Renaissance carved façade, and elegant tower with a carillon, dates from 1617. A former Franciscan church, the Broerekerk, has a moulded brick front from 1281, while the fifteenth-century Grote or Martinikerk has an older tower and some fine choir stalls and organ. From Bolsward, the route returns direct via Nijland and Ysbrechtum to Sneek.

The Wadden Islands

Stretching like a necklace across the northern coast of Holland, the islands, with the exception of Texel, lie in the Province of Friesland. Texel, the largest, lies within North Holland, but since they are all in the Waddenzee they will be grouped here for convenience.

Texel is completely different from the other islands, but has much to

**PLACES TO VISIT IN THE
WADDEN ISLANDS**

Texel
Old villages of Den Hoorn, Oosterend and De Waal. Natuur-recreatie centrum near De Koog, on west coast — natural history museum and seal nursery. Small museums in Den Hoorn, Den Burg, De Waal and Oudeschild.

Vlieland
Peaceful, virtually car-free island. Nature reserve. Tromphuys — Norwegian Folk art museum.

Terschelling
Quiet beaches and nature reserves.

Fifteenth-century lighthouse. Small local museum of costumes and craftwork.

Ameland
Het Oerd nature reserve. Old sea-captain's houses in villages of Nes and Hollum. Historical museum in Hollum, concerned with both the island and the whaling industry. Lifeboat launched with the aid of horses.

Schiermonnikoog
Small, car-free island, with nature reserves and good beaches.

offer in the way of beaches, dunes and nature reserves. At the end of the last Ice Age, the melting ice-cap left a gently-sloping hill covered with scattered boulders from Scandinavia, and it was here that the first settlers started to work. With 25km of sea beaches, wide dunes and forested areas, there are plenty of opportunities for recreation. At one point there is a gap in the dunes, and the water entering through a network of channels has formed a marshy area known as 'De Slufter', which provides a unique breeding place for masses of birds, and is now a nature reserve. Bulb-growing is an important industry of the islanders, the south being particularly colourful when the flower fields are at their best. There is a considerable contrast between the north and south due to the fact that originally there were two islands, Texel and Eierland. In 1630, dykes were constructed and the two islands joined together, with the creation of polders. These are typical of north Holland polderland, whereas the southern, older part of the island, has narrow winding lanes, old farms and sheep-folds. The main town of Texel is **Den Burg**, built in rings around the church. **De Koog**, on the North Sea coast, is the principal resort, while the villages of **Den Hoorn, Oosterend** and **De Waal** are conservation areas. The harbour at **Oudeschild** has a long history and was originally the ferry port before the service was transferred to 't Horntje at the south end of the island. It is still used as a yacht harbour and fishing port. There are four museums; a maritime museum at Den Hoorn, historical museum at Den Burg, an agricultural museum in De Waal and a Shipwreck museum in Oudeschild. In the Nature Recreation Centre there is a natural history collection, seal nursery and a bird hospital. At the extreme north of the island is the newest village, **De Cocksdorp**, developed for the tourist industry. By far the best way to explore is on foot or by bicycle. Although cars can be taken, the ferry is very expensive and it is not possible to book a car passage from Den Helder. The modern roll on-roll off ferries leave every hour, and tickets may be bought only at the departure place in Den Helder, and only for a return trip. A new boat is now in service, eliminating the long waits which were once the norm. Nature lovers might prefer to take a cycle in the off-season and make arrangements through the local VVV to visit some of the nature reserves. There are a number of camp-sites on the island.

Vlieland is the next island in the chain, and its peace and quiet is ensured by the fact that cars are banned. The only village is **Oost-Vlieland**, the old village of West Vlieland having been washed away by the sea in the eighteenth century. Some 20km long and about 2½km wide, the island, though small, has large unspoilt areas freely accessible to walkers. In addition, horses and ponies may be hired. A natural history museum deals with the local scene, while in the Tromphuys in Dorpstraat is a good collection of Norwegian folk art and many items from Lapland. Ferries leave Harlingen three times daily except during the winter when the service may be reduced. Ample car parking facilities exist at Harlingen.

Terschelling is, next to Texel, the largest of the Wadden Islands, with a length of 30km but still only between 2 and 5km wide. Beaches, dunes, extensive woodlands, heath and polders make up this outpost of Friesland, and a road links all the villages. Although cars may be taken on the ferry, it is expensive and bicycles are the best form of transport. The ferries dock at **West-Terschelling**, which together with the main village of **Midsland** and the other villages on the island, cater for tourists as their main occupation. The ferry service from Harlingen sails twice or three times daily, and it is essential to book in advance for cars. Ideally suited to those wanting a quiet holiday, there are nevertheless several places of interest, such as the fifteenth-century Brandaris lighthouse, and a small local museum showing craftwork, costumes and items relating to the whaling and shipping industries which were once the main source of the islanders' income.

Ameland is particularly noted for its flora and fauna, and is the only Frisian island upon which deer can still be found. The island is about 24km long and between 2 to 4km in width. The whole of the eastern end consists of a natural area of dunes and grassland, known as 'het Oerd', where rare birds and plants abound. The main village is **Nes**, near the centre of the island, and this is connected by road to **Ballum** and **Hollum** to the west and **Buren** to the east. Each village has its own characteristic charm. Once totally dependent on the whaling industry, now 95 per cent of the island's income is derived from tourism. However, this has been kept under some control so that the essential character of the island has not been destroyed. Nes is near the ferry landing, and a bus service connects with the other villages. The VVV office is in Nes, near the fine saddle-roof tower, which bears two dates. The first is 1664, and originally a fire basket stood on top to serve as a beacon for ships. Later, in 1732, the tower was made higher and a light was displayed from an opening under the clock. In the neighbourhood there are a number of so-called Captains' Houses, identified by an extra row of bricks in the gables, forming a small step. Near the tower is a little square in which the old town pump can still be seen, together with the old school room and post office. To the north of the village is an attractive octagonal thatched windmill, the only one remaining of four which once stood on the island. East of Nes is **Buren**, the only village with neither church nor cemetery. To the north of Nes and Buren, in the dunes, many holiday houses, beautifully secluded and sheltered, have been built so they do not intrude upon the landscape, and a cycle path runs right through to 'het Oerd' nature reserve. Recently, oil has been discovered here, but very strict conditions have been imposed on its extraction; work is only permitted between 1 October and 31 March, and all equipment has to be removed during the summer months. All buildings and permanent installations such as tanks must be painted to blend with the landscape. It is said that the first year this was done, the camouflage was so good that sea birds flew into the tanks and injured themselves, so the colours have had to be slightly modified. Certainly it is difficult to realise that modern industry has come to this place.

The villages of **Ballum** and **Hollum** stand in the western part of the island, with polders to the south. New farms were built here in 1950, with Government assistance, in the old Frisian style of 'kop, hals en romp' ('head, neck and body'), so-called from the layout of a living house connected to a large barn by a short connecting passage, all under one roof. The inhabitants of these two villages are Protestant, and at one time they never went to the other end of the island which was predominantly Catholic. Nowadays, however, the islanders mix more freely. Ballum is the quieter of the villages, and the family vault of the rulers of Ameland from 1424 to 1681 is in the churchyard. The 3m high figure of a knight standing between the columns gives an idea of the family's great power. The church itself contains a beautiful seventeenth-century pulpit. Hollum has an old church tower from the Middle Ages, and many Captains' Houses, in one of which is a small historical museum dealing with the island and the whaling trade. In the dunes just to the west of the village stands the 58m high cast-iron tower of the lighthouse, one of the most powerful in Europe, whose light may be seen over 100km away. Hollum also has what must be the only modern lifeboat still to be launched with the aid of 10 horses, who drag it from its boathouse in the village to the beach. Other interesting items of information about Ameland are, first, that in 1895 a dyke was built to the mainland in the hope that silt would collect against it to form a causeway, but most traces of it have now disappeared. The island is, however, connected to the mainland by a pipeline which conveys milk to the processing plants. The other interesting bit of history concerns the war between Holland and England in 1652-54, when the ruler of Ameland sent envoys to Cromwell to proclaim the neutrality of the island. The ferry service to Ameland starts from Holwerd, with 5 or 6 sailings per day, and more in the summer and on Saturdays. Advance booking is essential for cars, but these may be safely left in the car park at Holwerd. It is quite an interesting experience to make the passage at low tide, as the boat follows a winding course through the mudflats.

Schiermonnikoog is the most easterly of the five Dutch Wadden Islands, and is about 11km long and 2km broad. It also is closed to visitors' cars, and as the name implies, it was once owned by the monks from Klaarkamp, a Cistercian monastery in North Friesland, of which no trace remains. Apart from one village, which used to be called Oosterburen, the landscape consists of pine woods and sand dunes. The village is now usually known as Schiermonnikoog. The north-eastern corner of the island is very attractive, and the surrounding high dunes create a large bird sanctuary. The houses in the little village date mostly from the eighteenth century. The chief attractions for visitors are the beaches, pony riding, walking and cycling and the nature reserves. The ferry service departs from the new port of Lauwersoog, in north Groningen, with 3 or 4 sailings per day. Cars are left in the car park at the ferry terminal, and since there are only about 10km of road on the island, the ban on cars is not unacceptable.

South-East Friesland

South and east of **Drachten** is a countryside totally different from that of the Frisian lake district or the northern *terp* areas. It is a land of extensive woods alternating with sand dunes, heath and fens. Some very attractive scenery surrounds **Beetsterzwaag** and **Bakkeveen**, near the border with Drenthe province. A short distance from Bakkeveen is Zwartendijkster schans, an old fortification which is said to be the model on which Pieter Stuyvesant based the fort he built at New Amsterdam, in America, which later became New York.

Further south are the woods and heathlands of **Appelscha**, well provided with very pleasant cycle paths, and to the west is **Heerenveen**, a town which is described as being on the border between wood and water, referring to its position at the point where the lakes to the west meet the wooded country to the east, with its farms and fens. The name of the town shows that it is also in a land where peat was cut. To the east of the town are the woods of the Oranjewoud estate, with many waymarked footpaths and cycle paths through fine old beech woods. Formerly the property of the widow of Prince William IV of Nassau, in the seventeenth century, it is now freely open to the public. In the town itself are a number of fine old buildings, including the regional museum and the elegant Municipal offices in the seventeenth-century 'Crackstate' mansion. A restored cornmill dating from 1849 can often be seen working. Of special interest to many visitors will be the Batavus museum, which originated as a collection of bicycles starting with a model from 1817 and including the machine which holds the world one-hour record. In addition, the collection has been expanded to include motor-cycles and a unique collection of antique motor cars covering the years 1895 to 1926, together with many accessories.

Finally, to the south of Heerenveen is the small town of **Wolvega**, where there is a statue of Pieter Stuyvesant, who was born in the area. Wherever one goes in this part of Friesland, the wooden *klokkenstoelen* and typical Frisian farmhouses will be seen, with black and white Frisian cows in the fields. The farm barns have the ends of the gables finished off with decorated *uileborden* which also serve the purpose of protecting the entrances left for owls to enter and leave the loft space. Owls are always welcome lodgers in barns, as they help to keep mice and other robbers of the stored grain under control. The *uileborden* are a typical example of the combination of practical matters with decorative design.

All in all, Friesland deserves to be better known by visitors who can appreciate what it has to offer.

Typical Frisian
klokkenstoel *or wooden*
belfry, at Nijerveen

10 GRONINGEN -
THE MOST NORTHERLY PROVINCE

Groningen is seldom visited by overseas tourists from the West, perhaps because it has become associated with new industrial developments, or perhaps because it appears to be isolated in the far north of the country.

The truth is that there are rolling farmlands with cattle breeding and agriculture based on ancient manor farms, old villages built on mounds called *wierden* (*terps* in Friesland), fenland showing the results of peat-cutting over hundreds of years, rolling woodland, and extensive lakes and waterways ideally suited to recreational sailing. All this, together with the country's third largest port, one of the largest deposits of natural gas in the world, and deposits of salt for industry, add up to a fascinating part of the country which has been neglected too long by the visitor.

The city of **Groningen** is easily reached by two motorways, the A7 from the west and Amsterdam, and the A28 linking with the centre and south of the country. It lies at the centre of a network of trunk roads, and has good rail connections. It makes an ideal base from which to explore the province, and warrants some time spent looking around.

The city sprang up in 1040, as a trading settlement on the dividing line between the sandy country to the south and the claylands to the north, at a point where access to the sea was possible along the Reitdiep river. By the Middle Ages it had become a member of the Hanseatic League, and had extended its influence over the surrounding country, becoming an independent state. A University was established in the city in 1614. Extensive damage occurred during the last days of World War II, and after rebuilding much of the centre of the city has been pedestrianised, making walking and shopping easy.

The whole city centre is surrounded by water, showing how it was originally fortified, and parking up to four hours is possible at places around the canal ring. One such park is near the station, across Herebrug in Heresingel.

ROUTE 30   A WALK AROUND GRONINGEN

Start the walk from Hereplein, at the north end of Herebrug, and walk east along Heresingel, past the car park to the crossroads. Turn left into Verlengde Oosterstraat, and continue into Rademarkt, passing the old St Anthony Gasthuis or almshouse on the left. This beautiful old building dating from 1517 was once used as a hospital for plague victims, and in the last century as an asylum. At the top of Rademarkt, cross over into Gedempte Kattendiep, a filled-in canal, and a short way along, on the left, turn into Kleine Peperstraat, thence almost immediately right again into Peperstraat, to the beautiful Pepergasthuis (1405) with its chapel. It is possible to go through here into an alley at the back called Achter de Muur,

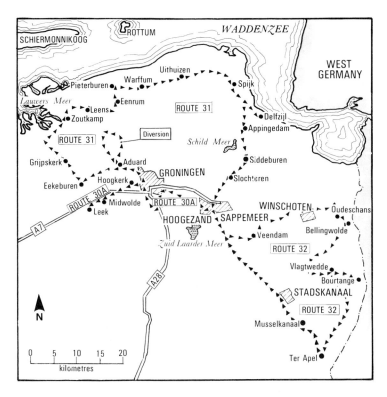

from which Poelestraat can be entered, and a left turn leads to the Grote Markt, where in the corner of the square is the huge Martinitoren. This may be climbed, and the effort is worth it for the view of the city and of the surrounding countryside on a clear day. The tower is almost 100m high, and dates back to 1469, although the top was destroyed by fire and rebuilt in the seventeenth century. The earliest record of a tower here is from 1215, and the present one belongs to the municipality. In the Martinikerk itself is an organ said to be one of the finest in Europe, and the choir dating from 1413 has some unique murals. The whole church was completely restored in 1975. Behind is the Martinikerkhof or former churchyard, a peaceful oasis surrounded by attractive old buildings of which the Provinciehuis, or seat of the Provincial Government, has parts dating from the sixteenth century.

Next to this is a house with a beautiful Renaissance façade from 1559. Go through the arched gateway in the corner of the churchyard into Turfstraat, then at the end turn left along Turfsingel to an ornate gateway which leads into the Prinsenhof garden. On the inside of the arch over the gate is a remarkable sundial (1731), and the garden itself has been restored to its seventeenth-century state with clipped hedges, sheltered walks, roses and a herb garden. The Prinsenhof was a house for lay brothers in the fifteenth century, then became the Bishop's home from 1568 to 1576. After that it had a long and complicated history, culminating in its present use as the site of the local radio station. After leaving the garden, turn left and left again into Kattenhage, and on into St Walburgstraat, where the Natural History museum is on the left. Ahead is a small square with restored houses. Turn right into Jacobijnerstraat leading to Oude Ebbingestraat, then left and right into Rode Weeshuisstraat; the carved doorway of the old orphanage may be seen on the left. Turn right into Oude Boteringestraat and on the left is the old city Watch House (1634) or Kortegaard, its name a corruption of the French *Corps de Garde*. Along this street are a number of elegant seventeenth and eighteenth-century houses, and at the end of the street, across the Boteringe bridge, is the 'new' town, built since 1625. The bridge leads towards the Ossenmarkt, with a number of attractive eighteenth-century houses. Walking westwards along Lopende Diep (North side), one can see high and low water quays; this was once the town moat and the link with the sea during the period of its membership of the Hanseatic League. The waters were tidal as far as the Spijlsluizen until 1877, when sea locks were built on the Reitdiep at Zoutkamp. Lopendediep leads to the strangely-named Kijk in 't Jatbrug. The name of this bridge is said to recall the siege of 1672, when look-outs were watching for the relief boats. On a house at the south-east corner is a carving of a head of an old man 'peeping into the creek'. Over the bridge, continue down Oude Kijk in 't Jatstraat past the tree-bordered forecourt of the former Harmonie building, once the home of the music society but now used by the University Law Faculty. Beyond here on the right is the fifteenth-century Mepschen almshouse, next door to one of the oldest houses in Groningen. Turn right through Kromme Elleboog and along Turftorenstraat to the Hoge der A. Many of the brick warehouses along the waterside have been converted into flats and apartments.

Turn left along the waterfront to Museumbrug, where on the left is the Groningen Museum, with a large historical collection, fine silver and Chinese porcelain, and exhibitions of modern art. Return along the waterside to the A-brug, turn right into Brugstraat, where there are two more excellent museums: the Northern Shipping Museum, and Niemeijer's Dutch Tobacco Museum. Both are housed in restored medieval buildings, in one of which are the remains of the first stone house in the city. Further along is the lovely A-kerk, originally consecrated in 1247, added to at various times since, and restored in 1981. Through the A-kerkhof is the the Corn Exchange building and the Vismarkt, and beyond, through Koude Gat, is the Grote Markt. The buildings here suffered much damage in 1945, the main survivors being the Town Hall, a neo-Classical building of 1793 to 1810, the Hotel de Doelen (1730) and the fine Goudkantoor from 1635, with the shell motif decoration that is typical of Groningen.

From the Goudkantoor, turn south along the pedestrian street of Herestraat, right into Kleine Pelsterstraat, and right again into Pelsterstraat, where on the left is the oldest almshouse in Groningen, the Heilige Geest or Pelstergasthuis. Originally a shelter for the sick, poor, and travellers, this beautiful twelfth-century building has been an almshouse since the sixteenth century. It has its own church, and by walking through beside this, a second courtyard can be seen, with one of the few remaining original town pumps. The walk ends by returning to Herestraat, turning right and regaining the car park via Hereplein.

ROUTE 30A AROUND GRONINGEN

About 4km out of the city, south towards **Haren**, is the Hortus de Wolf, the botanical garden belonging to Groningen University. Of interest to garden lovers, it contains many tropical plants in a huge glasshouse divided into sections according to climate. A short distance to the west, just across the motorway, is the Paterswoldse Meer, a lovely lake formed by generations of peat cutting, and now used for all kinds of watersport and recreation. A very picturesque road runs all round the lake, which is right on the border of the provinces of Groningen and Drenthe. Still on the provincial boundary, about 15km further to the west is the small town of **Leek**, in the neighbourhood of which is the Country Park of Nienoord. Leek is easily reached along the A7 motorway, although a more pleasant route is along the road through Hoogkerk, Oostwold and Midwolde.

At **Midwolde** is an interesting brick-built twelfth-century church, which has close historical links with the estate of Nienoord. The mausoleum of the former occupants of Nienoord, made in 1664 by the Dutch sculptor Verhulst, is to be found here, as is a very rare organ and a fine carved pulpit. The estate has pleasant waymarked walks and cycle paths, together with many attractions including a children's farm, playground, miniature railway, midget golf and outdoor swimming pools. On the lake are facilities for model boat enthusiasts, and an extensive model railway system offers similar facilities to model railway fans.

In addition to all this, the buildings of the old *borg* or manor house, which was founded about 1525 and rebuilt after a fire in the nineteenth century, now form part of the National Carriage Museum, the stable block accommodating a magnificent collection of historic coaches, etc. In the house itself is a collection of children's carriages, dog-carts, horse-drawn sleighs, and many travelling accessories from former days, including dressing cases, drinks cabinets, carriage commodes, and so on. All give a real insight into the rigours and pleasures of travel before the days of trains and motor vehicles. Many of the children's carriages come from the Royal Family and belonged to Queen Wilhelmina.

In the museum garden is a shell-grotto, its walls being richly decorated with shells and pebbles from all over the world.

On the estate there are plenty of refreshment facilities, an open-air theatre and a fully equipped campsite. From the lake, round trips by boat may be taken to the nearby Leekster Meer, where boats can also be hired.

ROUTE 31   AROUND THE NORTH OF GRONINGEN PROVINCE

This route runs past some of the interesting old *wierd* villages and *borgs*, and into the little towns of Zoutkamp and Appingedam.

Leave Groningen via the ring road Friesestraatweg (N46) on the northwest side of the city, thence taking the N355 Zuidhorn road. At **Aduard**, about 5km out, is an old abbey church situated in the former refectory. Opposite the church, on the Kaakheem, is an old-fashioned Post Office, still in use. From the village, a diversion may be made northwards to **Feerwerd** and **Ezinge**, where there is a good example of a *borg* nearby, at Allersma. Continue along the main road towards **Zuidhorn**, turn left at signpost 1544, cross the railway and follow the Grootegast road as far as **Eekeburen**. Just past here, turn off the major road to **Oldekerk**, where there is a good example of a *klokkenstoel*. Continue along minor roads, crossing the van Starkenborgh Canal beside the locks, and so to **Grijpskerk**. Turn left along the main road, and in 2km turn right, then right again at the beginning of Warfstermolen, following signs to **Zoutkamp**. The town is entered across a bridge beside the Friese Sluis, the sea locks where the Reitdiep enters the former Lauwers Zee. The little town of Zoutkamp was once a thriving fishing port, but since the closing of the Lauwersmeer in 1969 it now relies on the tourist industry. The newly-reclaimed land is being developed with this in mind, and the new road across the Pampusplaat to Lauwersoog is particularly good for bird watchers.

From Zoutkamp, take the main road north and at the T-junction (signpost 10091) turn right towards **Leens**. The church here is one of the oldest in the province, and has a very fine interior with a superb carved pulpit, pews and choir screen. The organ is an outstanding instrument built in 1733. Just beyond the village is the *borg* or mansion of Verhildersum, first inhabited in 1398, now owned by the local authority, and open to the public. A permanent exhibition entitled 'Wad and Land' illustrates the way in which the land and sea have been formed and have changed over the centuries, and how man has adapted and occupied the land. Changing exhibitions are staged here, and the gardens, restored to their former style, are well worth seeing.

The road from Leens continues east until the crossroads at **Mensingeweer**, where a left turn leads towards **Eenrum**. In this area are a number of typical farmhouses, but the special place of interest is the Arboretum, with more than 500 types of tree and shrub, all of which are best suited to the sandy soil. From the Arboretum, follow the road through the village towards the windmill, going right at the next junction, then left at the crossroads to **Pieterburen**. This small village behind the sea dyke is the centre for *Wadlopen* or walking over the mudflats of the Wadden Sea. The region off the coast is unique in Europe, and the extensive areas of mud which are covered and uncovered twice every day by the ebb and flow of the tides stretch for over 10km offshore. They provide a feeding and resting place for birds and other creatures, and an unusual and fascinating way of passing some hours in gentle exercise. However, it must be emphasised that walking out over the *wad* must not be undertaken without an experienced guide who knows the tides and the dangers, and who is trained and equipped to lead parties safely. A selection of walks is available, ranging from short introductory trips to long, strenuous walks to Ameland or Schiermonnikoog. Dates and times of departure, and all details, can be obtained from the organisers in Pieterburen. Also in the village, next to the Domies Toenhoes, is a botanical garden.

A long-distance footpath, the Pieterpad, starts at Pieterburen, and extends right through the east of the country to Maastricht in the extreme south, a total of 466km. Here it links up with the French GR5 via a connecting path through Belgium, and so a continuous walk is possible from the Wadden Sea coast to the Mediterranean.

From Pieterburen, take the minor road past the windmill via Westernieland and Den Andel to **Warffum**, which is an outstanding *wierd* village with an outdoor museum, 'Het Hogeland', depicting the way of life in the mound villages. From the church a network of small *kerkpaadjes* or footpaths radiate out through the town to outlying farms. These public footpaths are very unusual for the country. From Warffum the major road continues east to **Uithuizen**, on the outskirts of which is the beautiful moated manor house of Menkemaborg, with period rooms, and a park with a maze and lovely rose gardens, open to the public. The road continues through Uithuizermeeden and Roodeschool to **Spijk**, another outstanding *wierd* village whose thirteenth-century church, stands in the centre of a moated mound, surrounded by a ring road from which the streets fan out.

3km to the south of Spijk, the road forks for Delfzijl to the left or Appingedam to the right. **Delfzijl** is the largest port in the north of the Netherlands, and the third largest in the whole country, having developed rapidly since the discovery of huge deposits of salt and natural gas in the area. Originally a fortified town on the river Eems, a windmill stands on the oldest bulwark, and on the sea dyke is a good sea-water aquarium and shell collection. **Appingedam**, 4km inland from Delfzijl, is much more interesting, being noted for its 'hanging kitchens', built out from the houses and overhanging the water of the Damsterdiep in the old town centre. It is pleasant to walk around as many of the narrow streets are restricted to pedestrians, and the fine seventeenth-century Town Hall, thirteenth-

Hanging Kitchens, Appingedam

century St Nicolaikerk and the Regional Historical Museum are all worth seeing. Almost absorbed by recent development are the old villages of Solwerd and Opwierde, whose churches still stand intact on their mounds.

The main N33 road from Appingedam runs south to **Siddeburen**, where by turning right, the road leads to **Slochteren**. This town is on top of the largest natural gas deposit in Europe, but the installations are by no means excessively intrusive. Unlike the northern part of the province, where the villages are on mounds, set in between large landed estates and large farms linked by winding roads, the countryside around Slochteren is traversed by drainage ditches running either side of straight roads which follow sand ridges. Between these ditches lie narrow plots of land, sometimes as long as two to three kilometres.

On the edge of the town of Slochteren lies the sixteenth-century manor house and estate of Fraeylemaborg. Surrounded by a wide moat, the house contains various exhibitions of works of art, etc, and the grounds include stables and coach-house, and extensive wooded parkland laid out in the nineteenth-century English style. Within the estate there is a very fine restaurant in the converted coach-house.

Some 6 to 7km south-west of Slochteren is the large industrial area of **Hoogezand-Sappemeer**, where in spite of the industry, attempts have been made to provide some pleasant parks, recreation areas, and open spaces. In particular, there is the Zuidlaardermeer on the south of the town. This lake was originally constructed to act as an 'overflow' reservoir for when the river Hunze flooded, but it is now a very popular area for all watersports, with the Meerwijk recreation area at its north end. The town has shipbuilding yards along the banks of the Winschoterdiep, which is so narrow that boats have to be launched sideways into the water.

The return to the city of Groningen may be made either by the A7 motorway, or along the old road which runs beside the Winschoterdiep.

ROUTE 32   SOUTH-EAST GRONINGEN

This tour takes in the extensive peat area between the German frontier on the east, the border of Drenthe on the west, and the sandy ridge known as the Hondsrug which runs south from the city of Groningen, just to the west of the Zuidlaardermeer.

Hoogezand-Sappemeer was one of the first of the peat-cutting colonies in the province, and the road which runs south from the Hoogezand junction on the A7 motorway leads through typical peat-fen country.

A turning 7km south of the motorway leads left to **Veendam**, described as the garden city of the north owing to its many parks and lakes. Formerly a ship-building centre, it has several houses which were once the homes of sea captains. The most interesting place is the Veenkoloniaal Museum, depicting the history of the Groningen peat-cutting industry. Leave the town to the east, joining the main N33 road, which should be followed north to Meeden, then turn right towards **Winschoten**, through typical ribbon development along the roads between the drainage canals.

Winschoten grew from the monastery in neighbouring Heiligerlee, and has three fine tower windmills. In the centre of an agricultural area, the town lies on top of a very rich deposit of salt which serves the industry of Delfzijl. There is an exceptionally fine rose garden in the town park, with over 100 different species.

Leaving the town on the north side, turn right on to the N7 motorway, and follow to the next junction, then turn right through Klein-Ulsda to **Oudeschans**, a star-shaped fortress built about 1593, with a signed walking route around it. Continue along the same road to the next village, **Bellingwolde**, which is in complete contrast. The main street or Hoofdstraat stretches for nearly 3km, and is bordered on both sides by large farmhouses of a type common in this area. Unlike the 'kop-hals-romp' farmhouses of the west, in which the 'hals' was the dairy, the emphasis on crop-growing in the south-east caused the introduction of a seed loft above the *kophuis* or main part of the building. In the main street are the Oude Rechthuis or courthouse dating from 1643, and the regional museum 'De Oude Wolden', with a collection of old clothes-making appliances and implements. Continue along the main street, cross over the major road at signpost 3417, and carry on through Vriescheloo to cross the main road and into **Wedde**, where there is a fourteenth-century *borg* called Huis te Wedde or Wedderborg, and also a recreation park.

Through the village, turn left at signpost 2669, reaching after 4km the village of **Onstwedde**, on the edge of an area of sandy tracks, isolated farms

PLACES TO VISIT IN SOUTH-EAST GRONINGEN

Veendam
Veenkoloniaal Museum — history of peat cutting in the province.

Winschoten
Three fine tower mills. Beautiful rose gardens.

Oudeschans
Old fortress village, with waymarked route.

Bellingwolde
Long main street (3km).

Seventeenth-century *Oude Rechthuis*. Regional museum 'De Oude Wolden' related to the clothing industry.

Wedde
Fourteenth-century borg 'Huis te Wedde'.

Bourtagne
Outstanding restored fortified star-shaped village with moated ramparts, on German border.

and a network of winding waterways. The Saxon origin of the area can be seen in a number of early farmhouses to be found in the 'protected' hamlet of **Smeerling**, to the east of Onstwedde on the road to Vlagtwedde. In a countryside of heather, woods and wet grassland, an unusual feature is the tree-lined earth banks or *boomwallen*. At **Vlagtwedde**, pass the village and continue on the minor road eastwards, to the fortified village of **Bourtange**. The name comes from the word *tange* which means a sandy ridge, and the word *boer* or farmer. During the war with Spain, a road ran from Germany along a sandy ridge through the marshes towards Groningen, and in 1580 Prince William of Orange ordered an earthwork to defend this road. Owing to the surrounding marshes, the condition of the road itself, and the entrenchment, it was never overcome. It is interesting to note that Bourtange was the only fortified place in the north to be built solely for military reasons. During the seventeenth century, the defences were strengthened and extended, and again withstood siege, thus contributing to the safety of the city of Groningen which was also beseiged. In the eighteenth century the fortress was at the peak of its strength, with five bastions, connecting earth ramparts and other outworks, barracks, powder magazines, and so on, and a radial street plan leading from the town centre to the bastions. Towards the end of the nineteenth century it had outlived its purpose, many of the ramparts were destroyed, and the moats filled in. Bourtange became a forgotten town; but, in 1964 the town council of Vlagtwedde decided to rebuild and restore the fortifications and today we can see it as it was, complete with restored buildings, including the fine windmill on one of the five bastions. The whole complex forms a complete star-shaped pattern in the surrounding fields which now replace the former marshes.

Entrance to the fortress town of Bourtagne, across a moat

From Bourtange, return to Vlagtwedde and follow the road south. Here the route runs almost parallel with the German frontier, through pleasant scenery with fine farmhouses and old oak woods, many of which are protected as nature reserves, notably at Metbroek and 't Liefstinghsbroek. About 10km south of Vlagtwedde is the village of **Sellingen**, an area with excellent possibilities for walking and cycling. The wooded land continues all the way to **Ter Apel**, in the extreme southerly corner of the province where it joins Germany to the east and Drenthe to the west; it also lies on the edge of the peat area, and owes its origin to the digging of canals in connection with the peat cutting industry. To the north-west of Ter Apel, the town of **Stadskanaal** was once the longest peat village with double ribbon development, although now it has expanded outwards and is gaining new industries.

11 BEAUTIFUL DRENTHE

Drenthe is one of the earliest known settled areas in the Netherlands, as can be seen by the presence of more than fifty megalithic tombs or *hunebeds*. From north to south, right across the province, runs the sandy ridge known as the 'Hondsrug' (dog's back) where many of the *hunebeds* are to be found. For the traveller who enjoys beautiful country and peaceful surroundings, Drenthe has much to recommend it, with lovely moorland areas, small lakes, and many forests with miles of cycle paths and footpaths. The 'Pieterpad' runs the length of the Hondsrug, and it is possible to cycle for a whole day along secluded cycle routes with hardly another soul to be seen. For horse-riders there are plenty of *ruiterpads*, and small horsedrawn covered wagons known as *huifkarren* may be hired for the day to explore the sandy lanes through the woods and heathlands.

Apart from its natural attractions, Drenthe has a wide variety of museums, large and small, ranging from the huge peat colony village at Barger Compascuum to the small Kachelmuseum at Ruinerwold with its collection of antique stoves!

Large quantities of oil have been found in Drenthe, especially in the area around Schoonebeek, but the small pumps which bring the oil to the surface are far from intrusive, because of careful landscaping. They are known by the odd name of *Ja-knikkers*, which can be loosely translated as 'nodding heads'.

The provincial capital of Drenthe is Assen, which, with the towns of Emmen in the south-east and Meppel in the south-west make good bases for touring.

ROUTE 33   ASSEN and NORTH-WEST DRENTHE
The old town centre of **Assen**, as in so many of the small villages in Drenthe, is known as the *Brink*, meaning 'village green'. The town was developed from this point, and around the Brink are some attractive old buildings, including the former chapel of a Cistercian nunnery founded in the thirteenth century, which now forms part of the group of buildings housing the Drents Museum. This includes one of the finest archaeological collections in the Netherlands, with the oldest vessel ever found, a wooden canoe from Pesse, some 25km to the south of the town. Dated approximately 6,800BC, the canoe, like many other artefacts, had been preserved by the peat soil of the area. Other exhibits include material found in *hunebeds*, such as Beaker pottery and Bronze Age jewellery, together with Roman treasures from Beilen and other sites. The museum also has a fine collection of traditional costumes, as well as ceramics, silver and glass. In the Ontvangershuis (1650), formerly the official residence of the Receiver-General of Drenthe, are a number of beautiful period rooms, and nearby may be found remains of the thirteenth-century cloister, old

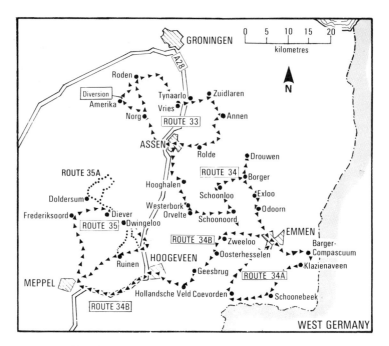

convent wall and pump.

Motor-cycle enthusiasts will know that Assen is the home of the Dutch TT races, held on the circuit just off the motorway to the south of the town, but the young enthusiast is also catered for in the Jeugdverkeerspark (Young People's Transport Park), located in the Asserbos near the town centre. This unique park contains roadways with all the appropriate traffic signs, on which children aged 6-12 may drive pedal cars and have great fun learning the rule of the road. For very young children there is a special bus, and a small playground exclusively for the under-fives.

Adults are catered for in the neighbouring Automuseum with its collection of vintage and veteran cars, including several Bugattis, motor-cycles, including a Royal Enfield from 1912, Indians from 1916 to 1942, and a Norton racing machine. All this plus a collection of mechanical toys should keep any family occupied for the day.

After looking around the town, leave on the road leading west across the ring road and motorway, signed to **Smilde**. In about 2km, turn right in the direction of **Norg** and **Roden**. At Norg is a thirteenth-century 'saddle tower' church, with choir, in which there are some thirteenth-century paintings believed to be the oldest in Drenthe. Here, too, is an old Brink in the centre of the village. From Norg, either continue north towards Roden, or make a diversion at signpost 1943 towards **Een**, where the road to the right (signpost 2422) is taken for 1km, then left at signpost 5051. This leads through narrow and pleasant lanes to **Een-West**, near which is the old fortification of Zwartendijkster schans. Just to the north is a small hamlet appropriately named Amerika, where *huifkarren* may be hired. More narrow winding lanes lead north via Nieuw-Roden into **Roden** itself.

On the Brink is the Nederlands Museum Kinderwereld, started originally as a private hobby, and since grown into an outstanding collection of all kinds of children's toys and games from the past 150 years. Here is everything from dolls and dolls' houses to toy soldiers and forts, from magic lanterns to model steam engines, a complete model railway layout operated by coin-in-the-slot mechanism, old spinning tops and hoops, and much more. Many of the toys and games can be tried out by today's children; a day out not to be missed by any child — or its parents!

From the centre of Roden, take the road leading eastwards to **Peize**, go through the town past the windmill, and follow the minor picturesque road on the right (signpost 10280) to Donderen and **Vries**, where there is a beautiful twelfth-century Romanesque church with one of the finest towers in the province. From the church, cross over the main road and follow the road for **Tynaarlo**, which crosses over the Noord Willems canal and under the motorway. Through Tynaarlo the road continues to **Zuidlaren**, near the border with Groningen province.

Standing on the Hondsrug, Zuidlaren is one of the prettiest *brink* villages in Drenthe, but it is also an impressive place, noted for its horse market. A fine old oak tree stands on the Brink, and the seventeenth-century manor house 'Laarwoud' is now used as the town hall. During the months of July and August, folklore markets are held, where local crafts and produce are on sale, demonstrations are given, folk dancing takes place and local costumes or worn. For the children there is the Sprookjeshof fairy-tale park. The whole area is ideal for cycling, there being many cycle paths through lovely wooded countryside.

Equally attractive is the road south from Zuidlaren (signpost 228 by the church) to Annen and **Anloo**, the latter being another very old village with an ancient church on the Brink, whose nave dates from the eleventh century. The little spire on top of the twelfth-century tower was added in 1757, and seems rather incongruous, but the nave is the oldest Romanesque building in Drenthe. The church contains wall paintings from three different periods.

Just to the south of Anloo, in the *Boswachterij Anloo* or Anloo Forest, is one of the many *hunebeds* to be seen in this locality, together with a pinetum. The *hunebed* lies just to the west of a sandy cycle track, and consists of a total of 18 stones. A minor road runs south from Anloo (paddestoel 21573) along the edge of the forest and a car park is located near the pinetum and *hunebed*. Follow this winding road south, passing two more *hunebeds*, then turn left at the T-junction and sharp right at paddestoel 21571, on the edge of the village of **Eext**. Cross the main road N33, and at the next junction, near signpost 3364, is another *hunebed* with

thirty-nine stones. Turning right at this junction, follow the road through
to **Rolde**, its fifteenth-century Gothic church with Drents-type tower being
one of the finest in the province. It possesses a fine pulpit and stained glass
windows by the artist Joep Nicolas (1964). Behind the church are two more
hunebeds, also tumuli. To complete the route, return to Assen along the
minor road past the church, or turn south past the mill and turn right along
the main road N33.

ROUTE 34   FROM ASSEN TO EMMEN
This route goes past the largest radio telescope in Western Europe, and an
old Saxon village where rural crafts are being kept alive; to a museum
which delves into the history of the *hunebedden*, and to a very fine modern
zoo.

From Assen town centre, leave by the road running south past the
railway station, Overcingellaan, and turn left at signpost 4022. This is not
the motorway, but the road which runs parallel, between the motorway
and the railway. After about 6km, in the village of **Hooghalen**, turn left and
follow a minor road north-east, towards Amen. In about 2km, is a car park
at the end of Melkweg Pad (Milky Way Path). Leave the car and walk

along this path for about 3km, to the largest radio telescope in Western Europe. Along the path are scale models of the solar system. Cars are not allowed owing to the risk of disturbing the sensitive electronic equipment. Not far from here is a memorial marking the site of the notorious Westerbork Transit Camp, which was used during World War II by the Germans to send Dutch Jews to Germany and the concentration camp at Auschwitz. A Memorial Centre has been built beside the road where the car park is situated, to record the facts of the transportation of some 100,000 Dutch Jews and other refugees in this way, and to remind all people of the terrible effects of such race hatred and persecution. The irony of this is that the camp was originally built in 1939 by the Dutch Government to accommodate many German Jews who had fled from Germany, to what they thought would be freedom.

Return to Hooghalen, turn left again along the road until the next turning on the left, at signpost 5560. This leads via a right fork through the hamlet of Zwiggelte to the village of **Westerbork**, where folklore markets are held some evenings in the summer. A museum farm, 'In de Ar', with old rooms and antique implements, and the Nederlands Museum van de Knipkunst, illustrating the art of paper-cutting, from the seventeenth century to the present day, with examples from all over the world are found here.

Continue in an easterly direction, to the next village of **Orvelte**, an old Saxon village in the care of a foundation whose purpose is to maintain the whole as a centre for traditional crafts such as milling and baking, wood carving, pottery, clog-making, and the blacksmith's art. The old houses are the homes of the craftsmen, and the Saxon origins of the village and its surrounding farmland are shown by means of way-marked paths around the area. Visitors' cars are not allowed in the village, but adequate free car parking is available. Several craft workshops may be visited. The farm is very interesting; by way of experiment, old and new methods of farming are followed side by side. During holiday times special demonstrations of cheese and butter-making, and other such activities, are given, and a very good restaurant is located in one of the enormous old barns. The whole place is worth more than just a passing visit.

From the car park, return to the road from Westerbork, turn left, then left again at signpost 1222, and then turn right towards **Schoonoord**. At the main road, turn left and in a short distance will be seen the entrance to yet another open-air museum, this time called 'De Zeven Marken'. Unlike Orvelte, which is a living village community, De Zeven Marken is a museum showing the life-style and work of a typical Drents farm and village at the turn of the century. Demonstrations of wood carving, pottery, weaving and other crafts are given at various times.

Some 4km south, along the road to Sleen, there is another *hunebed*, which has been given the name of the 'Papeloze Kerk' or church without a Pope. There are a total of 53 stones, of which 28 form a kidney-shaped outline.

PLACES TO VISIT FROM ASSEN TO EMMEN

Hooghalen
Largest radio telescope in Western Europe.
Memorial Centre 'Kamp Westerbork'.

Westerbork
Museum farm. Unusual paper-cutting museum, 'Museum van de Knipkunst'.

Orvelte
Old Saxon Village, maintained as a centre to keep alive traditional crafts.

Schoonoord
Open-air museum 'De Zeven Marken', showing the lifestyle and work of Drents people at the turn of the century.

Sleen
Hunebed known as the *Papeloze Kerk* (church without a Pope).

Borger
Largest *hunebed* in Holland, plus several others.
Museum ''t Flint 'n Hoes' — finds from the *hunebeds* and displays showing how the *hunebeds* were built.
Stone tower of church dating from the fourteenth century.
Drouwenerzand Natural History museum.

Recreatie Centrum 'het Drouwenerzand'.
'De Oude Waag' amusement and recreation centre.

Odoorn
Church with twelfth-century choir — evidence of stones from *hunebeds* used in the building.

Emmen
Noorder Dierenpark (zoo): Fine modern zoo, with animals in an uncaged environment, walk-through aviaries and butterfly houses.
Museum 'de Hondsrug': local history museum.
'Radiotron': Exhibition of radios and gramophones and telephone equipment.

Barger-Compascuum
Fen museum ''t Aole Compas'. Old fen village and living museum illustrating the history of peat-cutting from the mid-nineteenth century to the mid-1930s. Old turf huts, school and church, village bakery, etc. Original peat cutting machines demonstrated.

Schoonebeek
Historical farmhouse with 'sand-carpet'.

Coevoorden
Municipal museum in old arsenal. Twelfth-century castle.

Visiting this *hunebed* is a diversion, because from Schoonoord, the route continues north through peaceful forests along the Hondsrug, and at **Schoonloo** turns right towards **Borger**, an interesting village with plenty of scope for walking and riding in the neighbouring forests. Guided walks are organised during the summer months by the State Forestry Service. However, perhaps the most interesting sight is the largest *hunebed* in the Netherlands, one of the most concentrated group of such ancient monuments in the country, to be found on the minor road leading to Bronneger. The museum 't Flint 'n Hoes is housed in the former Workhouse, and has an exhibition of finds from the huge megaliths, and general displays about the Beaker Culture and how the *hunebeds* were built. The *hunebeds* themselves are made from huge stones or boulders which were carried to Drenthe by glacial ice during the Ice Ages. Because of the way in which these boulders were scraped along the ground, they usually have one flat side, which fact was used by the builders of the burial chambers. The original cap and roof stones have now collapsed in most instances, and of course many stones have long been removed for use elsewhere. The *hunebed* by the museum has 47 stones and is 21m long, and many of the cap stones are in position.

The church in Borger was built in the ninteenth century, but its stone tower is from the fourteenth century. About 4km to the north, along the main road to **Gasselte**, is a Natural History museum, at Drouwenerzand, which has many exhibits concerning underwater aquaria, both fresh and salt water. There are also two recreation and amusement centres in the neighbourhood, although they seem rather out of place in the countryside.

From Borger itself, leave by the road which runs parallel to the main road, going south through Ees to **Exloo**, where there is a museum farm and children's farm. On leaving the village, take the road to **Odoorn** from paddestoel 21544. The church in Odoorn was originally built in the twelfth century, with evidence to suggest that stones from *hunebeds* were used for the choir. The nave was built in 1856. The major road south from Odoorn forks in about 4km, and the left fork is taken into the town of **Emmen**.

Emmen is first mentioned in 1137, as a village lying on a spur of the 'Hondsrug'. However, men lived in the area a very long time before that, and hunters from about 6000BC must have used the stag-horn harpoon, the oldest find in the country, which was excavated from the peat just to the south of the town. During the following periods of changing climate, hunters and fishers gave way to farmers, through the Stone Age builders of the *hunebeds* and tumuli, and the Bronze Age to the earliest signs of peat cutting in the area, some 5000 years ago. The town lies right on the edge of the extensive peat countryside, with its network of small canals and drainage ditches dividing the land into square plots, so unlike the neighbouring Hondsrug with its forest and heath.

Since World War II, much light industry has been established here, and Emmen has grown rapidly into a modern but pleasant town.

One of the most interesting attractions is the Noorder Dierenpark Zoo, which has recently been completely reorganised into one of the most modern zoos of its kind, re-creating African savannah in which the animals roam freely. The zoo is also well known for its large pool for sea-lions, and the walk-through cage with over two hundred free-flying birds. The latest

Prehistoric megalith near Emmen, one of many hunebedden *in Drenthe*

addition is an enormous covered enclosure with free-flying butterflies from all over the world, amongst which visitors may walk.

Of more local interest is the small museum 'De Hondsrug', which illustrates the history and prehistory of Emmen and the surrounding country. In direct contrast is the 'Radiotron', a permanent exhibition of radio, gramophone and telephone equipment and apparatus from 1880 to date.

Emmen is one of the centres for the annual 4-day Drenthe cycle rides, arranged so that participants may ride at their own speed and enjoy the beautiful countryside. A glance at the area touring map will show just how much of this there is, and it is possible to cycle from Emmen to Roden along the Hondsrug, or from Emmen to Assen, along special cycle paths, most of which run through State Forestry areas (*Boswachterij*).

ROUTE 34A   SOUTH AND EAST OF EMMEN

To the east and south of Emmen is a corner of the province of Drenthe which lies against the German frontier, and in this corner are three places of interest easily reached from the town.

Leave Emmen by crossing the ring road to the south-east, signed towards **Klazienaveen**, and in 3km turn off to the left towards the frontier, across typical peat country. This leads to the village of **Barger-Compascuum**, and the open-air fen museum ''t Aole Compas'. The origins of the village can be traced back to around 1850, when peat workers and their families from the Frisian fenlands and from neighbouring Germany came and settled here to work. The living and working conditions were appalling, but gradually times changed and people became more aware that workers needed better conditions for themselves and for their children. In this living museum the way in which housing and amenities improved can be seen, from reconstructions of original turf huts to the later brick cottages of the early 1930s. School, church, bakery, windmill, all are here in their original or reconstructed form. There are displays of old turf-cutting implements, photographs, and a horse-drawn barge, once used to move the peat blocks, now carries visitors around the site. More modern transport for the hand-cut peat took the form of a light railway, which again now carries visitors to see not only the old workings, but areas where peat is still cut. On certain days, steam cutting machines are in operation, and the whole picture of the formation, cutting, drying and finally land restoration can be seen. The original churchyard with its simple graves still exists, and the old bakery is used to bake *krentebolletjes* (currant buns) in the turf oven. An exhibition hall is used for films and slide presentations, which include commentary in English.

Additional features and facilities are being added all the time, and refreshments and meals are available. During the year, the site is used for various events such as folk-dance festivals, and various other exhibitions.

From the museum village, take the road south to **Zwartemeer**, through Klazienaveen in the direction of Erica, where a left turn at the cross-roads leads to **Schoonebeek**. The first references to Schoonebeek date from the fourteenth century, and in the area there are a number of old Saxon farmhouses; in the town, opposite the Town Hall, is a magnificent example, fully restored and open to the public. Inside is an example of an old 'sand carpet', made by spreading fine sand on the floor to create patterns, which were changed as required for such purposes as to seek a good harvest, etc. Near the town are two unique huts, one just near the frontier south of Nieuw-Schoonebeek and the other actually in the town, where it has been rebuilt. These huts are known as *boeen*. A *boe* was a cattle-herder's hut, which in former times was built at some distance from the main farm; the cattle-herder lived there to look after the calves in winter. These are the only ones in the Netherlands, although once there were some thirty or forty in the Dutch-German frontier region.

Today things have changed for Schoonebeek, with the discovery of oil. Since 1943, when the first well was sunk, some 600 wells have been drilled, about half of which are in production, indicated by the little nodding pumps which have already been noted. The remaining bore-holes are for injecting steam or water to help force the thick oil to the surface. The whole operation is largely screened by trees and bushes, to minimise the effect on the landscape. Guided tours around the installations are possible, for groups, by arrangement with the VVV.

From Schoonebeek, the road westwards, parallel with the German frontier, comes in 9km to the border town of **Coevorden**, with its restored twelfth-century castle, open to visitors at certain times. The municipal museum is located in the magnificently restored musket and cannonball armoury of the old Arsenal, which is currently used to house the public library, and the old fortifications on the northern side of the town are now a garden. Exhibits in the museum include two silver chalices from 1672, and a model of the fortifications, together with maps and plans etc from around 1550 to the present day. Old photographs of the town during the late nineteenth and twentieth centuries are also on view.

Other places of interest in the town include a seventeenth-century Greek church with a magnificent pulpit, and an eighteenth-century Synagogue, at present in use as a music school. In the town centre is an attractive statue of the Goose Girl.

The return to Emmen may be made either north along the main road, or along the parallel minor road through Dalen.

The area to the west of Emmen consists mainly of farmland and small villages, interspersed with wooded areas, and some of this can be seen on the way from Emmen to **Meppel**, in the extreme south-west corner of the province.

ROUTE 34B   EMMEN TO MEPPEL

Leave Emmen by the main road to the west, and cross over the major junction (signpost 11370) continuing for about 8km to the turn-off to **Zweeloo**, on the left. This is a particularly attractive village, with lovely old farmhouses close together and a thirteenth-century church with an unusual pagan altar. Follow the road through **Aalden**, passing a windmill on the right, then at **Meppen** turn left to the outskirts of **Oosterhesselen**, where there are old Saxon farmhouses. Turn right at signpost 7057, through **Gees** where there is a *zwerfkei* or ice-borne boulder weighing 35 tons. On reaching the road junction beside the canal, turn to the right towards **Geesbrug**, fork left and left again to cross the main road (signpost 7784), from where signs should be followed to **Schoonhoven** Recreation Area at Hollandscheveld. This is a very well-laid-out man-made country park with swimming facilities, beaches, woodlands, etc. When excavating the lake, the spoil was used for a hill from which a good view of the surroundings can be obtained. There is a restaurant near the lake. Follow signs to the village of **Hollandscheveld**, and thence to **Hoogeveen**, a modern town where traditions die hard. Every Sunday morning at 9.30, the people of the town are called to church by the *trommelslager* or drum beat, rather than by the sound of church bells, a 300-year-old tradition. The museum 'Venendal' is located in a seventeenth-century gentleman's house, and contains period rooms, costumes, ornaments and other items relating to the history of the town and surrounding area. Built on top of an old fen, the wide streets follow the lines of old drainage canals. The earliest of these was filled up in the seventeenth century, thus laying the foundations of the modern town. A short run along the motorway brings one to **Meppel**, a convenient base for further travels in south-west Drenthe.

ROUTE 35   MEPPEL and THE VILLAGES OF SOUTH-WEST DRENTHE

Lying as it does in the extreme corner of Drenthe, **Meppel** makes a convenient base for excursions into parts of Overijssel. The town is dominated by the impressive tower of the fifteenth-century church. There are some rather attractive seventeenth-century houses and it is the main shopping centre for the area, so it is often possible to see women wearing the unusual local costume from Staphorst. In the summer boat trips may be taken to the 'broads' of north-west Overijssel.

Leave the town by way of Steenwijklaan, which runs beside the railway, then at the major road junction on the north-east of the town, take the minor road across the N32 motor road towards **Ruinerwold**. Here is a museum farm dating from 1680, with seventeenth-century wall cupboards and tile pictures; also a most unusual Kachel-museum with a collection of more than 120 antique stoves, cookers and fireplaces. Continue along the same road for about 10km to the village of **Ruinen**, whose fifteenth-century church on the *brink* contains some sixteenth-century wall paintings. During the summer, a folklore evening is held each week, with demonstrations of old crafts.

On the outskirts of the village to the north is a *schaapskooi* or sheep-fold. In this part of the world, a sheep-fold is a very large shelter into which the flocks of sheep are herded for the night. At around 5-6pm every evening the sheep may be seen being driven in from the heathlands to the fold. In the summer months a Visitor Centre is opened here with information on the Drents heathlands, the flora and fauna.

From Ruinen, cyclists have an advantage over cars because they can ride through the woods and over the heath to **Dwingeloo**. Turn left in Ruinen at signpost 1763, and follow the cycle routes via paddestoel 21293, right towards the Schaapskooi and Visitor Centre, and straight on to paddestoel 21368. Here the path turns left, after 2km passing the radiotelescope site. Continue to the junction at 24268, thence via **Lhee** to **Dwingeloo**.

Cars will have to continue through Ruinen to Eursinge, then follow the minor road beside the motorway, which is crossed to **Pesse**. The minor road then runs north to **Spier**, then left again, back across the motorway and through the woods to Lhee, and so to Dwingeloo. The village centre, the *brink*, is very attractive, with a number of cafés and restaurants, all overlooked by the church, a fourteenth-century Gothic building with an unusual onion-shaped tower, known locally as the *Ui* (onion). On summer evenings on the *brink*, demonstrations of old crafts and old-style harvesting methods are given.

The next village is **Diever**, reached by crossing the canal, the Drentse Hoofdvaart, at Dieverbrug. On the *brink* at Diever is the Schultehuis, built in 1604, and now a small museum of household goods and furniture. The Glass Museum, 'De Spiraal', has a permanent exhibition showing how glass is worked and has been used through the centuries. A modern studio has been added, and in summer demonstrations are given showing glass-blowing using traditional methods. The village also has two potteries and a smithy, all of which give demonstrations at various times. Diever is an ideal place for walking and cycling. *Huifkarren* may be hired nearby at **Vledder**, **Doldersum** and **Zorgvlied**.

ROUTE 35A   A FOREST RIDE FROM DIEVER

This is a route intended for cyclists, but part of it, where sandy tracks run beside the cycle paths may be suitable for *huifkarren*. Hire centres will advise on any restrictions.

Leave Diever on the Vledder road, and at paddestoel 21504 fork right along the small road which soon becomes a sand path with an unmade path (*fietspad*) alongside. At the next junction (paddestoel 21642) turn right and follow the track through woods and along the edge of heathland. After about 2km the cycle track becomes a metalled path, and at this point anyone on foot may turn sharp right and return to Diever. After another 1km, turn right again, crossing over a road and in 3km, paddestoel 23770 is reached. Turn left along an unmade cycle track, crossing the next road after about ½km, and continue straight ahead. Just past the fire watchtower, at paddestoel 23772, turn left again, beside the nature reserve. Keep straight on, bearing slightly right at paddestoel 23773, then across the road at paddestoel 22736, taking the cycle path to the left towards the Zorgvlied to Diever road. Cross this and continue on the cycle path to the cross-tracks at paddestoel 22578. Bear left to Doldersum, and at the road (paddestoel 22156) go left to the memorial on the *brink* in Doldersum. Bear left again to paddestoel 22577, cross over the road and take the minor road, forking right almost immediately. After crossing the little river Vledder Aa, the road makes a right-angled turn to the right, but keep straight on along the cycle track through the woods, returning to the starting point in Diever.

The main route now continues from Diever, along the road to **Vledder**, where there is a fifteenth-century church with fourteenth-century 'saddle-roof' tower. The road turns left in Vledder, coming to **Frederiksoord**, where there is a museum with a collection of clocks and watches made between 1500 to 1900. The horticultural school in the village has a garden which

Meppel
Fifteenth-century church tower.
Seventeenth-century houses in town
centre.

Ruinerwold
Museum Farm with old furnishings
and tile pictures.
'Kachel Museum': collection of
antique stoves and fireplaces.

Ruinen
Typical Drents sheepfold and Visitor
Centre.

Dwingeloo
Fourteenth-century church with
onion-shaped dome. Attractive
brink.

Diever
Schultehuis, built 1604, containing
small museum. Glass museum (De
Spiraal) and glass-blowing
demonstrations.
Huifkarren or horse-drawn wagons
for hire (at Vledder, Doldersum and
Zorgvlied).

Frederiksoord
Museum of clocks and watches.
Horticultural school garden open to
public.

Havelte
Restored *hunebeds*. Fifteenth-
century church.

may be visited in summer, with a variety of roses, shrubs and trees. In the neighbourhood are a number of Saxon farmhouses, also tumuli.

The road running south leads towards **Havelte**, past two *hunebeds* on the left side of the road. These were completely destroyed during World War II, during the construction of an airfield by the German forces, but fortunately a local archaeologist had made a scale model of them, so they have now been restored exactly to their former state. Havelte has a fifteenth-century church with a Drents tower dating from 1410.

Leaving the town, the road runs south from the land of woods and heath, joining the main road where it crosses the Drentse Hoofdvaart or canal, and in 7km Meppel is reached at the end of the tour.

12 AROUND HILVERSUM AND AMERSFOORT

Geographically speaking, this is one of the oldest parts of the Netherlands. The two towns, although in different provinces, are linked by beautiful heaths and woodland extending from the shores of the Gooimeer and Eemmeer in the north, to the Utrechtse Heuvelrug in the south. To the north of Amersfoort lies the Eemland polder and the old twin villages of Bunschoten/Spakenburg, and to the east is the Gelderse Vallei. Many historic buildings, including castles and palaces, are to be seen, also the best-preserved fortress town in the country and Napoleon's pyramid at Austerlitz. The whole region is particularly pleasant for cycling along the paths which criss-cross the heathland of 't Gooi, north and east of Hilversum, and the State Forest area of Vuursche to the south and east, linked through quiet minor roads and paths to Amersfoort and the extensive heath and wooded areas south of the town.

ROUTE 36   AROUND HILVERSUM

Hilversum was originally a poor heathland village, first noted in 1424. With the coming of the railway from Amsterdam to Amersfoort, bringing as it did the growing textile industry, the village and its surrounding suburbs grew slowly. The present town is relatively modern, and most of the buildings date from the nineteenth century. The St Vitus Church, with its 98m tower, was designed by the architect Cuypers, who was also responsible for both the Central Station and the Rijksmuseum in Amsterdam. A very good example of twentieth-century design is the fine Town Hall, built in 1931 to a design far ahead of its time by the city architect W.M. Dudok. The VVV in Hilversum can supply a leaflet and guide to the buildings he designed for those interested, also a guide to the many sculptures around the town. Probably Hilversum is best known as the centre of Dutch radio and television broadcasting. Other interests are catered for by the Pinetum Blijdenstein, with 450 species of conifer, and the Dr Costerus botanical garden specialising in wild plants and herbs. The VVV is in Stationsplein, and not far away from the station and bus station is a large three-storey shopping centre, the Hilvertshof, which includes a car park.

From the town centre, it is necessary to follow local signs owing to a complicated one-way system, but the route leaves along 's Gravelandse Weg, in the general direction of **Weesp** and **Amsterdam**. On approaching **'s Graveland**, turn right beside the canal and take the next turning to the left across the canal towards **Ankeveen**, where the road bears right alongside the lake, joining the main road at signpost 942, and turning left to **Weesp**. Cyclists may prefer to follow a winding route across the lakes from Ankeveen to Weesp. This village is now much industrialised, but the little

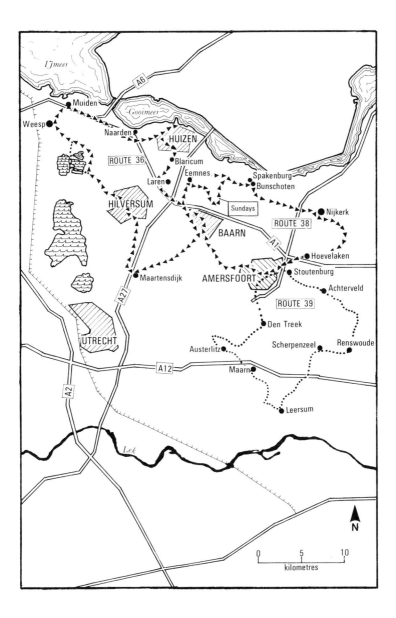

IJmeer

Muiden

Weesp

Naarden

HUIZEN

ROUTE 36

Blaricum

Eemnes

Laren

Spakenburg

Bunschoten

HILVERSUM

Sundays

ROUTE 38

Nijkerk

BAARN

Hoevelaken

Maartensdijk

AMERSFOORT

Stoutenburg

Achterveld

ROUTE 39

Den Treek

Renswoude

UTRECHT

Austerlitz

Scherpenzeel

A12

Maarn

Leersum

Lek

0   5   10

kilometres

N

Gooimeer

eighteenth-century Town Hall contains an exhibition of Weesp porcelain dating from the eighteenth century. Follow the road beside the river, under the railway by the station, and follow signs to **Muiden**, going under the motorway. Cyclists may cross the river Vecht in Weesp and follow the river to Muiden if they prefer. The locks at Muiden are very old, dating back to 1694, but are still in daily use, with many boats passing through on their way from the IJ-meer to the lakes along the Vecht. The narrow streets of Muiden make parking difficult. The most interesting sight here is the castle or Muiderslot, a medieval brick building at the mouth of the river. Built in 1285 by Count Floris V, who was later murdered here, the castle was razed to the ground but rebuilt in the fourteenth century on the original foundations. Fully restored in 1948, it is now open to the public.

Return to the locks in Muiden, turn left and follow the narrow road alongside the canal, the Naarder Trekvaart, keeping the canal on the left. On reaching the Hakkelaarsbrug (about 2km) cyclists should cross the bridge and continue on the other side of the canal, then follow signs for **Naarden-Vesting**. If they do not cross at this point, a long diversion will be necessary. Motorists should rejoin the main road, as the canal road is not a through road for cars. Follow signs for Naarden-Vesting, and, after leaving the main road, Parking-Centrum, crossing the bridge over the moats. Visitors, particularly cyclists, arriving at about 1pm may be startled by a loud report, as a gun is fired daily at this time.

Naarden-Vesting (Fortress Naarden) is a perfect example of a seventeenth-century fortified town, but its history goes back further than that. In the tenth century it was in the possession of the Abbey of Elten; this strategic spot was then given to Count Floris V in 1280. After a stormy period of development, the present town layout of streets in an oval shape with a church in the centre was evolved, and is shown in a drawing dated 1560, when the usual walls with gates, towers and moat existed. In 1572 the town was completely destroyed by the Spanish, rebuilt in 1596 with six bastions, five gates and an artificial harbour, and was captured by the French in 1672. Retaken by William III, the whole system was rebuilt in 1688.

Finally, during World War I, the fortress was again put on a war footing even though Holland was neutral.

In one of the casemates there is a museum which shows in detail all these developments, together with other interesting facts about military methods and history, culminating with an exhibition dealing with the experiences of Naarden in World War II. Because of the double ring of moats and the star-shaped fortifications, access to the town is limited, but once inside, park by the VVV, and explore the narrow cobbled streets of the town and the paths along the ramparts between the double moats.

The fifteenth-century St Vitus or Grote Kerk, stands in the centre of the town. There is a sixteenth-century choir screen inside, and the tower may be climbed for a fine view, across to Flevoland, and over the town fortifications below. Next to the church is the Stadhuis, built in 1601,

Hilversum

Neo-gothic church of St Vitus, designed by P.J. Cuypers.
Exceptionally fine twentieth-century town hall.
Pinetum 'Blijdenstein' with 450 species.
Dr Costerus botanical garden — wild plants and herbs.

Weesp

Eighteenth-century town hall with exhibition of Weesp pottery.

Muiden

Seventeenth-century locks in village.
Fourteenth-century castle 'Muiderslot'.

Naarden-Vesting

Perfect seventeenth-century fortified town. Vesting museum in casemates under ramparts. Collections and displays concerning the fort and military history in general.
Walking and cycling routes through ramparts.

St Vitus church: sixteenth-century choir screen.
Stadhuis: built 1601.
Comenius museum — containing relics of the philosopher and educationalist.

Huizen

Old fishing harbour and yacht marina.

Laren

Singer museum of modern art.

Soest

Soestdijk royal palace (no admission).

Groeneveld National Forest Centre — various exhibitions. Park open to the public.

Laage Vuursche

Kasteel Drakensteyn (no admission). Beautiful woodland area for walking.

---

although this is not the original Town Hall. That was in Turfpoortstraat, on the site now occupied by a house built in 1615, and now housing the Comenius Museum. This commemorates the seventeenth-century philosopher who advocated the use of illustrations in children's school books, and who lived and is buried here in Naarden.

Leaving the fortress by the exit towards the south-east, turn left along Huizer Straatweg, under the motorway and follow Naarder Straat through an area of country estates to the centre of **Huizen**, then turn left along Karel Doormanlaan to the harbour area. Formerly an old fishing port on the shore of the Zuiderzee, this is now a rapidly developing yachting marina and centre for watersports.

Cyclists from Naarden may leave the fortress via the ramparts and along Oostdijk, under the motorway, then follow cycle routes along the coast of the Gooimeer. This continues all the way to Huizenharbour. The eastern part of Huizen is being developed very rapidly and it is therefore very difficult to find the way, because roads seem to be built overnight, and maps cannot keep up!

South of Huizen is an area of heathland crossed by a number of foot and cycle paths, and from Huizen cars can follow Ceintuur Baan and Blaricummer Straat to **Blaricum**, and the twin village of **Laren**. These are pleasant residential areas, rather exclusive, with shady roads lined with holly hedges, and old farm houses situated between large and small villas.

Entering Laren via Toren Laan, on reaching the *brink*, turn right down Naarder Straat, and on the left at the cross-roads at Oude Drift is the Singer Museum, a cultural and art centre with collections of paintings by nineteenth and twentieth century French and Dutch Impressionists, and by the founder W.H. Singer (1868-1943). Returning to the town centre, bear right along Sevenaarstraat into Hilversumse Weg which leads to the motorway junction. Join the motorway A1 in the direction of Amersfoort, and be prepared to leave it again at the turn-off for **Soest**, in about 4km. This leads along the N221 road, which runs through some very pleasant wooded country with fine estates. Just near the motorway turn-off is the mansion of Groeneveld, which is now the National Forest Centre. Its park is open to the public, and in the house various exhibitions are arranged and regular concerts held. At Soestdijk, (signpost 850) turn right; at this junction, on the right of the road, is the Soestdijk Palace, which until 1980 was the home of the Queen of the Netherlands. Built originally as a hunting lodge for Stadhouder Willem III, it is not open to the public, but a very fine view of the front of the building may be obtained from the road.

In the area around Soest there are plenty of opportunities for horse riding, with many stables and equestrian centres.

Continue along the road from the Palace, and take the right turn at signpost 860 towards **Maartensdijk**. At the next cross-roads a diversion to the right may be made to see Kasteel Drakensteyn, the former home of Queen Beatrix when she was Crown Princess. The castle is not open to the public. Return to the road junction (signpost 596), turn right and continue to Maartensdijk, then turn right again to **Hollandsche Rading** and so back to Hilversum.

ROUTE 37   A WALK THROUGH OLD AMERSFOORT

Long before receiving its first charter in 1259, the lovely medieval town of Amersfoort originated as a settlement on a ford (voorde) on the river Amer, which is now called the Eem. It is said to be the only European town whose centre is surrounded by a double ring of canals, and it contains many exceptionally fine historic buildings.

Parking inside the town is not easy. It is possible to park at the railway station, near the VVV office, and take a bus into the town centre (P+R car park). The walk described here takes in those buildings of greatest interest. Many of the sights are widely scattered, and those with more time to spare can obtain a booklet in English from the VVV with a detailed description of a longer town walk.

A walk of about 15 minutes through uninteresting streets will be saved by taking the local bus from the station to Hellestraat near the modern Town Hall. With this on the left, walk across Westsingel and cross the canal, turning right into Breestraat. Ahead is the great Onze Lieve Vrouwe Toren, all that is left of the former church, built in the fifteenth century and blown up accidentally in 1787 when used as an ammunition store. According to legend, the church was built as a place of pilgrimage after miracles occurred as a result of a simple peasant girl's action in throwing a statuette of the Virgin Mary into the canal. The remains of the statuette are now kept in the old Catholic Church in 't Zand, on the north of the inner town. From the tower, walk across the churchyard to the Visbank, still in regular use on Friday mornings by fishmongers from nearby Spakenburg. On the corner of the churchyard is the Kapelhuis, once used for the administration of the church, and now used as a gallery. On the other side turn right along Lieve Vrouwestraat, cross over Langestraat, and continue opposite along Scherbierstraat, at the end of which is Muurhuizen. These unique 'wall-houses' almost completely encircle the inner town, and are built on the town walls. Turn left along Muurhuizen to Korte Gracht, where across the canal, on the right, is the house Tinnenburg, a beautiful wall house, the oldest known such building, dating from before 1414. At the side of the house are the remains of the old water gate. Also, by looking down past Tinnenburg to the next canal bridge, under Zuid Singel, the so-called 'House with the purple window panes' may be seen. The window glass has not been painted, but has changed colour with age. Just beyond the trees, further along the same canal, may be seen the pointed turrets of the Monnickendam, a water gate on the second town wall, built between 1380 and 1450. Although the walls were demolished during the last century, the gate was preserved, and it stands at the confluence of a number of small streams from the Gelderse Vallei which flows into the river Eem.

Continue to walk along Muurhuizen, and on the right is the tower known as the Plompe or Dieventoren, built in the thirteenth century as part of the first town wall, and used as the town prison for many years. It is also known as the *Latijntje* because in 1860 the little steeple on top was placed there, having been taken from the old Latin School. The passage through the base of the tower was made in 1942. There are many other fine old houses along this part of the wall, and at the far end of Langestraat is the Kamperbinnenpoort, all that remains of a much larger gate in the first town wall, and which was restored in 1930. Nearby is a pewter workshop which may be visited.

From the gate, continue again along Muurhuizen to Kerkstraat, on the left, and through here to the Appelmarkt, where the beautiful 'Onder de Linde' is situated. Dating from the sixteenth century, this building with its lovely stepped gable and attractive windows is now used as a pub, a quite different use from its original purpose as a home for the canons from the nearby church of St Joris. The original church was consecrated in 1248, but nothing remains of the first building. The tower dates from the thirteenth century, and the main building was completed in 1534, and contains a lovely sixteenth-century rood screen and a very fine organ. The outside of the south porch, built around 1500, is particularly beautiful, with much carved stonework around the windows. Nestling against the wall of the church is the little seventeenth-century Botermarkt where local butter used to be weighed and sold.

The large square known as the Hof is surrounded by old houses with attractive gables. From the corner of Hof, follow Lavendelstraat to Havik, site of the town docks in the Middle Ages. Looking to the right gives one of the most attractive views of Muurhuizen, with the sluice where the canal water ran below the houses into the harbour. Turn left along Havik, cross over the bridge into Nieuweweg and along to 't Zand, turn left again, and on the left, on Westsingel, are the three old wall-houses which now house the Museum Flehite, so called after the old name of Eastern Utrecht. One of the houses retains its original form, while the other buildings had neo-Renaissance gables added during restoration in the nineteenth century. The exhibits deal with the history of the town from prehistoric times to the present day.

On leaving the museum, return towards 't Zand and turn left along Kleine Spui towards the imposing Koppelpoort, a combined land and water gate built over the river Eem around 1427, and showing the boundary of the town after its fifteenth-century expansion. Two arches span the roads and a central arch over the water has a wooden gate lowered by means of two treadmills which still exist. The town centre may be reached again along Westsingel. From here, either return to the station by bus, or look around the shops in the pedestrianised Varkensmarkt and Utrechtse-straat. Amersfoort is known for its jewellery shops, which sell beautifully-worked traditional silver ornaments. From the Varkensmarkt (Pig Market) walk down Arnhemse-straat to the wide ring road, and on the left will be seen a huge boulder, mounted on a plinth. This is the famous 'Amersfoortse Kei', weighing some 9 tons. Legend has it that a seventeenth-century eccentric wagered that some inhabitants of Amersfoort were so stupid that he would get them to drag this relic of the Ice-Age from nearby Leusderheide into the town. In 1661, 400 Amersfoorters did so, hence the nickname *Keientrekkers* (boulder-haulers) given to people from the town.

The wide road where the boulder stands is known as Stads-ring, and was once the outer moat which ran around the south and east of the town. To the north the moat is still in existence and the whole ring has been landscaped for most of its length, with trees and small parks making it very attractive. The town is a garrison town, and some old barracks still exist, some being classified as listed buildings.

To the south-west, the large area of heathland known as the Leusder-Heide is a military training ground, and at Soesterberg, about 7km out of

Onze Lieve Vrouwe Toren
All that remains of a fifteenth-
century church.

Huis Tinnenburg
The oldest (fifteenth-century) and
probably the best of the 'wall houses'
built on top of the town walls, for
which the town is well known.

Plompe Toren
Thirteenth-century tower, once used
as the prison.

'Onder de Linden'
Beautiful sixteenth-century house
with fine gable and windows.

St Joris Kerk
Sixteenth-century church with
particularly beautiful South Porch.

Botermarkt
Seventeenth-century butter market
hall adjoining the church.

Museum Flehite
District museum housed in some fine
old buildings, with exhibits depicting
the history of the town from
prehistoric times.

Monnickendam
Fifteenth-century water-gate.

Kamperbinnenpoort
Restored thirteenth-century town
gate.

Koppelpoort
Magnificent combined water and
land gate, built in 1427, at north-
west entrance to the town.

Soesterberg
(7km west) Dutch Air Force
Museum. Historical collection of
service planes, etc.

Amersfoort on the road to Utrecht, is the Air Force Museum, displaying a
collection of aircraft and other material showing the history of the Dutch
Army and Naval air forces and the evolution of aviation.

Amersfoort makes a good centre for exploring the east and south of
Eemland and the Gelderse Vallei, so two routes are described, starting from
the town.

ROUTE 38   THE EEMLAND POLDER

Leave Amersfoort in the direction of **Soest**, and just after crossing the railway
near Soestdijk station, turn off the main road, on to Stadhouders Laan and
Toren Laan, into the centre of **Baarn**. This was once described as a
'fashionable village' and the description could still apply, particularly as
regards the surroundings and the Baarnse Bos. On the Brink is a fifteenth-
century Dutch Reformed Church with a fourteenth-century tower, and in
nearby Java Laan, are the Peking Garden and the Hortus Botanicus, both
open to the public. The latter is the Botanical Garden of Utrecht University.
From the town centre, follow Eemnesser Weg towards the motorway

Traditional fishing boats at Spakenburg

junction, then turn right, under the motorway and along Wakkeren Dijk to **Eemnes**, passing a number of old farms along the way. The village is situated on the edge of the polder, in pleasant surroundings, and has a fifteenth-century church with tower, dating from the time when this was a much larger community. The road which has been followed now runs on as Meentweg, still going past old farms. A short way past the village is a turning on the right which runs out across the polder to a small ferry (*pontveer*) across the river Eem to **Eemdijk**. This ferry does not run after dusk or on Sundays, when Eemdijk may be reached by way of Baarn and **Eembrugge**.

The road to Eemdijk along the other side of the river will come to the ferry landing again, from whence the straight road to the centre of **Bunschoten/Spakburg** is followed across the polder. On reaching the main road, follow signs for 'Centrum' which lead to Spakenburg, a very old fishing village with narrow streets and an inner harbour in which traditional boats may be seen, often with eel nets hanging from their masts to dry. The dyke at the entrance to the harbour gives good views across the Eemmeer, and there is a fine new marina for sailing enthusiasts. The fishing village of Spakenburg is joined to the twin village of Bunschoten, an agricultural community first granted a charter in 1383, where old farmhouses stand close together on either side of the long street.

The most notable feature of these twin villages is the unique traditional costume worn by many of the women as a matter of course, not as a tourist

PLACES TO VISIT IN AND
AROUND THE EEMLAND
POLDERS

Baarn
Peking Garden and Hortus
Botanicus of Utrecht University.

Bunschoten/Spakenburg
'Twin' fishing and farming villages.
Old fishing harbour. Colourful
costumes worn daily.
Local museum in Church rooms.

Nijkerk
Fifteenth-century church with fine
eighteenth-century organ. Carillon
concerts.
Waag building containing
Netherlands Electricity Museum.

attraction, and remarkable for their preservation of details from the late-medieval dress. The outstanding feature is the huge starched shoulder-piece known as a *kraplapp*, made from brightly-coloured pieces of material which are sewn on to a special linen; the whole is treated with starch to make it stand out. Some of these *kraplapps* are hand-painted, and it is possible to see them being made. During the summer an exhibition of historical costumes, model boats, furniture, etc is held in the church room behind the Noorderkerk.

Returning along the main street of Bunschoten, turn left at signpost 3016 and go across the polder, cross the motorway bridge and enter **Nijkerk**, an attractive old town on the edge of the Gelderse Vallei. The Grote or Catharinakerk was originally built in 1222, burned down in 1450 and rebuilt in 1461. The beautiful eighteenth-century organ is used for recitals by visiting organists during the summer months, and on Thursday evenings in summer the carillon is played. Exhibitions about the old town are held in the old Waag building, which also houses the Netherlands Electricity Museum. The view along the canal, the Arker-vaart, towards the Nijkerkernauw from near the Town Hall is very attractive, and the canal is often busy with pleasure craft.

The return to Amersfoort may be made by leaving Nijkerk along the road running south through **Driedorp**, and just past the windmill 'De Hoop', turn right (signpost 4903) and follow the winding road through **Zwartebroek** to **Hoevelaken**. This is a prosperous village on the outskirts of Amersfoort, which had its origins in the twelfth century. The manor Huis te Hoevelaken accommodates art exhibitions. Continue under the motorway junctions back into Amersfoort.

ROUTE 39   A CYCLE RIDE SOUTH OF AMERSFOORT
South and south-west of Amersfoort is a very attractive area of wooded and parklike country with big estates, stretching across to the Utrechtse

Heuvelrug. It is particularly suited to exploring by bicycle, and a circular signed route known as the 'UMO Route' takes in part of it; the route given here follows part of this signed route. One word of warning: in places, the cycle paths are rather sandy.

Leave the centre of Amersfoort along Arnhemseweg and Leusderweg, signed to Maarn. On reaching the motorway junctions, follow the cycle-path signs for **Oud-Leusden** to the left. This road follows alongside the motorway for about 1km, then at paddestoel 20743 turn right along the cycle track. Keep on this path, following paddestoels signed to Den Treek. There are many paths in this big estate and sometimes extra ones are opened to cyclists. The whole area is known as 'Den Treek', but the signed route will lead to the old mansion 'Huis Den Treek'. Nearby is a little shop belonging to a wood carver, where all kinds of craftwork is sold. Follow the cycle path past the mansion to a T-junction, then turn right in the direction of Treekerpunt, following the path known as Treekerweg. At the main road (signpost 10047) turn left, and at the next large crossroads, cross over to the right at the cycle traffic signals, in the direction of **Austerlitz**. Down the hill on the right is the Pyramide restaurant and amusement park, behind which a path through the woods leads to the Pyramide van Austerlitz. This artificial hill was built in 1804 by French soldiers encamped nearby, and was named after the battle of Austerlitz in Czechoslovakia, where the French gained a victory over Russian and Austrian troops. Now 20m high, the pyramid had a tower added in 1894, and an access stairway built. A small fee is charged for ascending to the balcony on the mound, but the view on a clear day is well worth the effort. Anyone who thinks Holland is a flat country is in for a surprise.

From the Pyramide restaurant, continue along the road for another ½km, then fork right along the minor road at paddestoel 20083, past a car park and keeping to the cycle track beside the forest road. On the right of the path just beyond paddestoel 20082 is a small stone memorial commemorating the founding, in 1918, of the Utrecht and District cycle-path society (UMO) which pioneered the establishment of the network of cycle paths in this area. At the memorial, turn about and retrace the route back to paddestoel 20092, about ½km, where the signs for the UMO-Route will be seen. Follow these signs right, and along a zigzag route through the woods, crossing the main road and passing the village of Austerlitz before continuing through the woods to Maarn. Cross the road, railway and motorway at the traffic lights and follow the route along a pleasant tree-shaded road to Huize Maarsbergen, from where the route runs to the right again, through quite a hilly stretch towards the main road at signpost 1580. At this point, leave the UMO-Route, turn left along the road to the next main junction (signpost 2889), turn left, and in about 500m fork right on to a cycle track (paddestoel 22433). At paddestoel 22414 take the left-hand track through the Leersum forest and nature reserve. At paddestoel 21043, fork left and cross over the motorway and the railway, turn right and follow alongside the railway, turning left at the next paddestoel (23742). Continue straight on, then bear right and continue towards Lambalgen, a country estate on the edge of the Gelderse Vallei area, where the typical landscape of small streams and attractive hedgerows becomes apparent. Ahead lies the little town of **Scherpenzeel**, where the nineteenth-century Huize Scherpenzeel, once a stately home, has been restored and is in use as the Town Hall. From here, follow the main road east to **Renswoude**, where there is a fine seventeenth-century moated castle, built on the foundations of an earlier building. The gardens and estate are open to the public, although the castle itself is not normally open to view. From Renswoude, take the road north to the windmill at **Walderveen**, then turn left along the winding road to **Achterveld**. This part of the country is criss-crossed by narrow roads over pleasant rural landscape, totally different from the wooded estates and heathland at the beginning of the route. Ride through Achterveld and follow the cycle track beside the main road through **Stoutenburg** back to the ring road around Amersfoort.

13 THE LOVELY LAND OF THE VELUWE

The Veluwe is one of the largest areas of open countryside in Western Europe, being some 50km from north to south and about the same in width. It is one of three regions in the Province of Gelderland, and is mainly parkland, woods and heath. Bounded on the north by the Veluwemeer, by the rivers IJssel and Rhine to the east and south, and by the Gelderse Vallei on the west, the largest towns are Arnhem and Apeldoorn, but a number of other interesting towns and villages exist, mainly around the edges. The region is divided across the centre by an east-west motorway passing by Apeldoorn, to the south of which are two National Parks.

ROUTE 40   THROUGH THE NORTH OF THE VELUWE

On the northern perimeter of the Veluwe, on the coast of the IJsselmeer, lie the old sea ports of Harderwijk and Elburg. To the east is the old Hanseatic town of Hattem on the western bank of the river IJssel, and to the south are the towns of Heerde and Epe. Crossing back towards Harderwijk, across woods and heathland, the route passes through Vierhouten, Elspeet and Uddel.

Harderwijk may be reached from Amersfoort via Nijkerk and the motorway, or from Flevoland across the Harderbrug. Parking is possible at a number of places around the town, most convenient being along the Strand Boulevard. An old Zuiderzee and Hanseatic port dating from 1231, and the departure point for many ships sailing to the East Indies, the port was no longer able to flourish due to the silting-up of the Zuiderzee in the eighteenth century. Remains of the medieval ramparts may be seen at the Vispoort on the Strand Boulevard, and in Smeepoortstraat near the *Kazerne* (Barracks), originally a convent and later the Munt, before being converted to accommodate Colonial troops. The Veluwe Museum van Oudheden in an eighteenth-century gentleman's house in Donkerstraat houses collections illustrating local history and geology from prehistoric times to the present day, and the former Town Hall (1727) in the Markt is now the district Music School. Near the old harbour is the Dolphinarium, one of the biggest of its kind in Europe.

Leave Harderwijk by the old road past the approach to the Harderbrug, towards **Nunspeet**, a popular seaside and country holiday resort. Next the road passes through **Doornspijk**, one of the oldest villages in the North-West Veluwe, before reaching Elburg.

Elburg is a beautiful thirteenth-century town on the former Zuiderzee, planned in an almost perfect square surrounded by moat, ramparts, dry moat and walls. Parking is strictly controlled, and a notice at the approach to the town advises motorists to 'go further on foot'! There is a car park near the harbour, approached from the road leading into the town from the Elburgerbrug. From here, the town is entered via the old Vispoortbrug, a

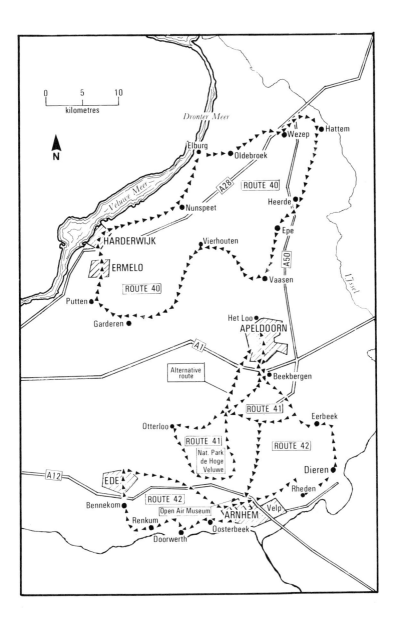

ROUTE 40

ROUTE 41

ROUTE 42

lovely square tower with turrets at the corners and an ornate spire. Dating from 1233, the town centre still retains much of its old character, with old brick walls, round bastion towers and casemates between the outer ramparts and the town itself. The inner moat is now dry in most places, and is used for car parking, gardens, allotments, etc. As the town is entered, through the Vispoort, a beautiful *trapgevel* may be seen on the left, on the corner of Ellestraat. Vispoortstraat leads straight ahead, to cross Beekstraat into Jufferenstraat. The junction forms the market place of the town. Beekstraat is a wide tree-lined street with a small canal running through the centre. In this street are several beautifully restored *trapgevels* and *klokgevels*. Continue into Jufferenstraat and take the first turning on the left (Schapensteeg), at the end of which, on the left, is an old decorated door. Turn right into Van Kinsbergenstraat. On the corner is the old fourteenth-century castle, and next door the former Stadhuis, or town hall.

The VVV (situated in Jufferenstraat opposite the Abbey), can supply a detailed Town Walk with map, which is especially interesting to those who like details of old architectural monuments. Most visitors will, however, prefer to wander at leisure through this lovely little town, where all the streets except one, the Krommesteeg or Crooked Alley, are completely straight. A walk along the footpath round the ramparts will give good views of the historic buildings. Of special interest are the old Abbey buildings, containing the town museum and the National Organ Museum. An annexe of the museum is housed in the Vispoort, from where it is also possible to visit the casemates under the town walls. In Ledigestede is the impressive Feithenhof, built in 1740 as an almshouse for twenty-four elderly people. Along Noorderwalstraat and Oosterwalstraat are old houses built into the walls themselves, best seen from the ramparts on the east of the town. Near the Vispoort, in the dry moat on the west side, is an open-air rope-walk. The fascinating craft of ropemaking is rarely seen these days, and visitors are welcome to watch.

Leaving Elburg, the road swings away from the shore past **Oldebroek**, an old farming village with eighteenth and nineteenth-century farmhouses along the road. Here it is possible to see the old Veluwse costume being worn. The church tower dates from 1200, and inside are some painted ceilings in the choir vaults, an old oak pulpit and some seventeenth-century silver. The local museum is in the Town Hall. In this part of the country the farmhouses are quite different from those in the north, being smaller, often completely thatched, with roofs coming very low at the sides. The living area is at the front, and the animals are kept in the rear and side parts, all under one roof.

Keep to the main road, and in 8km pass under the A28 motorway to **Wezep**, where the road makes a sharp turn to the left, thence through **Hattemerbroek**, under another motorway, then a right turn to **Hattem**, an old fortress town on the boundary between North Veluwe and the IJssel Valley.

It is best to park the car along the Bevrijdingsweg or Kleine Gracht, on

the edge of the town. The VVV can supply a plan and notes on interesting
sights but the walk described here will cover most points of interest.

ROUTE 40A   A WALK IN HATTEM

The first mention of Hattem is in 891, and town rights were granted in 1299.
Of the four town gates, only the fourteenth-century Dijkpoort remains.
The walk starts from this gate, a fairytale-like tower with four turrets on the
corners. Through the archway, Kruisstraat leads to the Markt, dominated
by the church, a sixteenth-century basilica originally dedicated to St
Andrew and St Catherine, and now the Reformed Church. In the square is
the large Stadhuis, built in 1619, with ornate decorated gables, and a pump
dated 1776. Between the Stadhuis and the church is Kerkhofstraat, at the
end of which is the beautiful sixteenth-century Daendelshuis, birthplace of
a former Governor-General of the Dutch East Indies. Turning left, on the

159

corner of Ridderstraat is a Bakery Museum where on Saturdays bread is baked in the traditional way of the Middle Ages. Continue across Kruisstraat into Achterstraat, at the end of which is the Regional Museum, incorporating the Anton Pieck museum and the Voermanhuis. At the end of the street, where it joins Molenbelt on the right and Zuiderwal on the left, is the original Town Pump, erected in 1733. Looking to the right, the huge tower mill will be seen. Built in 1852 and recently restored, it is still in working order. Walk back along Kerkstraat to the Markt, to an old seventeenth-century house, on the right. Opposite is Korte Kerkstraat, a small street with some very attractive old houses, looking almost like a small village street in the middle of the town. At the end is the Hoge Huis, built on top of the town walls in 1580. If time permits, walk along the footpath beside the town walls and the moat, then return to the car park along Kruisstraat.

Rejoin the main road near the river, and continue south through the hilly wooded country around **Heerde**, which is a centre for tree and rose nurseries, and on to **Epe** after passing under the motorway. Epe is a popular holiday resort which also has a district museum with an exhibition of the local costumes from the Eastern Veluwe area.

Beyond Epe, to the south, is **Emst** and **Vaassen**, where a turning on the right will lead to Kasteel De Cannenburgh, a very fine moated castle originally built in 1543, and enlarged in later years. Through the centuries it has been lived in continuously, and is now in the care of a foundation which aims to preserve castles in Gelderland. Both the castle and its grounds are open to view.

The route now leaves the main road and heads across the heath and forest areas to the east. Much of this is Crown Land, and at certain times some roads are closed to cars, so it is important to watch for closure and diversion signs. The route to be taken should avoid these problems. From Vaassen, follow through the village past the swimming pool then keep right and then straight on at paddestoel 22808 for 1½km. Turn right at paddestoel 20177, and bear right at the car parking place (20176) at Niersen. Continue along this road to **Gortel**. Here, turn sharply back to the left at signpost 2870, crossing some lovely heathland and wooded country to **Vierhouten**, a very popular country holiday resort with almost unlimited opportunities for walking and cycling. At Vierhouten, turn left and pass signpost 6918 in the direction of **Elspeet**. The road passes between the Vierhouter Bos on the left and the Elspeeter Heide on the right, part of the latter being a military training area.

Elspeet is another village in the middle of a very pleasant area for walking and cycling, and all these roads are picturesque in every respect. There are frequent parking places, from which walks can be taken along the many paths, and deer and wild pigs roam freely, although one is lucky to see them. Cyclists may be more fortunate in this respect as they can move faster and silently.

Old locks and Harbourmaster's House, Hindelopen

Town Hall and windmill, Dokkum

Old Amersfoort

At Elspeet, continue south at signpost 196, to the village of **Uddel**, where the road bears right, passing Uddelermeer (swimming is possible here) and on to **Garderen**. The church tower dates from the eleventh century, and was in former times a beacon for fishing boats on the Zuiderzee. In the village is a farmstead originally dating from 1326, although now with a nineteenth century appearance. At signpost 3030, take the road for **Putten**, and in the town centre (signpost 2939) turn right and follow signs to Ermelo and so back to Harderwijk.

From Harderwijk, a drive of some 30km brings one to the town of **Apeldoorn**, 'Royal Apeldoorn' as it is sometimes called. Well situated and with first-class facilities, it is noted as a holiday and congress town in the centre of an area of beautiful natural scenery. The town itself, although very pleasant and a good shopping centre, is mostly used as a starting point for tours in the surrounding countryside, details of which may be obtained from the VVV office by the railway station. Some of these tours, which last about $2\frac{1}{2}$ to 3 hours, go through what is virtually the State Game Reserve, where wild animals may be seen. Cars are not allowed, and booking on the tours is essential.

Within walking distance of the town centre is the Royal Park of the Palace *Het Loo*. From the station, the entrance may be reached by following Nieuwstraat, Loo Laan and into Amersfoortseweg, from where the Park and Palace entrance, with free car park, can be found. Originally, William III, Prince of Orange, purchased a small medieval manor house called *Het Oude Loo* for use as a hunting lodge, then in 1684 it was established as the Palace *Het Loo*. The English Princess (afterwards Queen) Mary Stuart, wife of William III, laid the foundation stone, in 1685, of *Het Nieuwe Loo*, the gardens of which were even finer than those of Versailles. Members of the House of Orange inhabited the Palace, from the time of William III to Queen Wilhelmina, who ruled for fifty-seven years until her abdication in favour of her daughter in 1948. It is no longer used by the Royal Family, and has been fully restored, following the seventeenth-century plans. Together with the restored gardens, it is now a National Museum. Visitors can see how the Royal Family lived here during three centuries, and how the House of Orange Nassau was linked to the Netherlands. The Royal Mews are also open, and house a collection of carriages, coaches and sledges. The Park is open to pedestrians only, with several waymarked routes. The old castle *Het Oude Loo* is in the park, but only the exterior may be seen.

In and around Apeldoorn are many reminders and memorials to those lost, both at home and abroad, during World War II, including the many resistance fighters who operated in and around the countryside here.

On the outskirts of the town to the west is the large Recreation Park 'Berg en Bos', with both natural and man-made attractions. Within its boundaries is the 'Apenheul', where apes of many kinds are free to move among the trees and among the visitors. A group of gorillas roams freely on an island within the park. At the nearby Julianatoren there is a playground offering many attractions for children.

Another attractive way of spending a day is to take the steam train from Apeldoorn south along the eastern edge of the Veluwe to Dieren. During the summer a combined excursion trip may be taken on the train, continuing with a 3½-hour *huifkar* ride through some of the beautiful forest scenery. Another trip combines the steam train ride with a boat trip from Dieren up the river IJssel to Zutphen, returning to Apeldoorn by normal train service. Both trips are available as day-trips from any station in Holland.

This chapter started by saying that the Veluwe is one of the largest areas of open countryside in Western Europe. It is, in fact, unique for its variety of scenery and wild life. Within this large area are two National Parks, the National Park De Hoge Veluwe and the National Park Veluwezoom. The former is the most famous of the two, and from Apeldoorn a very pleasant circular drive may be made to include a visit to the park, within whose boundaries is the Kröller-Müller Museum of Modern Art.

ROUTE 41   A DRIVE AROUND THE HOGE VELUWE

Leave Apeldoorn by Arnhemseweg, under the motorway, and at Beekbergen turn left at signpost 216, and follow signs for **Loenen**. About 1km after crossing over the motorway, there is a car park on the left, near Holland's highest waterfall. 15m high in total, there are three falls which cascade through the woods, with broad flights of steps on either side leading to pleasant woodland paths. Continue along the road to Loenen, and turn right at signpost 2454, taking the road across heathland to join the main N50 road to Arnhem. By the junction is a sober memorial to 117 Dutchmen who were shot in March 1945 at Woeste Hoeve in retaliation for an attempt on the life of a German SS officer.

Turn right on to the main road, then after 500m take a left turn on to a narrow road winding through the forest to **Hoenderloo**, where there is one of the entrances to the National Park De Hoge Veluwe. Having paid the entrance fee, which covers all the exhibitions within the park, drive straight to the Visitors' Centre (*Bezoekerscentrum*), where there is plenty of car parking space. Maps, explanations and other exhibits will repay some study before setting off to explore the park, which covers a total of over 13,500 acres. About one half of this is heath, grassland and shifting sand. One quarter is planted woodland and the remainder is naturally-seeded Scots Pine. The woodland is mixed, and as far as possible the original character of the Veluwe landscape has been retained. Wildlife includes many varieties of wild bird, such as sparrowhawks, kestrels, and woodpeckers. Foxes, badgers, pine martens and weasels exist, together with deer, wild boar and mouflons, the longhaired sheep imported from Corsica. Fences in certain parts of the park divide off areas where these larger and wilder animals can roam at will, but normally cars can drive through the network of about 32km of road, subject to a speed limit of 50kph (30mph). Certain roads are one-way routes, so watch out for signs.

The Hoge Veluwe National Park

A network of about 40km of cycle paths, together with an extensive network of footpaths, all waymarked or signed, covers the area. An unusual touch for visitors other than the Dutch themselves is the provision, at the restaurant near the Visitor Centre, of 400 'White Bikes', which may be borrowed free of charge. The park itself is open all the year, from 8am to sunset, although some of the facilities might be closed.

PLACES TO VISIT IN THE HOGE VELUWE

Beekbergen
Holland's highest waterfall, 15m high.

Hoenderloo
National Park Hoge Veluwe with many walking and cycle routes. Visitors' Centre.
Kröller-Müller Museum of modern art, with collection of Van Gogh works. Sculpture Gallery. St Hubertus Hunting Lodge.

Otterlo
Tile Museum.

Arnhem
John Frost Bridge, named after Commander of British Paratroops who held bridge for three days and four nights in 1944.
Airborneplein — sunken garden in roundabout near bridge, with memorial.

Within the park is the State Museum Kröller-Müller, a modern purpose-built complex which houses the world-famous collection of works by modern artists, including the renowned Van Gogh collection of 276 works. The exhibits were originally the property of Mr & Mrs Kröller-Müller, the founders of the park. Adjacent to the museum is the Sculpture Garden with works by many of the world's best-known modern sculptors. Plenty of time should be allowed to look around the gallery, as there is a complicated system of rooms and passages. Different people will have differing views on the works of art on display here and around the park, but whatever one's views, they are certainly interesting.

Near the northern boundary of the park is the 'St Hubertus' hunting lodge, the country house of the Kröller-Müllers, with a splendid garden, open all the year round.

A leaflet in English gives general information about the park, the best places to see the various birds and animals, and sets out the rules for admission. However, it should be noted that captions on exhibits in the *Bezoekerscentrum* are only in Dutch, although brief recorded descriptions in four languages are available. Likewise, walking routes through the park are only described in Dutch, although the maps are easy to follow, with coloured spots corresponding with coloured posts on the ground. Note also that the museum is closed on Mondays.

After exploring the park, return to the car and leave by the Otterlo gate on the west side of the park. In **Otterlo** is a Tile Museum with a unique collection of 7,000 tiles from the thirteenth century to the present day.

Take the road south along the edge of the National Park, to **Schaarsbergen** (the third entrance to the park) and keep to this road as far as signpost 4716, turn left, and continue through **Deelen** to Hoenderloo. Turn right through the village, and at signpost 3239 take the road on the left which leads through the forest to **Beekbergen**, where a left turn will lead along the main road back to Apeldoorn. An alternative route from Hoenderloo is to continue ahead to the major road, turn right at signpost 3499 and follow this road along the edge of Ugchelse Bos under the motorway, through Ugchelen to Apeldoorn. Although a main road, this is a very pleasant route through attractive countryside.

Either from Apeldoorn, or after leaving the Hoge Veluwe National Park, easy routes can be taken to Arnhem.

Arnhem is the capital of the Province of Gelderland, and a look at the geography of the area will soon show how it grew in importance. Built on the banks of the river Rhine, on the north side, and backed by steeply rising hills of the Veluwe, it is halfway between the densely-populated western part of Holland and the industrial Ruhr area of Germany, with the river providing a natural highway. Add to that the motorway and rail links, and it follows that Arnhem has become an important centre for industry and business.

The natural location of the town, with its major river crossing by bridge, also gives the clue to its importance during the final stages of World War II. The hilly wooded country behind the town, to the north of the river, also explains the great difficulty of the task facing the Allied forces who tried unsuccessfully to capture the vital bridge intact and to hold it until reinforcements could reach them overland. Looking at the scene today makes one wonder how the airborne troops managed to achieve what they did, when everything was clearly on the side of the defenders, sited on rising ground with plenty of cover on the northern bank of the deep and fast-flowing river.

During and after the unsuccessful airborne operation, until its eventual liberation after bitter fighting in April 1945, Arnhem was subjected to heavy shelling from across the Rhine, and the present town has been almost completely rebuilt since the war.

The first record of a settlement here was in 893; in 1233 the town received its first charter, and in 1433 joined the Hanseatic League. No stranger to fighting during its long history, the town ramparts were finally levelled in 1853, being replaced by boulevards. The bridge to the west is a modern structure, while that to the east was known as the Rijnbrug, now renamed John Frost Bridge after the commander of the 2nd Battalion of the 1st British Parachute Brigade, who held the bridge for three days and four nights during the fighting in 1944.

The older buildings have all been restored or rebuilt since the damage during the war, and include the oldest building, St Pieters Gasthuis (1407) in Rijnstraat, at one time the mint. The Grote or Eusebius Kerk was built between 1452 and 1650, the 98m high tower being a replacement for that destroyed in 1944. Nearby is the former Stadhuis, originally built in 1545 as the mansion of Maarten van Rossum, also called the Duivelshuis on account of the carvings on the front. In the Markt is the eighteenth-century Waag, near to the Huis der Provincie, the first public building to be erected after the war (1954). The Sabelspoort is the only remnant of the fortifications of 1440. Near the Stadhuis is the Walburgiskerk, a Gothic church from 1422 and the oldest church in Arnhem. Just to the east is Airborneplein, a sunken garden in the centre of a busy roundabout, in which is a broken column from the ruins of Arnhem, bearing the date 17 September 1944.

ROUTE 42   AROUND ARNHEM and THE VELUWEZOOM

A number of interesting places may be visited in the Arnhem neighbourhood, including the unique Outdoor Museum and the Veluwezoom National Park. Although these have been included in one route, it is really too much to cover in one day, if the attractions are to be enjoyed to the full. Leave the town along Utrechtsestraat from the Stationsplein, where the VVV office is located. Bear left into Utrechtseweg. The Municipal Museum is on the left, and not far beyond here, signs will direct towards 'Elektrum', down a left fork into Klingelbeekseweg. Elektrum is a museum which is a joint enterprise of the electric power industry in Arnhem, showing a collection of old materials, equipment and tools related to the development of electrical engineering. There is ample free parking space. From here, continue under the railway viaduct, turn right, then left again along Utrechtseweg, in the direction of **Oosterbeek**. In about 1 km will be seen the Airborne Monument, and opposite, on the left, the entrance to the former Hotel Hartenstein, in a large park open to the public. The building was, during the airborne operations of September 1944, the headquarters of 1st British Airborne Division under Major-General Urquhart. In May 1978, the house was opened as a museum and contains displays of equipment, much of it actually used here at the time, models, photographs and dioramas, which with spoken commentaries, explain the whole operation and its consequences. The exact conditions within the Command Post in the cellars have been reproduced, with life-sized models of the people involved. On the north side of Utrechtseweg, in what is still rather a select residential suburb, is the beautiful landscaped and maintained War Cemetery, resting place for nearly two thousand British and Allied soldiers.

In Oosterbeek-Laag, the lower village along the river bank below the hilly part where the Hartenstein house stands, is the little church which was the rendezvous point for the remaining airborne troops after the order was given to withdraw at night across the river, an operation carried out by British and Canadian sappers which resulted in saving about 2,200 men. The church was badly damaged but has since been rebuilt, during which some remains of the original building were uncovered.

By way of complete contrast, along the river a short distance to the west is the Rhine Terrace Westerbouwing, a small leisure park on a hill overlooking the river and the country to the south, equipped with children's playground, cable-cars, scooter-tracks and a restaurant. The road along the hillside through pleasant wooded country runs past Kasteel

Doorwerth, a thirteenth-century castle, rebuilt after the war, with superb views over the river, and in fine weather as far as Nijmegen. Now the castle houses the Netherlands Jachtmuseum, a museum devoted to hunting and wild life.

Beyond the castle the road bears sharply right, joining the main road leading left into **Renkum**, formerly a place of pilgrimage. A picture of a Madonna and Child dated 1380 is in the church.

The road along the river leads next to **Wageningen**, one of the most important centres for agricultural studies in the world, with gardens, arboretum and visitor centre all open to the public. The town itself has a twelfth-century church, and was granted a charter in 1263. On 5 May 1945, in the former Hotel de Wereld, General Foulkes, commanding the 1st Canadian Corps, received the surrender of all the German forces in western Holland.

Taking the road north from Wageningen, at signpost 7355 fork right towards **Bennekom**, a rural village between the natural landscape of the Veluwe and the agricultural fields of the Gelderse Vallei. In Kerkstraat is a museum going under the name 'Kijk en Luister', which simply means 'Look and Listen'. In the museum are two collections. One by the Old-Bennekom Society shows costumes, tools used by craftsmen and photographs of Bennekom in former times. The other collection comprises all kinds of mechanical musical instruments such as small organs, music boxes, early phonographs, etc.

North of Bennekom is the motorway A12, which is crossed underneath on the way to Ede, in an area with a number of military barracks. On the nearby Ginkelse Heide to the east is the area where many of the British airborne forces were dropped before trying to reach the Arnhem bridges. Along this road, the Amsterdamse Weg, is a memorial to these events, near a sheep fold where flocks of sheep can be seen grazing. Follow this, the old road into Arnhem, past the points where it crosses over the A12 motorway and under the A50 motorway, into a section of dual carriageway, leading towards the outskirts of Arnhem. A left turning (signpost 2277) will be signed to Burgers Safari Park and the Openluchtmuseum.

In about 2km along this road, Schelmseweg, is the entrance to the Zoo, considered to be one of the best in Europe, and employing the most modern ideas of keeping animals in surroundings as near to their natural habitat as possible, yet still enabling visitors to watch them in safety. Aviaries are also included, and for the larger animals, the adjoining Safari Park with its safari train can provide a memorable experience.

About 1km further along Schelmseweg is the entrance to the renowned Openluchtmuseum, the Open Air Museum which has formed the pattern for many other such enterprises all over Europe. Set in a lovely park and gardens, dozens of farmhouses, cottages, mills, and houses have literally been transplanted from their original locations and have been furnished and equipped with authentic articles. Here in one place the different styles of farmhouse unique to the various regions of the country, with the typical furnishings and all the detailed items from everyday life in the past, may be seen. An example of every type of windmill has been re-erected here, together with sawmills, a boat-yard from Marken, and a number of old craft workshops in which demonstrations may be seen. A separate hall accommodates a fascinating display of regional costumes from all over the Netherlands, together with very fine embroidered household linens. The whole complex really demands at least a day to see and enjoy everything. It should be noted that on Mondays, as is the case in many such places, the buildings and halls are closed, although the grounds of the museum remain open.

After leaving the museum grounds, continue along Schelmseweg, across the bridge over the motorway, and after about 1½km, is Kasteel Rosendael on the left. Its round tower with dungeon dates from the fourteenth century, and the building houses the museum of the International Castles

Institute. The gardens, commenced in 1722, include terraces, streams, ponds and waterfalls, and a famous 'shell-gallery'. From the castle the road continues along the northern edge of the Beekhuizen estate, from the steep slopes of which clear streams provide the water power for papermills along the valley. The road becomes very winding and steep, as it enters the National Park Veluwezoom. This name means the edge of the Veluwe, and it comes as a surprise to many to find roads with repeated hairpin bends and gradients which will test the most careful driver. Follow the signs for **Posbank**, but after a particularly steep and winding bit of road, a turning on the left at signpost 10931 leads to the highest point of land in the Veluwe, 110m above sea level. From the neighbourhood, fine views can be obtained, and a network of cycle paths lead off in all directions. It should be noted that it is forbidden to ride or drive along some of the roads in the area after sunset. Continue to Posbank, then follow the road signed to **Rheden**. At signpost 2570 will be found a Visitor Centre, the 'Bezoekerscentrum De Heurne', where there is also a sheepfold and a horse-riding centre. The road now descends to the main road, where one can cross into the town of **Rheden**, which lies between the slopes of the Veluwse highland and the shores of the Gelderse IJssel.

The main road continues alongside and parallel with the railway, to De Steeg, with Kasteel Middachten and its French-style gardens. The castle is only open when exhibitions are staged.

About 3km further on, the small town of **Dieren** is reached. The old village centre is on the right of the road, between it and a bend in the river, at the place where the Apeldoornse Kanal leaves the river. The annual pole-jumping over the canal attracts hundreds of spectators. From Dieren the steam railway runs north to Apeldoorn. Turning along the road north through the fast-growing new part of the town, the route runs along the edge of farmland.

About 2km out of Dieren, a turning on the right at signpost 212 goes towards the canal, and on the canal bank take the left turning alongside the water, for about 3km. Here is an old oil-mill powered by a waterwheel. From the mill, several turnings to the left will regain the main road beyond Eerbeek. Turn right and continue to Loenen, where at signpost 2454 turn left again, continuing to the main road at Woeste Hoeve, where a left turn is made to return to Arnhem.

14 WEST AND CENTRAL OVERIJSSEL AND THE IJSSEL VALLEY

The very large province of Overijssel is divided into three administrative areas, namely West Overijssel, Salland and Twente. The first includes the north-east polder of the IJsselmeer, but we deal only with the remainder of West Overijssel together with the whole of the IJssel Valley, including that part which lies in the province of Gelderland.

ROUTE 43   THE OLD COASTLINE and THE BROADS

The old sea-dyke of the former Zuiderzee still exists, and it is possible to drive along the road on top of the dyke all the way from Vollenhove in the south to Lemmer in the north. Our route takes in a large part of the dyke, passes through the reed-fens of the Weerribben to Steenwijk, then to the broadlands around Giethoorn. The area around Staphorst is then explored before returning to the starting place at Hasselt which is conveniently accessible from Zwolle, the provincial capital. Part of this route follows the ANWB signed 'North-West Overijssel Route'.

Hasselt is an old fortified Hanseatic town on the Zwarte Water, chartered in 1252. Scattered throughout the town, but, particularly along the picturesque tree-lined Herengracht and in the Hoogstraat, are some attractive seventeenth-century houses, and the Waterpoortje in Ridderstraat is a remnant of the fourteenth-century town walls. In the Markt is the Stadhuis, parts of which date back to 1500, with a fine collection of old weapons and paintings, and archives relating to the history of the town. Nearby is the Grote or St Stephanuskerk, with a massive tower, dating from 1466. There is an early sixteenth-century wall painting of St Christopher on one of the supporting pillars of the tower. An attractive park along the Zwarte Water contains a corn windmill dated 1784; it stands at the beginning of a stone dyke built in the eighteenth century against the onslaught of the water from the former Zuiderzee.

Leave Hasselt in the direction of **Genemuiden**. It is best to follow the signed ANWB route at this point, because there is a double bridge leading out of the town and it is easy to lose the way. The route goes across the main road bridge towards **Zwolle**, then in about 1km turn left at signpost 1429, and left again back towards Hasselt. This road brings one almost to the bridge (signpost 11359) then goes left once more, under the main road bridge then straight ahead on the road signed for Genemuiden. Cyclists will have separate signed routes as this road is for motor vehicles only.

Genemuiden, a town dating from 1275, lies on the Zwolse Diep, and its inhabitants have for centuries made their living from the rushes used for making high-quality rush matting. This cottage industry is now mechanised. From Genemuiden, cross the Zwolse Diep, by ferry and continue left along the dyke road towards **Vollenhove**, an old fishing port first mentioned in 944,

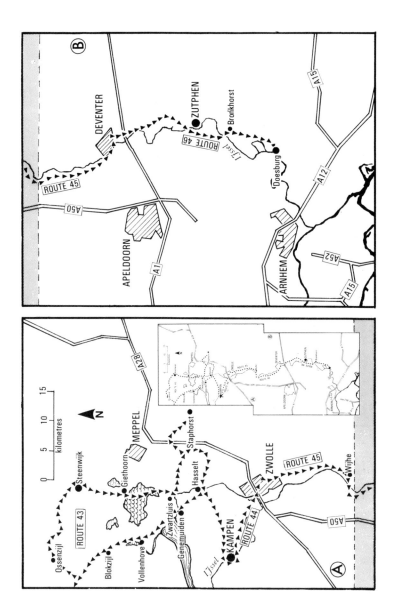

and known for its fine old buildings and picturesque harbours. The old Town Hall (1621) near the inner harbour is now a restaurant, and next to it is the Grote or St Nicolaaskerk dating from the end of the fifteenth century. Inside is an organ dated 1686, and many monuments to the noble families who came to the town in the fourteenth century when it was the country seat of the Bishops of Utrecht. Opposite the church is the seventeenth-century Latin School building with a most lovely *trap-gevel* and high arched windows, which, during the summer houses the VVV office. Next door, the former French School building is now a hotel.

On the east side of the town, at signpost 7768, turn north along the Vollenhovermeer. The road runs along the former sea dyke to **Blokzijl**, an old fortress town established in the fifteenth century by Dutch merchants, which still retains its character. The name Blokzijl dates from 1438, and its charter was granted in 1672. Since the enclosing of the Zuiderzee, the busy traffic of trading vessels has changed to that of pleasure cruisers. The harbour basin, lies in the centre of the town, where there is an old 'high water' cannon, which used to be fired as a warning against floods. It was placed here in 1813 and was last used after the disastrous floods of 1825 when a vast area of Overijssel was under water. Take a short walk through the narrow streets to see the beautiful old merchants' houses with their high decorated gables, many of which have been bought by the Hendrik de Keyser Foundation which aims to save them from falling into disrepair. The old orphanage, Prins Maurits Weeshuis in Brouwersstraat, is now used as an exhibition centre. The fortifications are still in in fairly good condition, and inside the fine seventeenth-century church is a pulpit dated 1663 and a model of the seventeenth-century armed merchant ship 'De Zeven Provincien'.

From Blokzijl, continue along the dyke road, still following the ANWB signs. Small ponds to the right show where the sea has broken through in the past. Beyond the hamlet of **Blankenham**, either follow the dyke road straight ahead to the next junction (signpost 333), or follow the signed route to the left then right, along to the Kuinder Bos picnic and recreation area, where a break may be taken. Waymarked footpaths are provided through the woods. The road junction on the old dyke may be regained by going through the tiny township of **Kuinre**, which originally consisted of just one street with fortified houses.

From signpost 333 on the dyke road, turn towards **Ossenzijl**, where a Visitor Centre ('Bezoekerscentrum De Weerribben') provides information about a most interesting nature reserve, consisting of fenland, with reed beds and small waterways. Many species of bird, including a colony of blue herons, breed here, and old fen-workers' cottages and a small windmill of the type known as a *tjasker* can be seen. The area within the reserve is very extensive.

From the centre, continue towards **Oldemarkt**, but before the village, take the turning on the right (ANWB signs) then the second turning on the left, followed by the next on the right. This comes on to a picturesque road for 1km, after which the road takes a sharp turn to the left and heads towards **Paasloo**, a very small village with an interesting church, set among trees. Dating from 1336, the nave bears a striking resemblance to an Overijssel farmhouse and the door is Norman. It is one of the oldest churches in Overijssel.

From Paasloo, follow the road for about 3km, and turn right at signpost 12172, through **Steenwijkerwold** to the old fortress town of **Steenwijk**, so named on account of the large quantities of stones found in the ground. A large part of the old town wall and moats remain intact, forming a pleasant walk. One of the most interesting buildings in the town is the old Boterwaag (1642) in Waagstraat, and there is a small local museum with antiquities, pottery, old weapons, etc in the Markt. The two churches, the Grote or St Clemenskerk, and the Kleine or OLV Kerk, both date from the fifteenth century. Just outside the walls is the park and nineteenth-century villa of Rams-Woerthe, now the Town Hall.

Leave Steenwijk by the road running south, turning right at the T-junction on the edge of the town, then in 2km turn left (signpost 4367) towards **Giethoorn**. Park at the northern end of the village and walk through to the pretty paths running beside the waterways. The village originated in 1280, when land was given to a group of religious fanatics, who, whilst digging peat, uncovered horns of wild goats, so named the settlement 'Geytenhorn' or Goats' horn. Peat-digging, and storm floods, in particular the disastrous break-through of the Zuiderzee in 1776–77, formed many ponds and lakes which today give the area its characteristic appearance. The waterways were originally dug to transport peat, and now the whole village is intersected by these canals, crossed by numerous little bridges to give access to the houses. It is now very much a tourist attraction, with many reed-thatched houses open as gift-shops. The best way to see the village is to hire a small motor or rowing boat. The whole area resembles the East Anglian Broads, and that name is given to many of the stretches of water in this area. The large lake nearest the village is called the Bovenwijde (*wijde* = broad). On this broad is the large 'Smits Paviljoen', with pleasant terraces and a restaurant with superb views over the water; a complete contrast to the nearby village, known in Holland as the Venice of the North.

Most of the small roadways between the canals are closed to motor vehicles, although cycles are permitted on some paths. One small museum in the village, the 'Oude Aarde', includes a collection of precious, semi-precious and other stones and minerals. Naturally the whole area is a paradise for pleasure boating.

From Giethoorn, do not follow the ANWB route, but continue south from the car park, along Beulakerweg, passing on the right a *klokkenstoel* dating from 1633 beside the church. After leaving the village, the road crosses the beautiful broads of the Beulakerwijde and Belterwijde, where parking bays enable one to stop to admire the scenery, and to watch the masses of water birds which breed in this area. Passing Schutsloterwijde on the right, the road bears right at signpost 6070, and heads towards **Zwartsluis**. This attractive little sixteenth-century fortress town ('Fortresse Swartersluys') came into prominence during the eighty-years war, and was known as the 'Poort naar het Noorden', or gateway to the north. Situated on the Zwarte Water, where two waterways, the Meppelerdiep and the Arembergergracht joined to run into the Zuiderzee, it still provides the gateway for pleasure and other craft to enter the extensive recreation areas of the broads.

In the Town Hall hangs a painting of the town as it was in 1680, together with a plan of the early seventeenth-century fortress; and the sixteenth-century church has a pulpit dating from 1668. Outside is a *klokkenstoel* still with its bell from 1606.

On the south of the town, turn left along the water side, and by the

The Koornmarktspoort, one of Kampen's three town gates

pumping station, at signpost 7942, turn left again, taking the road across the polder which in about 7km reaches the Staphorst to Rouveen road. **Staphorst** and **Rouveen**, together with **IJhorst** to the north-east, form one municipality. the origins of which go back to the thirteenth century. The village street, the Diek, is about 12km long, and on each side are fine farmhouses, painted traditionally in green and blue, with reed-thatched roofs. Of the 1,100 or so farmhouses in the whole parish, some 300 are listed buildings. Formerly this area was quite isolated and the traditional local costumes have been retained until the present day. Most of the women still wear the unique dress, but visitors are specially asked not to take photographs without permission, and not on Sundays. In Staphorst itself there is a ban on photography. Although the essential character of the village itself is being preserved as much as possible, it is nevertheless developing, with new housing and some industry coming into the area. One of the 150-year-old farmhouses has been restored and houses a municipal museum, open during the summer months, showing in great detail the everyday life of the inhabitants, and the work of the farmers who lived here. An exhibition room has examples of the costumes of Staphorst, Rouveen and IJhorst, and in the rear of the farmhouse is a hand-weaving workshop.

The road through Staphorst is closed to through traffic on Sundays during the times of church service, but at other times one can drive through.

The close spacing of the farmhouses, often with one or two others behind the main house on the road, derives from the custom of dividing the farms among the sons of the family, and the old strip-farming system still persists. A diversion may be made from Staphorst by crossing the railway in the direction of IJhorst, and immediately turning right beside the railway. After about 3km a sign on the left directs travellers to 'Zwarte Dennen', in the Staphorst Forest. This is a recreation area with parking, picnic tables, a lake and a number of walks, all provided by the State Forestry Service.

Returning to Staphorst, turn left again, along the main street through Rouveen to the junction with the A28 motorway. Turn right along the minor road beside the canal towards Hasselt, the starting point of this route. Go through the town and follow the start of the route again to signpost 11359, left again under the main road bridge and turn left towards **Mastenbroek** and **IJsselmuiden**, finally crossing the bridge into **Kampen**.

The river IJssel is the only major river in Holland which runs from south to north. It connects the river Rhine at Arnhem with the IJsselmeer near Kampen, and is about 50km in length. The river crosses Gelderland from Arnhem to Deventer, the country to the east of the river being known as the Achterhoek. North of Deventer the river forms the boundary between Gelderland and Overijssel. Our journey along the IJssel valley will be described from north to south, and it forms an ideal link route between north-east Holland and the great river plains of the south. It passes through a number of interesting towns, and will be described in three sections.

ROUTE 44   KAMPEN and ZWOLLE

Kampen is an old Hanseatic town at the mouth of the IJssel, which received its charter in 1230. The quayside is always busy and a number of traditional Dutch sailing vessels are based here, many being available for hire. The most interesting of the three Town Gates is the fourteenth-century Koornmarktspoort, on IJsselkade, its twin towers with steeples standing on either side of a tall central building.

The spires and towers of the other gates, the Broederpoort and the Cellebroederspoort, may be seen from the streets in the town. Kampen lost its importance when the river silted up in the seventeenth century, but now, because of its position in relation to the new polders, it has regained its place as a centre for trade and communications.

The old town is confined on the west side by a moat and on the east by the river. In Oudestraat there are narrow alleys known as *steegs*, with buildings on either side which lean towards each other and are prevented from collapse by buttresses of wood or steel. For this reason, the alleys are called *balksteegs*. At the northern end of Oudestraat is the Town Hall, consisting of the Oude Raadhuis (sixteenth century) and the Nieuwe Raadhuis (eighteenth century). The adjoining 'Gotische Huis' accommodates the district museum. Nearby stands the beautiful seventeenth-century Nieuwe

Toren, with a carillon. The sixteenth-century St Nicolaaskerk stands on the foundations of an original thirteenth-century church, whilst the restored OL Vrouwekerk was originally built in the fourteenth century. By way of contrast, in Botermarkt is the Kampen Tobacco Museum, with an exhibition of cigar-making tools and machines, and the biggest cigar in the world, 5m in length.

Leave the town and cross the bridge, latest in a succession of bridges dating back to at least 1448, to **IJsselmuiden**, from the waterside of which a fine view may be obtained. Follow the main N50 road to **Zwolle**. Note that there is now a new road bridge south of Kampen which enables IJsselmuiden to be bypassed. This may avoid traffic jams on the older bridge.

Zwolle, another Hanseatic town, has an exceptionally well-preserved town centre and fortifications, and is capital of the province of Overijssel. The town received its charter in 1230, and parts of the old town walls dating from about 1250 still remain. In 1621 the fortifications were strengthened, with a typical star-shaped perimeter and moat, most of which still exists, enclosing the centre of the town. The street plan remains exactly as originally laid out, and car parking is confined to signed places outside the walls. The best place to park is on the northern 'island', near the Friesewal or the Assiesplein, then walk across the bridge from Dijkstraat to Vispoortenplas, along Roggenstraat to the Grote Markt. This is the centre of the old town.

The Grote or St Michaelskerk dates from about 1040, and the present building is early sixteenth century. The organ, dating from 1721, is one of the finest in Holland. On the side of the church in the Grote Markt stands the Hoofdwacht or Guardhouse of the town, built in 1615. Over the doors are carved the words 'Vigilate et Orate' ('Watch and Pray'). Behind the church, in Grote Kerkplein, is the VVV office. From here, walk between the old Stadhuis, and the Wheeme, originally the clergy house of the Grote Kerk, into Lombaardstraat and thence to Goudsteeg, where on the left is the Huis met de Hoofden, a fifteenth-century residence now used as the municipal music school. The Gothic building takes its name from the 'heads' on top of the brick supports on the gables. Goudsteeg leads to Koestraat, where by turning left, the turreted Sassenpoort will be seen. This is the only remaining town gate from 1408, and bears a tablet commemorating 700 years of the town's existence. Close by are the beautifully-landscaped bastions of the southern bulwarks, from which a fine view may be obtained of the towers of the Sassenpoort above the trees. From the gate, walk up Sassenstraat, to Nieuwe Markt and on the left is the Reventer or Reventorium, the refectory of the former Bethlehem monastery. Continue ahead up Sassenstraat to the Bethlehemskerk, dating from 1308 and also part of the monastery.

Sassenstraat winds to the right, and then to the left. On the right there is a house, known as Karel V Huis, on account of a medallion bearing his head and the date 1571 on the Renaissance gable. Just beyond, on the right, a

PLACES TO VISIT IN KAMPEN, ZWOLLE AND DEVENTER

Kampen

Three old Town Gates.
Harbour with traditional sailing craft.
Narrow alleys in town. Sixteenth-century old Town Hall.
Gotische Huis district museum.
Seventeenth-century Nieuwe Toren with carillon.
Tobacco Museum with world's largest cigar.

Zwolle

Old fortified town with much still remaining.
Sixteenth-century St Michaelskerk with very fine organ.
Seventeenth-century Guardhouse.
Fifteenth-century Clergy House and Town Hall.
Sassenpoort — fifteenth-century Town Gate.

Old monastery and abbey buildings.
Provincial museum.

Deventer

Preserved town centre.
Sixteenth-century Waag with historical museum.
Sixteenth-century merchant's house 'De Drie Haringen'.
Albert Schweitzer Museum.
Twelfth-century Bergkerk (Church on the Hill) with nearby old Overijssel houses.
Seventeenth-century Muntentoren — now Space Navigation museum.
Thirteenth-century Stadhuis.
Sixteenth-century Municipal Library — the oldest in Western Europe.
Toy Museum.
Grote (St Lebuinuskerk) with cupola-topped tower and fine carillon.

small street, Rode Eeuw Straat, leads into Oude Vismarkt, where a left turn will lead across Grote Markt into Voorstraat. Along this street on the left is Drostenstraat which leads to Ossenmarkt and the church of OLV ten Hemelopneming (Our Lady of Heaven) with its distinctive 'pepper-pot' tower.

Cross back over Voorstraat, along Melkmarktstraat and into Melkmarkt. Turn left, and on the left, at No 41, is the Provincial Museum, with a good selection of period rooms and exhibits specifically relating to the Province. It has an eighteenth-century façade but dates back to the sixteenth century, the back of the building being particularly attractive. The nearby Vrouwenhuis (No 53 Melkmarkt) has an interesting frontage. At the end of Melkmarkt turn right to Rodetorenplein. Standing on its own here is a fine seventeenth-century building, the 'Hopmanshuis', known locally as the house with ninety-nine windows.

Continue along Buitenkant beside the moat, where remains of the thirteenth-century town walls may be seen. Cross the Stadsgracht by the bridge, turn right into Thorbeckegracht and look back over the water to the old defence towers between the walls, each with three weapon slits and various lookout openings. The walls of the towers are more than one metre thick. Continue on to the footbridge, from which an excellent view can be obtained of the Broerenklooster and Broerenkerk (1465), owned since the Reformation by the Dutch Reformed Church, and now being restored.

ROUTE 45   THE IJSSEL VALLEY TO DEVENTER

Leave the car park in Zwolle and cross back over Achter Gracht, turning right along Zamenhofsingel and Diezerkade, following signs for **Raalte** and **Almelo**. At the junction with the main N35 road, turn right (signpost 2088) on to the N337 road signed to **Ittersum** and **Wijhe**. This road runs parallel with the river and the railway, which it crosses about 10km south of Ittersum. After another 3km, the small riverside town of **Wijhe** is reached, situated in an ideal area for walking and cycletouring. At this point, cross the IJssel by car ferry, to continue along the other side of the river, which is a more pleasant road. The road runs south through **Veessen**, where there is a windmill dated 1775. Good views over the river are obtainable from here. Continue along the river valley to the villages of **Welsum**, and **Terwolde**, which has a church dating from about 1350.

As the road comes opposite **Deventer**, a fine view of the town can be obtained over the river to the left. After passing under a railway bridge, the main road into the town is joined and the river is crossed by the Wilhelminabrug. yet another old Hanseatic town with a well preserved centre, its importance derives from its position on the river, a major trade route, and the fact that since the fifteenth century there has been a bridge, connecting west Gelderland with Overijssel. Parking places are reasonably plentiful, and those on the Brink or on Broederenplein, off Smedenstraat are centrally placed for sight-seeing.

The first records of a settlement here date back to about AD770, and in 881 the town was plundered by Viking raiders. From the tenth century, Deventer began to grow in importance as a trading centre, which made it necessary, in the twelfth century, for the old walls to be replaced by new ones.

ROUTE 45A   A WALK IN DEVENTER

A walk around the town can best be started from the Brink, a large open space in the town centre. At the end is the magnificent Waag, dated 1528, which now houses the local historical museum. Among other exhibits, this has a collection of old bicycles, a typical 'Salland' kitchen, and some of the furnishings from the old Burgerweeshuis (orphanage). The fine merchant's house behind the Waag, on the left, is known as De Drie Haringen. Built in 1575, it is now the VVV office. Further down the street, at Brink 47, is an excellent toy museum, with one of the largest public collections of old toys in existence, containing every type of toy used by children in the days before television.

Beyond the Waag the square narrows, and in the corner is a fine old building known as the Penninckshuis, which has six statues on the façade representing Faith, Hope, Love, Prudence, Strength and Modesty. Inside is the Albert Schweitzer Museum and a Mennonite Chapel, and in front stands a statue of the famous doctor. Continue around the Brink and turn into Bergstraat, which leads through the old Bergkwartier to the twelfth-century Bergkerk, the 'Church on the Hill', its twin spires standing high over the town. On the Bergkerkplein are some lovely old Overijssel façades. This part of the town has been renovated with the aid of a grant from the Dutch Government, as it is considered to be so important architecturally. At the end of Bergkerkplein, near where Bergstraat enters the square, is a steep alley, Kerksteeg, on one of the walls of which is a stone with an iron ring, placed there in the sixteenth century. Iron chains were fastened to the ring and hung low over the street in times of war. Continue ahead into Bergschild, then right into Rijkmanstraat. Turn left into Achter de Muuren which leads to a small square. Through a gate in the wall is a yard in front of the Muntentoren, where Deventer's coins were minted in the seventeenth and eighteenth centuries. Now the building houses a small museum devoted to Space Navigation. Continue through the passages back into Rijkmanstraat, turn left and return to the Brink. Cross over into Kleine Overstraat with more interesting houses, and on the left turn into Vleeshouwersstraat, crossing into Grote Poot then into Kleine Poot by the Church entrance. The Grote or Lebuinuskerk is the oldest church in Deventer, built on the site of a wooden church of AD765. The foundations for the present building were started in 1040, and the crypt is still in existence. In the cupola-topped tower is a fine carillon. At the other side of the square is the rather unusual Botermarkt, with cast-iron pillars supporting the roof of the colonnade. Returning along Kleine Poot to Grote Kerkhof, the Stadhuis is seen ahead. Dating back to the thirteenth century, much of the present building is of later date. Walk to the end of the square, around the end of the church and turn left down Vispoort to the waterfront.

A really good panoramic view of the town can be obtained by crossing on the small pedestrian ferry to the opposite bank of the river, where there is a small park. On the town waterfront near Vispoort will be seen a round brick building, part of the restored town defences. Returning on the ferry, go up IJsselstraat into Achter de Muuren with remains of the old and newer town walls, and characteristic old houses and buildings. At the end, turn right into Muggenplein, right again along Noordenbergstraat, then on the left is the restored building of the Athenaeumbibliotheek. This houses the Municipal Library, dating from 1560 and the oldest municipal library in Western Europe. In the basement is an exhibition of old books and prints. This walk has given a brief look at the town, which has much more to offer given more time.

ROUTE 46   THE IJSSEL VALLEY TO ZUTPHEN and DOESBURG
Leave Deventer by following signs for **Gorssel** and **Zutphen**, which will lead to the main N48 road. About 2km south of the town, this road crosses

The seventeenth-century Muntentoren, Deventer

under the A1 motorway at the boundary between Overijssel and Gelderland. The river IJssel winds through a broad flood plain to the right of the road, and in the neighbourhood of Gorssel there is plenty of scope for cycling or walking. At **Eelde**, the road crosses the Twente Canal, a major and very busy waterway, then crosses the railway line to enter the town of **Zutphen**, standing at the confluence of the Berkel and the IJssel rivers. It owes its importance as a trading centre to the communications by water with France, Germany and Scandinavia during the Middle Ages. Originally a castle was built in the eleventh century on a rising piece of land where the two rivers met. Town rights were granted in 1190, and it became known for its many towers, both on the churches and on the town gates.

Parking is possible in Stationsplein or on the IJsselkade, as well as at various other places within the town. Confined on the west by the river IJssel, and on the north and west by the river Berkel, the inner or old town is bounded on the remaining sides by canals and fortifications, many of which remain intact.

ROUTE 46A   A WALK IN ZUTPHEN

A walk around the town may start in Kerkhof, by the Grote or St Walburgskerk, which has a magnificent tower. Inside are some beautiful wall paintings and a fine organ on which recitals are given. In the past a nightwatchman lived in the tower, and in case of fire or other danger, would sound the alarm. The top has been burned several times, the last being in 1948, and was restored in 1970. The Chapter House adjoining the church contains a very rare chained library from 1561, unique in Western Europe. Over 400 old hand-written books and manuscripts are here.

Opposite the church is the oldest square in Zutphen, where the outline of the foundations of the old 's Gravenhof, the original castle around which the town developed, are incorporated in the pavement. Around the corner, in Waterstraat, is the Bourgonjetoren, part of the medieval defences of the town, whose walls are 4m thick. Return through 's Gravenhof and walk along Martinetsingel, to the Drogenapstoren, built in 1446 as the Saltpoort, one of the town gates. Ten years later it was taken out of use as a gate, and gained its present name from that of the town trumpeter who lived there in 1555. The building was also the first water tower for the town. Walk through Drogenapssteeg into Zaadmarkt, and on the right, a short way along, is the Bornhof, a fourteenth-century hospice for elderly poor people. Further along on the other side is the Henriette Polak Museum devoted to modern art, in one of a number of houses with attractive façades along this street. Continue on into Houtmarkt, and across Lange Hofstraat into Groenmarkt. On the corner to the left is the Wijnhuistoren, built on the site of the fourteenth-century town inn. The tower contains a carillon dated 1648. Badly damaged during fighting during the last days of World War II, it has now been restored and houses the VVV office. Walk up Korte Hofstraat, bear right along Turfstraat, then right again into Oude Wand. On the left is the entrance to the fourteenth-century Agnietenhof, formerly a nunnery, now almshouses. At the end, turn left along Komsteeg to the Hagepoortplein, on the other side of which is the fifteenth-century Berkelpoort over the water, with its turrets. In times of war gates were lowered to prevent shipping from passing through, and defenders could drop pitch and boiling oil from the battlements.

Cross over the river Berkel and along Isendoornstraat, at the end of which, on the right, is the Nieuwstadspoort, dating from 1536, through which the town was invaded by the Spanish in 1572. Returning left and back over the Berkel and right into Rozengracht, there is a museum dealing with the history of the town and district. It has just been undergoing rebuilding and renovation. Ahead and over the water on to Berkelkade, a right turn to Stationsplein will reveal the old mid-fourteenth-century powder tower, part of the old town defence works, which now houses a very large collection of lead toy soldiers, mostly in original colours, set out in parade and battle formations. The tower forms the north-west corner of the town walls. From here, return across the bridge, right along Barlheze, past some more fine façades, and left into Groenmarkt. At the end, turn right at the Wijnhuistoren, down Lange Hofstraat, where the fifteenth-century Stadhuis is on the left. The original building dates from 1450, with later additions, and next to it is the Burgerzaal (1452) with a very fine oak roof. The walk ends back at the Grote Kerk.

To leave the town, drive north along IJsselkade, towards the railway, then turn left across the IJsselbrug, left again on to the main N345 road. This gives a fine view back across the river to the town. Follow signs for **Dieren** and **Arnhem**, past the junction where the road becomes N48. About 6km from the IJsselbrug, on the outskirts of **Brummen**, take a left turn (signpost 9054) to the ferry for **Bronkhorst**. Cross the IJssel into the little town, which is officially the smallest town in Holland, although it is barely the size of a village. It has a chapel dating from 1344 which was once part of the castle. The Hoge Huis, a seventeenth-century manor house, is seen best from the dyke after leaving the ferry. In Bronkhorst, turn right at signpost 2336 and go towards **Steenderen**, passing a windmill (1844) on the right. The church here dates from the twelfth century, and beside the town hall is a war memorial with an inscription referring to an RAF pilot. From Steenderen, pick up the signpost 961 in the centre of the town, and follow minor roads to **Doesburg**. The road runs very near to the river on a big loop, and joins the main road on the edge of Doesburg at signpost 7086, at which point a right turn leads into the town.

Doesburg once again demonstrates how an early settlement at a strategic position on the river system grows into an important trading centre, fortified to protect it against outside interference. Originally the river IJssel ran from within Germany through Doetinchem in eastern Gelderland, turning north to run via Zutphen and Deventer to the Zuiderzee. At the point where it turned north, an early settlement arose. There is some doubt as to whether the Romans had much influence here, but certainly by AD1000 a permanent settlement existed on the banks of the river IJssel, at the place now known as Doesburg. Although the whole system of major rivers in Holland is very complicated, it seems unclear when and how the connection between the Oude IJssel and the Rijn was made. One suggestion is that the Roman General Drusus caused a canal link to be made from the IJssel at Doesburg to the Rijn near Arnhem. Such a link exists, but actual evidence for the Roman involvement has yet to be found.

Town rights were granted to Doesburg in 1237, it was later fortified with walls, gates and canals, and joined the Hanseatic League in 1447. At the end of the fifteenth century, wars and silting of the river IJssel began a decline in the town's importance as a trading centre, since when farming, cattle-raising and later, industrial development arrived, although the character of the town has not been affected. Serious damage occurred at the end of World War II, but this has now been repaired.

The layout of the town centre depends on the now-familiar star-shaped fortifications of the early eighteenth century, much of which still survive. On entering the town, keep straight ahead to 'Centrum', along Kraakselaan to Meipoort. Bearing left along Meipoortstraat, then right into Kerkstraat brings one to the Markt, in the oldest part of the town. The tower of the Grote or St Martinikerk, was destroyed by the German forces during 1945, but it has now been rebuilt. The original carved seventeenth-century pulpit was rescued from the ruins and is now restored to use. Beyond the church, in Roggestraat is the Roode Tooren, built in 1789 on the site of a former prison which had been built on a site previously occupied by the Red Tower, part of the town wall defences destroyed by the French in 1673. Today it is a museum, illustrating the history and development of the town. At the corner of Roggestraat and Koepoortstraat is the Stadhuis or Town Hall, which now occupies a group of buildings dating from the fourteenth to the seventeenth centuries. In Koepoortstraat itself is the Waag, another impressive building, dating from the sixteenth century. Along this street are a number of dignified and elegant houses. In Gasthuisstraat, leading from the junction of Kerkstraat and Koepoortstraat, are some sixteenth-century almshouses.

One interesting fact about Doesburg is that the church tower is one of the tallest in the country. Because the ground beneath contains iron, the tower has been struck by lightning on a number of occasions. In 1783, the first lightning-conductor in the country was installed here by General Krayenhoff.

There are many more interesting buildings to be seen in the town, and a good descriptive leaflet in English may be obtained from the local VVV, whose office is in Kerkstraat, near the turning into the Markt. Many of the eighteenth-century fortifications have been restored and laid out as a park, on the south and north-east of the town.

Exits from the town towards Arnhem are via the Coehoornsingel, the ring road around the north of the town which crosses the IJssel to join the A48 and N48 roads.

15 IN THE BACK CORNER

To the east of the IJssel Valley, stretching to the frontier with Germany, lie those parts of the provinces of Overijssel and Gelderland collectively known as Twente and Achterhoek. Twente is the most easterly of the three regions of Overijssel and the Achterhoek, or 'back corner', is the eastern region of Gelderland. We also include parts of the central Salland region. Ideal country for walking and cycling, at the same time there are modern industrial towns which have developed rapidly since World War II. This is 'old' land, away from the low-lying polders, and has its own particular attraction. In the north, **Ommen** lies half-way between Zwolle and the German frontier, and makes a good centre for our first route.

ROUTE 47   IN and AROUND OMMEN

Ommen, in the Salland region of Overijssel, is an old town with a rich history, lying on the river Overijsselse Vecht, which runs from within Germany by a very circuitous route to join the IJssel north of Zwolle. The first bridge over the Vecht was built here in 1492, and the town has since become one of the leading tourist centres in the country. The church dates from 1300, and in the town are three old corn mills, now owned by the municipality. One, 'D Oordt', together with a former Toll House, houses the municipal museum which contains collections of Stone, Bronze and Iron-Age finds, and furniture and other items in a room from old Ommen, Documents, books, costumes, pictures and photographs give a good picture of the town's history. Another mill, 'De Lelie' may be visited on application to the miller.

Around the town are many picturesque roads and waymarked cycle-tracks and footpaths, and this route follows some of them.

Leave the town by crossing the river on the road south, signed to Nijverdal, then immediately turn right, passing the windmill and taking the road parallel with the river towards **Vilsteren** from where pleasant cycle and walking routes lead to the river. Continue for about 4km, and Kasteel Rechteren, an imposing fourteenth-century building with an interesting defence tower, can be seen on the right.

A further 2km brings the road to **Dalfsen** station, the town being on the other side of the river, crossed by a bridge. Turn left (signpost 410) past the station, and take the road past Huize Den Berg (eighteenth century) to follow the very twisting but picturesque route signed to **Heino**. Cross the main N35 road into the town, with its thirteenth-century church tower and pump in the square, and follow the road to the railway station. Cross the railway to Kasteel 't Nijenhuis, parts of which date from the sixteenth century. The castle is not normally open to visitors, but the coach-house contains an exhibition of old and modern art, including old Chinese and Japanese porcelain.

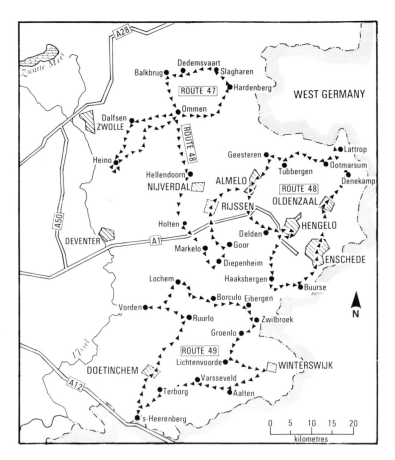

Return to Heino, re-cross the main road and take the turning on the right towards Lemelerveld. After about 6km, at signpost 1802 continue straight ahead across the canal until the road enters the wooded estate of Rechteren, where, at signpost 7932, turn right towards **Dalmsholte**. Cross the main road N48, and in about 500m turn left (signpost 7929), and follow the winding road to **Giethmen**, one of the many hamlets in the area with old thatched farmhouses typical of this region. From Giethmen, turn right then left to **Nieuwebrug** on the little river Regge. Turn left on to the main road towards Ommen and at the next main junction turn right (signpost 219) through the woods to **Eerde**. Where the road turns to the right towards Den Ham, turn left along a minor road through the forest where there is very pleasant walking and a number of car parks. Cross the railway, turn right through the woods to **Beerze**, another typical Salland hamlet.

Continue to the main N36 road, cross over, and at **Marienberg**, turn left at signpost 2166 to cross the river Vecht at the sluice, to the Boswachterij Hardenberg. Follow the road which bears right at signpost 10821 and continue through to **Heemse**, a suburb of the town of **Hardenberg**.

Hardenberg was chartered in 1362, an industrial town in an agricultural region offering beautiful countryside and recreation facilities. Part of the town wall can still be seen, a windmill stands high above the town. A small historical museum is housed in the former Town Hall (1805) and has a Saxon farmhouse kitchen, costumes and other exhibits.

From Hardenberg, cross the main N34 road at signpost 6755 and continue to **Lutten**. At the major cross roads (signpost 3343) turn right on to the dual carriageway and on the right by the windmill is the entrance to the Slagharen Ponypark, a large amusement park with many attractions from Shetland ponies to the latest 'space-age' rides.

Return to Lutten, and turn right along the minor road to **Dedemsvaart**. which has some so-called Patricians' Houses, set among pleasant trees, and a modern covered shopping centre. Tuinen Mien Ruys, twenty beautiful gardens within an area of 20,000 square metres, each illustrating a different type of plant or flower for various purposes is open to the public during the summer months and is intended to show gardeners and others what is possible. The idea of the garden designer Mien Ruys, it took over fifty years to create, and is an ongoing project. Even for those with no intention of making a garden, it provides two hours of delightful wandering in peace and quiet. From Dedemsvaart the road continues to **Balkbrug**, site of one of the most modern cheese factories in Europe. Turn left at the cross roads (signpost 391) and a short distance along the road are the remains of Ommerschans, an old earthwork with ditches and trees. The road continues directly back to Ommen, crossing under the motor road just outside the town.

ROUTE 48   THE SALLANDSE HEUVELRUG and TWENTE

To the immediate south of Ommen a belt of small hills known as the Sallandse Heuvelrug stretches towards the border with Gelderland. This route follows the ridge, then makes a circuit of the eastern region of the province, Twente.

From Ommen, cross the river and follow the road south to **Hellendoorn**. The road runs between the hills to the right and the winding river Regge on the left. The church has a nave built about 1150, and Gothic choir and side chapels from 1484. There are two windmills and a historical museum situated in a centuries-old Saxon farmhouse. In the neighbourhood, on the road to **Luttenberg**, is the Hellendoorn Avonturenpark, with many unusual attractions for all ages. South of the town, the road crosses the railway and the main N35 road into **Nijverdal**. Unlike Hellendoorn with its 900-year history, Nijverdal was only established in 1836. Carillon recitals are given in the Town Hall. From here go west along the main road for a short distance, then turn left at signpost 3819 on to the road through the forest. In about 1km, is the visitor centre, 'Bezoekerscentrum Noetselerberg'. This gives information about the Sallandse Heuvelrug and the work of the State Forestry Service, together with details of all the walking routes in the area. There is a large car park. The road south towards **Holten** follows a beautiful route through the forest, where there are several cycle routes. On the Holterberg road is 'Bos Dierenwereld', a natural history museum with displays and dioramas telling the story of the wildlife of Europe.

At the road junction on the south of Holten (signpost 29) a road runs south-east, crossing over the A1 motorway to **Markelo**, one of the oldest villages in Twente. Three typical Twents farm taverns with antique interiors are in the village. Leave by the road south via **Beusbergen** and **Stokkum**, then cross the railway, the Twente Kanaal and the main N346 road, before entering an area of large country estates. On the right is Westerflier, a manor house first named in 1046, with the present house dating from 1729; the woods of the estate are open to walkers. The road bears around to the left to the little rural town of **Diepenheim**, whose church existed in 1214. Nearby is the Rosarium De Broenshof, with more than 1,000 varieties; it is open to visitors free of charge. Around the neighbourhood are other castles and estates, including Huis te Diepenheim, Het Nijenhuis, and Huize Warmelo, whose grounds and estates are open to walkers. An old Saxon farmhouse from 1475, 'Erve Broaks', and a small museum of old implements in 't Ambachtshuuske, are of interest. Just to the south of the village, on the road to **Markvelde**, is a thirteenth-century watermill, 'Den Haller', which is still in use.

From Diepenheim, the minor road leading north-east from signpost 2563 comes to the seventeenth-century Huize Weldam, a nobleman's stately home, surrounded by water. The park, in eighteenth-century style, is open to view. From here, cross the main road, and enter **Goor** past the station. This is another old town, surrounded by pleasant woods and heath, with many large estates. A parish church stood here in 800, but the present building was started in about 1600. In the churchyard is a family vault and memorial to an Englishman, Thomas Ainsworth of Lancashire, who died in 1841 in Nijverdal. An inscription reads 'To a useful man, Thomas Ainsworth, from Grateful Overijssel'. The story behind this rather extraordinary memorial is that Ainsworth introduced the English power-loom system and taught young workers how to use it to treble the output from their existing hand-thrown shuttles. The important textile industry of Twente was thus revolutionised.

From Goor, take the road towards Markelo, and on the edge of the town at signpost 2960 turn right and folow the pleasant route to **Rijssen**, another typical little town dating back to 1243. The twelfth century church has a sandstone font from about 1200. A large oil windmill stands by the river Regge on the north-east side of the town.

The main road north-east is now followed via Wierden to **Almelo**, the third largest town in Twente. Parking places are fairly plentiful, and a convenient spot is near Markt Plein. The town has a good shopping centre, and the Grote Kerk has a crypt dating from 1236, bells from the seventeenth and eighteenth centuries, and Venetian glass chandeliers. A number of small old streets and houses, combined with open parks and modern buildings create a lively and growing town. The former Town Hall in Grote Straat was built in 1690, with a cupola, and is now used as a restaurant. The Waaggebouw, built in 1914 in Oudhollandse style as a market hall, is used as an exhibition centre. The moated Huise Almelo, begun in 1135, the property of the Count of Rechteren Limpurg, stands in a tree-lined park near the town centre. The castle and grounds are not open to the public.

Leave via the inner ring road, taking the turning on to the A35 road signed for **Enschede**. In about 2km, at signpost 3968, turn left on the road through **Bornerbroek**, crossing the A1 motorway and passing through more very pleasant wooded country with typical Twickelse farm houses with black and white shutters. Cross the main N346 road into **Delden**, a small town whose centre is about 600 years old. The St Blasiuskerk on the Markt has a tower of local sandstone, and dates from 1347. Inside are frescoes, hand-painted windows and church treasures. Nearby are some characteristic houses including the Oude Posthuis, formerly an inn dating from 1764, a merchant's house from 1860, and the old Town Hall (1792). Just to the north of the town lies Kasteel Twickel, dating from 1347. The castle is not open, but the extensive park, with a French garden laid out by the famous designer Marot in 1690, later extended with an English garden and orangery, may be viewed during the summer.

The road from here leads into **Hengelo**, a modern town and centre of textile, metal, machine and electronics industries. The central shopping area is pedestrianised. Some eighteenth-century town houses exist, not far from the Stadhuis, a modern building, with a carillon of forty-seven bells, one of the largest in the country. There are some old salt bore-holes with towers in the industrial area south of the town. On nearby Twekkelerweg, is the recreation park 'De Waarbeek', alongside the Twente Kanaal.

Leave by the Haaksbergen road, crossing the Twente Kanaal on the south-west side of the town, and immediately after passing under the A35 motorway turn sharp right towards **Oele**. A short way along is an old restored watermill, a corn mill named 'De Olde Meul'. Return to the major road, near the motorway junction, and turn right for Beckum and **Haaksbergen**, another pleasant town well situated for a holiday centre in beautiful countryside. The old railway station has been purchased by the Museum Buurt Spoorweg (MBS), a railway preservation society, and has been restored to the style of 1900. The goods shed will house a museum, and

Sixteenth-century Oostendorper
Watermolen (double undershot
watermill, beautifully restored).

Buurse
Pewter workshop Tingieterij
'Wibor'.

Enschede
Church with fine organ and Delft
glass windows. Eleventh-century
font preserved from original church.
Rijksmuseum Twente — local and
general historical and cultural
subjects.
Natuurmuseum — natural history,
with vivarium and aquarium.
Textielindustriemuseum — all
aspects of local textile industry.
DAF Automobile Museum.

Oldenzaal
St Plechelmusbasiliek — huge
thirteenth-century tower and carillon
— largest bell tower in Europe.
Many church treasures.
Het Palthehuis — historical
museum.
Het Hulsbeek recreation park.

Denekamp
Thirteenth-century church tower.
Huize Keizer — nineteenth-century
shop and dwelling house in original
condition.
Kasteel Singraven — fifteenth-
century castle open to public, with
interesting watermill in grounds.

Lattrop
Saxon farm with small museum, 'De
Gerrie Hoeve'.
Brecklenkamp — moated
seventeenth-century castle, now a
Youth Hostel.

Ootmarsum
Beautiful thirteenth-century RC
church.
Eighteenth-century Town Hall.
Farm museum 'Het Los Hoes'.
Kuiperberg viewpoint 70m above sea
level.

Vasse
Watermills 'De Mast', 'Bels' and
'Frans'.

Geesteren
'Erve Brager' farmstead.

work is in progress to restore to working order one of the very few
remaining Dutch State Railways steam locomotives. Meanwhile, a steam
service is operated on certain days during the summer from Haaksbergen
to Boekelo, a distance of 7km.

From Haaksbergen, cross the main road to the south at signpost 7091,
and follow this road for about 2km, to where it crosses a small river, the
Buurserbeek. Here stands a sixteenth-century watermill, the Oostendorper
Watermolen, built on local sandstone, with brick walls and tiled roof. It
has two waterwheels; one operates a corn mill and the other drives an oil
mill. Just beyond the mill, take a turning on the left and follow a narrow

road parallel with the river for about $3\frac{1}{2}$km, then cross over the river towards the left, then right along the road signed to **Buurse**. In this small village is a pewter smith working in the traditional manner, the only one still working with sand moulds in the Netherlands. Each piece is unique, and the workshop, the Tingieterij 'Wibor', may be visited on request. There is also a cheese factory which may be visited. From Buurse, follow the road north to the river, cross over, and take the road to the right which runs parallel with the German frontier. In about 6km, a junction is reached at signpost 10351. Turn left and follow the road into **Enschede**.

The largest town in Overijssel, an important industrial and cultural centre and still largely concerned with textiles, it has become, in recent years a leading centre for the micro-electronics industry. The Twentse Technical Highschool, a modern establishment on the lines of the American open campus is located here.

Originating in Saxon times, with the first Grote Kerk on the Markt dating from 1050, a disastrous fire in 1862 destroyed almost everything in the town. The only building which survives is Het Elderinkshuis, built in 1783. The Grote Kerk was rebuilt, a fine organ installed in 1893 and the beautiful stained glass windows made in Delft were fitted in 1928. Historically, the eleventh-century Romanesque font is its most valuable possession. The impressive Town Hall was built between 1930 and 1933. In the Markt stands a monument commemorating the great fire, whilst in the public park near the railway is a War Memorial to victims of World War II.

In Enschede are several outstanding museums. The Rijksmuseum Twente is the largest museum in eastern Holland, in the garden of which is an example of a farmhouse of the eighteenth-century 'Los Hoes' type from Twente. The Natuurmuseum, deals with natural history, and has a vivarium and aquarium. The Textielindustriemuseum deals with all aspects of the Twente and Achterhoek textile industry, including demonstrations of weaving, linen production and lacemaking. In the same building is the DAF Automobile Museum.

Leave the town centre via Oldenzaalse Straat, under the railway, following signs for Lonneker and Oldenzaal. In **Lonneker**, turn right off the major road to the windmill in Lonnekermolenweg, a corn mill built in 1851 on the highest point in the rural district of Enschede (69m). Return to the **Oldenzaal** road and continue to that town, the oldest in Twente, which is busy with traffic across the frontier into Germany. The main N1 road now forms a ring road on the north side of the town. The St Plechelmusbasiliek has a huge thirteenth-century tower with a carillon of forty-six bells hung in a so-called floating belfry. The bell tower is the largest in Europe, and the church itself, built of sandstone in the twelfth century, has many treasures, including an early sixteenth-century monstrance and a beautiful baroque pulpit. In Marktstraat is the seventeenth-century 'Het Palthehuis', a historical museum with typical Twentse interiors, an old pharmacy, and the private library of the Palthes family. To the west of the town is a recreation park, Het Hulsbeek, whilst to the east, towards the frontier,

Harbourside, Terschelling

Windmill, Terschelling

Waterpower, Singraven

there are many footpaths and cycle tracks worth exploring. The main N342 road leads north to **Denekamp**, whose massive sandstone church tower dates from the thirteenth century. In the town the St Nicolaasmolen dates from 1859 and the Huize Keizer is an old shop and house from 1880, fitted and stocked in the original style. The Maria Kloeze is a small Saxon half-timbered house, formerly the home of the so-called *klopkes*, old women who, at the time of the Reformation, roused or knocked up the Catholics so they could attend the secret services during the night.

About 2km west of the town is Kasteel Singraven part of which dates from about 1415. The house contains a fine collection of seventeenth-century paintings, furniture, Chinese porcelain and Gobelin tapestries, and guided tours are possible. An interesting double watermill dating from 1448, and still in use as a sawmill and corn mill stands in the grounds. Entrance tickets for the castle may be obtained at the restaurant by the mill. The estate is very extensive and free walking is permitted.

From Denekamp the road runs north for about 6km through pleasant scenery, and reaches **Lattrop**, where a Saxon farm 'De Gerrie-Hoeve' houses a small museum and collection of antiques. To the north is the manor house of Brecklenkamp, a beautiful moated house from 1635, which is at present in use as a Youth Hostel.

From the village of Lattrop, return south to the junction at signpost 3633, then turn right and right again at signpost 2284, following signs to **Ootmarsum**, a small town surrounded by pleasant woods and heathland. The town itself is very old, and apart from archaeological finds dating back to Neolithic times, there is said to have been a chapel here in AD917. The thirteenth-century Roman Catholic church is the only one of the so-called Westphalian 'hall' type in the country. Its treasures include a fifteenth-century monstrance, a huge organ (nineteenth-century), old crypt and a lovely carved nineteenth-century pulpit and canopy. Some handsome old restored half-timbered houses with gables, and a town hall from 1778 with a gable decorated in rococo style and stained glass windows, can be seen. A farm museum, 'Het Los Hoes', gives a good insight into the lifestyle of former times, with exhibits dealing with spinning and weaving. Farm and agricultural implements and machines are on view, and an annex contains a geological museum. Outside the town on the Almelo road is the Kuiperberg (70m above sea-level) the highest point in Twente, where the ANWB has erected a direction indicator. Fine views over the surrounding countryside of Twente and Germany are obtained from this point. From the town, take the road north-west towards **Vasse**. In the area to the left of the road, the Vasser Grafveld, are some prehistoric tumuli. About 3km further, on the left, is a watermill, 'De Mast'. From Vasse, a diversion may be made along the road to the right (paddestoel 22193) to two more watermills, 'Bels' (1830) with a restaurant, and 'Frans' (1870). Return to Vasse and take the road south-west to **Tubbergen**. The rolling parkland in this area reminds one of English countryside. In the neighbourhood of Tubbergen there are several tumuli, and also half-timbered farmhouses. In

Lochem
Seventeenth-century Town Hall.
Fifteenth-century St Gudulakerk
and brass rubbing centre.

Zwiep
Village with legendary 'White
Women', mill and Highland Cattle.

Borculo
Old lock, weir and watermill (now
restaurant).
Museum commemorating cyclone of
1925, and Fire Service museum.
Farming museum, 'De
Lebbenbrugge'.

Eibergen
Watermill and mill house.
Local museum.

Zwilbroek
Natuurpark 'De Leemputten' —
variety of trees and plants, wild
animals and waterfowl in abandoned
clay workings.

Groenlo
Fortified town with cannon on
ramparts.
Thirteenth-century church with
remains of wall paintings.
Grolsch Museum with local history
and folklore exhibits in seventeenth-
century farmhouse.
Stoomhoutzagerij 'Nahuis' working
steam sawmill museum.

Lichtenvoorde
'Erve Kots' museum — open air
museum about life in the
Achterhoek.

Winterswijk
Seventy-two estates in area available
for free walking.
District museum 'Huize Freriks'.

Grotestraat, there is an interesting sundial. From the town centre take the
road to the right towards **Geesteren**. where there is a large farmstead, the
'Erve Brager', with two barns, and a bakehouse and granary with plastered
walls. There is also an exhibition farm, ''t Vleerhoes', with ornamental and
useful handicrafts on display. At signpost 2951, take the road to the left
which leads via **Harbrinkhoek** and **Mariaparochie** back to Almelo.

ROUTE 49   THE ACHTERHOEK

A convenient starting point to explore the Achterhoek is the town of
Lochem on the south bank of the Twente Canal. It may be reached quite
easily from Almelo via the motorway A35 south, then on to the A1 west to
the junction signed **Lochem,** which is 12km to the south. The town lies in
pleasant farming country, and has a Town Hall built in 1634 and a late-
Gothic church with carillon. In the tower of the church is a brass-rubbing
centre. From the market square, at signpost 157, leave by the minor road
leading east to **Zwiep.** Just after leaving the town, the sixteenth-century
mansion Huize De Cloese will be seen on the left which is now used as a

police training school. The village of Zwiep has one of the few herds of Scottish Highland Cattle in the Netherlands; also a fine corn windmill, still in service. Both the cattle and the mill are owned by the same family, who have lived here for 130 years. They also own the local bakery and a restaurant with gardens, known as the 'Witte Wieven' or White Women. There are many legends about a deep hollow in the nearby woods of the Lochemse Berg, which is called the Witte Wieven Kuil. From Zwiep, the road swings south to **Barchem**, with the woods on the right offering very good walking. Turn left in the village to **Borculo**, a small town on the river Berkel. An old gate from 1598, and an old lock and weir from 1628, recall the former barge traffic on the river. In the town there is also an old undershot watermill from 1628, with mill pool and two waterwheels. The late-Gothic church was severely damaged in a terrible cyclone which caused much destruction in the town in 1925. A museum commemorates the occasion, and is annexed to a Fire Service museum with an interesting collection of old fire pumps, the oldest from 1670.

To the south-west towards Ruurlo, is a farming museum, 'De

The old watermill, Eibergen

Lebbenbrugge', with an old farm hostel from about 1850 (possibly older), kitchen, dairy, weaving shop, baking oven, stable, barns and other interesting items. Recreation facilities, are plentiful around Borculo. From the town, take the road running east via **Haarlo** to **Eibergen**, through a very pleasant and varied landscape of fields, hedges, copses and streams.

Eibergen also lies on the river Berkel, and has an old watermill with sluice-gate and mill house, dating from 1753, which was associated with the barge traffic. There were installations here as long ago as 1188. A small historical museum, 'De Scheper', in the town has exhibits relating to old farming and other country crafts.

To the east of the town, on the major road, at signpost 2163, take the minor road signed for **Zwilbroek** and **Winterswijk** via **Meddo**, and where it crosses the road from Groenlo towards the German town of Vreden will be seen signs for the Natuurpark 'De Leemputten'. This landscape was formed from old clay pits (*leemputten*) which have been in existence for a hundred years or so, and have been abandoned to nature. A unique and attractive area has been created in which free entry for walking or just sitting and watching the wildlife is possible.

From the claypits, take the road from signpost 5766 towards **Groenlo**, an old walled town with moats and ramparts, on which stands a captured Spanish cannon of 1627. The old St Callixtuskerk, contains remains of wall paintings from about 1400, and the font is dated about 1200. During the restoration in 1956, a carillon of thirty-eight bells was installed. The

Grolsch Museum is situated in a seventeenth-century farmhouse, and contains local historical and folklore material and works of religious art. Somewhat different is the Stoomhoutzagerij 'Nahuis' on the Winterswijkseweg. This is a working museum located in an old steam sawmill. An engine dated 1897, imported from Germany in 1918, is supplied with steam from a boiler 9m long and fired by wood to drive a total of sixteen saws. The 28m high chimney was built in 1918. A smaller steam engine from 1892, of a unique type, is coupled to a 100volt dynamo to supply light to the factory and dwelling house. The whole establishment is operated by a trust as a unique monument to technical and industrial achievements.

Leave Groenlo by the minor road running south-west signed for **Lievelde**, and watch for signs to 'Erve Kots' (paddestoel 21453). This is an open-air museum illustrating the life of farmers and peasants in the Achterhoek in former times, and there is also a restaurant. Back on the road, turn right, across the railway, through Lievelde, over the main road and into **Lichtenvoorde**, thence from signpost 9385 along the minor road to Vragender and Winterswijk.

On the right in **Vragender** will be seen the windmill, 'De Vier Winden', and to the left of the village are ruins of St Janskapel dating from 1444. The road enters the outskirts of **Winterswijk** near the water tower, and the town centre is reached by crossing the main road and railway. The town lies at the centre of an area of quiet meadows, woods and small rivers, with a network of footpaths and cycle tracks, and no less than seventy-two estates in the area which permit free walking. An unusual feature is the Steengroeve (stone quarry), about 3km to the east, where it is possible to dig up specimens of rocks and fossils. In the town, the district museum Huize Freriks in Groenloseweg has departments of history, natural history and geology. The church stands on the site of a wooden chapel of AD800.

Leave the town by passing the water tower, and at signpost 429 take the left fork along the road to **Bredevoort**, a small old fortress town with many old buildings, some of which are half-timbered. Remains of the old ramparts still exist, also a wall windmill from 1850. Between Bredevoort and **Aalten** is the former manor house of Walfort, part of which remains in use as a farm. The fifteenth-century church in **Aalten** has a twelfth-century Romanesque tower and a beautifully-restored organ. Behind the district museum 'Frederikshuus' is 'De Freriksschure', an old Saxon farm with wooden façade.

The road from Aalten to **Varsseveld** runs between the railway and the small river Slingerbeek, through pasture and woodland. Through Varsseveld the road swings slightly to the south to **Terborg**, where it crosses the Oude IJssel river to **Etten**, then continues to the junction with the road from Doetinchem to Emmerich, in Germany.

At the junction, signpost 2315, turn left to **'s-Heerenberg**, an old frontier town whose church was originally the castle chapel of 1259. Remains of ramparts may be seen nearby, and the attractive Town Hall with its Gothic tower was built in about 1500. The castle, Huis Bergh, is one of the largest

Typical Achterhoek landscape

and finest in the country. The earliest parts date from the thirteenth century, with the finest parts from the fifteenth and seventeenth centuries. The castle contains furniture and art treasures, and is now a historic monument. The wooded estate is a nature reserve. On the south of the town, on Emmerikseweg, is the Recreation Centre Gouden Handen, an exhibition of works by all kinds of artists and craftsmen. It is difficult to describe, but includes an exhibition of dolls, sculpture, models, children's attractions and dioramas.

's-Heerenberg lies within an area known as Montferland, consisting of the extensive woods of the Bergher Bos on the German frontier. This hilly ground was formerly a coniferous forest used for timber, but has now been made into a nature reserve, open to walkers.

Returning north through the town, the road leads to **Zeddam**, where there is an old windmill dating from about 1450, also the 'Rosmolen', a corn mill driven by a horse. Built in 1546, it has been restored and is used as a museum. The road continues north towards **Doetinchem**, and just after crossing over the A15 motorway, the Toren De Kemenade (1413) may be seen on the right standing at the confluence of the Oude IJssel and the Waalse Water. Doetinchem, chartered in 1237, is the principal town in the Achterhoek. The Grote or Catharinakerk, has a choir dating from the fourteenth century and a modern carillon. In the town is a music school with one of the most modern purpose-built premises in Europe. A local museum is housed in the eighteenth-century former prison.

Leave the town towards the east, following signs for **Ruurlo**, and follow the road through **Zelhem** with its Lamberti-kerk dating from about 1200. Approaching Ruurlo the Kasteel Ruurlo, first mentioned in 1326, is on the right. It has been in the unbroken ownership of one family for more than 500 years, and is now used as the municipal offices. It can be visited on request, and the gardens and the extensive wooded estate are freely accessible to the public. The church in the town dates from the fourteenth century, and in the town centre stands a seven-branched oak tree several hundred years old, called the 'Kroezeboom'. To the north of the town is a windmill driving a sawmill, dating from 1851, and the Kaasboerderij 'n Ibbink is open to visitors to see how genuine farmhouse cheese is made.

The main road, N319, leads to **Vorden** a town ringed by a total of eight castles with their estates. The oldest, Kasteel Vorden, dates from 1208; many of the parks, gardens and woods are open to walkers and cyclists, with varying conditions. An eighteenth-century corn mill driven by a waterwheel is in the grounds of Kasteel Hackfort, but it is not open to the public.

From Vorden take the main road back across the railway, and turn left at signpost 3457 to follow the pleasant road back to Lochem, the starting point of this route.

16 ALONG THE GREAT RIVERS

The busiest waterways in Europe stretch across the centre of the Netherlands from the German frontier in the east to the great delta area of the west. These are the Rhine, the Waal and the Maas, but the situation is complicated by the fact that they follow very winding courses, divide and join, and even change names at various points along their routes. The Rhine changes its name to Waal as it enters the Netherlands and continues westwards until just before it reaches Dordrecht. At the same point it connects by a canal to the IJssel near Arnhem, then flows towards Rotterdam, changing its name to Lek at Wijk bij Duurstede. The southernmost of the three, the Maas, has the longest route in Dutch territory of any river, flowing from the extreme south in Limburg parallel with the German frontier, turning west at Grave, south of Nijmegen, eventually coming to the sea south of Dordrecht. Even this is an over-simplified account of the Great Rivers, because the system is made more complicated by cross-linking canals, divisions in the rivers themselves, and smaller tributaries. Despite the fact that the great rivers carry large amounts of freight traffic, the whole area is extremely interesting and attractive, including as it does the fruit-growing district of the Netherlands. The country between the rivers lies mainly in Gelderland, with parts in South Holland, North Brabant and Utrecht provinces.

The most important towns are Nijmegen, Tiel and Gorinchem, all lying along the Waal, the widest of the rivers. In late springtime the area is particularly attractive when the fruit trees are in blossom, but at other times the wide water meadows and twisting dyke roads with old houses tucked behind make ideal subjects for the photographer or painter. Cyclists will enjoy riding along the old dykes but local traffic is sometimes faster than might be expected, and the roads are narrow with little in the way of verges on which to take refuge. Many ferries cross the rivers, taking the visitor to some fascinating places which would be missed if the motorways and main roads are followed over the bridges which now cross the area.

Europe's largest inland locks, and the historic city of Nijmegen, and many smaller towns with interesting medieval buildings and castles lie 'along the Great Rivers'.

Nijmegen is one of the two oldest towns in the Netherlands, with a history going back to a Roman siege in AD69. Subsequently, the Emperor Trajan established a frontier town and fortress called Novio Magus or New Market, from which the present name is derived. The Emperor Charlemagne often stayed here, and the twelfth-century Emperor Frederick Barbarossa built a stronghold on what is now called the Valkhof. Because of its strategic position and economic importance on the bend of the river Waal, Nijmegen has often been the scene of sieges and battles, culminating in the

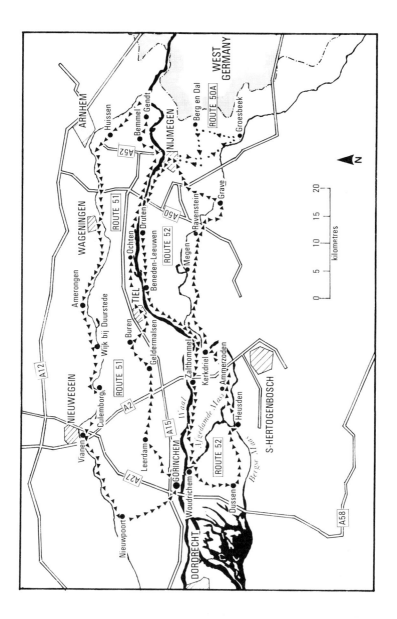

WEST GERMANY

ARNHEM

Huissen
Bemmel
Gendt
NIJMEGEN

Berg en Dal

ROUTE 50A

Groesbeek

A52

WAGENINGEN

ROUTE 51

Amerongen

Ochten
Druten

A50

Beneden-Leeuwen

ROUTE 52

Megen

Ravenstein

Grave

Wijk bij Duurstede

TIEL

Buren

Geldermalsen

Zaltbommel
Kerkdriel
Ammerzoden

A12

NIEUWEGEIN

ROUTE 51

Culemborg

A2

Waal

Afgedamde Maas

Vianen

Leerdam

A15

GORINCHEM

Woudrichem

Heusden

ROUTE 52

S-HERTOGENBOSCH

A27

Nieuwpoort

Bergse Maas

Dussen

DORDRECHT

A58

N

0   5   10   15   20
kilometres

201

well-known action to secure the vital river crossing during 1944 as a prelude to the abortive attempt to seize the bridge at Arnhem, about 15km to the north.

During the fighting in 1944-5 much of the town centre was destroyed, but it has now been rebuilt in modern style, with many well-kept parks and gardens. The river bank rises steeply into the town. The original fortifications were demolished in 1878, their position now being marked by a boulevard linking two large roundabouts, the Keizer Karelplein on the south-west of the town centre and the Keizer Traianusplein to the east. Leading off Traianusplein is St Jorisstraat, and at the roundabout end of this street is the VVV office, a convenient starting point for a town walk.

ROUTE 50   A WALK IN NIJMEGEN

Turn left on leaving the VVV, and across the road a small wooden former tram shelter will be seen, with to the left some remains of the fifteenth-century town wall. Walk along the top of the wall, across a footbridge, then along a path to the Belvedere, an old wall tower from which a wonderful panorama of the river, the bridge and the surrounding countryside may be obtained. Below is a huge flowerbed forming the emblem of the town, best seen in late spring. In the nearby Hunnerpark a capsule containing documents relating to 'Operation Marketgarden' was buried beneath a plaque on 18 September 1974, in the presence of the Queen of the Netherlands and Allied military leaders. The capsule is not to be opened until the year 2044, one hundred years after the battle to seize the bridges in September 1944.

From the Belvedere, go down the path, across a stone bridge leading to the high ground of the Valkhof, where the settlement of AD69 was situated. Here, Charlemagne built a palace, later made into a fortress by Barbarossa, which stood here until demolished in 1796. The only remaining fragments are the ruined twelfth-century 'apse' and the octagonal Carolingian Chapel, Nijmegen's oldest building, dating from the eleventh century. It is now preserved and used for small exhibitions.

From near the chapel a flight of steps leads down, and past a mosaic of the Holy Mother and St Olav, into Steenstraat, with the Waalkade or quay along on the right. During sewer-laying work in 1985-6, Roman remains were uncovered here, causing great interest among archaeologists. Turn right at the end of Steenstraat, then immediately left along the retaining wall built to protect the lower part of the town from floods, to the Lage Markt. Along here are some seventeenth and eighteenth-century dwellings and warehouses. From Lage Markt a left turn leads into Priemstraat and on to Ganzenheuval, where some steps on the left lead to St Stevenskerk. Parts of the original building from 1254 still exist, and the main parts date from the fourteenth and fifteenth centuries, but almost complete reconstruction was needed after war damage in 1944-5. Other interesting buildings are situated near the church. In the Grote Markt is the old Laeckenhal or Cloth Hall, and the Waag, which is now a restaurant.

Walk between the two buildings, and across Smidstraat to the Commanderie van St Jan, the twelfth century hospital of the Knights of Malta later used for the first University of Nijmegen, then as a Walloon church until the war damage of 1944-5. After restoration it became the City Museum showing the history of the town from Roman times to the nineteenth century. Return to the Grote Markt and into Burchtstraat to the Town Hall, which has stood on the same site since the fourteenth century. Continue straight along Burchtstraat and St Jorisstraat back to the VVV office.

The State Museum G.M. Kam, mainly concerned with archaeological finds and named after a distinguished amateur archaeologist is situated in Kamstraat, not far from the Keizer Traianusplein. Smaller but still interesting is the Velorama Museum of vintage bicycles, cars and accessories, on Waalkade.

ROUTE 50A   AROUND NIJMEGEN
South of Nijmegen is Heiligland Stichting an open-air museum devoted to the Holy Land and the story of the Bible, with village and town buildings and other exhibits depicting life in the Middle East.

From here a road leads through pleasant woodland with waymarked walks and cycle paths to the village of **Groesbeek**. In this area American Airborne forces landed prior to their capture of the bridge at Nijmegen in 1944.

Take the road north to Berg en Dal and the Afrika Museum, which includes a reconstruction of an African village, and an indoor exhibition illustrating many aspects of African life, work and culture. Return to

Nijmegen along the main road N271, (St Annastraat) which leads back past the University into the town.

ROUTE 51 A TOUR IN THE BETUWE

The Betuwe is that part of Gelderland which lies north of the river Waal. Betuwe means 'good land' with rich vegetable and fruit growing areas, in contrast to the Veluwe, which is 'bad land', agriculturally speaking.

Starting from Nijmegen, cross the river by the Waalbrug and immediately turn off the main road to the right, following signs for Lent and **Bemmel**, and at signpost 9647 turn right and follow the road to **Gendt** and **Doornenburg**, where Kasteel De Doornenburg lies on the point of land where the Rhine and Waal divide, built mainly in the fourteenth and fifteenth centuries. In 1936 a trust was set up to care for the property as a historic monument, but in March 1945 a German commando completely destroyed the castle. It was rebuilt and is now available for conferences and receptions, and a collection of weapons is on display in one of the towers.

From the castle, follow minor roads north to Angeren and **Huissen**, which until 1816 belonged to Cleve in Germany. Formerly the river Rhine ran past the town walls, although now it is about 1km away. Take the minor road north-west to Elden, cross the A52 motorway, and pick up signs for **Driel**, crossing over the dual carriageway at signpost 6300 to follow the road alongside the river. This small town on the south bank of the Rhine, opposite Oosterbeek, was where the 1st Polish Parachute Brigade was dropped during the operations to capture the bridge at Arnhem, and is the point to which the remaining forces were withdrawn across the river when the action was abandoned.

Continue along the river dyke, towards Heteren; there are fine views across the river towards Doorwerth with its imposing castle. Further along the dyke road is Randwijk, beyond which a turning to the right leads to the ferry to **Wageningen**. Follow signs into the town, then turn left at the main N225 road and continue to **Rhenen**, an old fortress town in which remnants of the town walls still exist. A white tower windmill stands high above the houses on one of the walls, and nearby is the district museum containing many prehistoric and Roman finds. The Cunerakerk has a fine tower, from the top of which may be obtained a fantastic view over the river and surrounding countryside.

Continue along the N225 road through Elst to **Amerongen**. Turn off left through the town to Kasteel Amerongen, standing on the site of a building first mentioned in 1286. The original castle was burned down in 1672 and was rebuilt in the Dutch Classical style. From 1918 to 1920, Amerongen was the residence of the exiled Kaiser Wilhelm of Germany, and here he signed the act by which he gave up the German throne. The castle contains a large collection of works of art, porcelain, silver, glass and tapestry. In the town itself is a Historical Museum located in a former tobacco warehouse, with varying exhibitions.

Continue along the road past the castle, cross straight ahead at signpost

1506 and follow the dyke road towards **Wijk bij Duurstede**. On the left, in about 4km will be seen the strange shape of the *stuw* or sluice to control the flow of water. It is associated with locks to allow passage of shipping.

Wijk bij Duurstede is a fascinating old town. The original town of Dorestad probably arose from a Roman settlement at the point where the rivers Kromme Rijn and Lek divided. In the seventh and eighth centuries it was one of the largest trading towns in Europe, and in 850 it was, for a short time, the capital of the Norse Kingdom of Frisia. Interesting buildings include Kasteel Duurstede, whose eleventh century keep stands within a park and has now been restored. In the Markt stands the Grote or St Janskerk, with a massive tower, built to rival the Dom in Utrecht, but never completed owing to lack of funds. Old pumps, the Town Hall (seventeenth century) and many fine old houses may be seen, and of special interest is the windmill 'Rijn and Lek', which stands over one of the town gates, on Dijkstraat. The mill which figured in the famous painting by Jacob van Ruysdael in the seventeenth century no longer exists, but its foundations stand behind a fence on Langs de Wal, a street along the inside of the town wall.

Beyond the town, the dyke road swings to the right towards the massive Prinses Irene locks, where the Amsterdam-Rijn Kanaal crosses the river Lek, at what is perhaps the busiest point on the European waterways system. The road crosses the canal near the locks, where a side road enables one to see the complex structure and watch the passage of shipping. Continue along the dyke road past Den Oord, and at signpost 2083 fork left and keep along the dyke to signpost 1258, just before the railway. Here turn left to the ferry across the river to **Culemborg**.

Typical of so many of the old towns along the lines of the great rivers, this is another fortified town, which was chartered in 1318. The centre is encircled by a canal. At one end of the Markt stands the Town Hall (1534–9), while at the other end is the Binnenpoort dating from 1557. The Grote or St Barbarakerk is mainly fifteenth century. The local museum is in the Elizabeth Weeshuis and of interest is the former home of Jan van Riebeek (1617–77) who founded the colony which became Cape Town.

From Culemborg, continue westwards along the river dyke, where fine views over the river to the right and over the surrounding countryside to the left make it well worth travelling slowly — but watch out for other less leisurely traffic. Just before passing under the end of the motorway bridge over the river, another lock and sluice complex will be seen on the right, all part of the extensive system for controlling water traffic and regulating the flow of flood water. Beyond the bridge the road becomes very narrow and crosses the canal by the locks, then turns left into **Vianen**, situated at another major waterway junction, between the Lek, the Lekkanaal to the north and the Merwede Kanaal to the south.

A very broad main street runs from the turreted fifteenth-century Lekpoort past the Stadhuis, a fifteenth-century building housing a local museum, to the fourteenth-century church. The town sits in a triangle formed by the river Lek and two motorways, which join at a massive junction south of the town. To reach the dyke road, leave the main street by passing through the old gate, turn left, under the second (west) motorway, then along the dyke road running parallel to the main road, to Lexmond. The dyke road continues close to the river as far as Sluis, where it crosses a small canal (signpost 900). Immediately over the canal turn right through the small town of **Ameide** with pleasant seventeenth and eighteenth-century gentlemen's houses at the foot of the dyke.

Continue alongside the river to **Tienhoven**, then a long stretch of dyke road leads into **Nieuwpoort**, a particularly attractive small fortified town lying directly opposite the town of Schoonhoven. Nieuwpoort which has a Stadhuis (1697) built over the canal which runs through the town centre, forming a water gate, is surrounded by old ramparts which are planted with trees.

Leave Nieuwpoort by joining the main road south at signpost 8833 and follow the road into **Gorinchem**, which lies on the north bank of the river Waal at the point where it is joined by a branch of the Maas, to become the

Nieuwpoort
Old fortified town.
Seventeenth-century Stadhuis built
over canal forming watergate.
Old ramparts.

Gorinchem
Sixteenth-century fortified town.
Sixteenth-century Dalempoort town
gate.
Fifteenth-century church tower.

Leerdam
National Glass Museum.
Museum, 't Poorthuis, in old town
gatehouse.

Buren
Small town completely enclosed by
ramparts.
Town mill on ramparts.
Fourteenth-century St
Lambertuskerk.

Sixteenth-century Stadhuis.
Beautiful seventeenth-century
Weeshuis, now museum of Royal
Marechaussee or Military
Constabulary.
Farm Wagon museum in
Culemborgsepoorthuis.

Tiel
Prins Bernhardsluis: Largest inland
locks in the world.
Twelfth-century fortress town, much
rebuilt.
Fifteenth-century St Maartenskerk.
District museum De Groote
Societeit — old period room, crafts,
silver, tiles, etc.
Remains of Stadswallen — town
walls.

Dodewaard
Twelfth-century church on dyke.

Merwede. Fortified in the thirteenth century, most of the existing town walls and moats date from the sixteenth century, including the only surviving gate, the Dalempoort. St Janskerk has an impressive fifteenth-century tower. From the waterfront near the Dalempoort a fine view over the river towards Slot Loevestein may be obtained.   At Gorinchem, the river Linge runs into the Waal, having followed a parallel winding course through the Betuwe from Doornenburg. Follow the road through Gorinchem, under the A15 motorway, to the town of **Arkel** and at signpost 380, turn right along the picturesque high dyke road beside the river Linge to **Leerdam**. Since 1765 this has been a centre of the glassmaking industry and is the location of the National Glass Museum on Lingedijk. Remains of the walls and towers from the Middle Ages stand along the riverside, and the local museum, in 't Poorthuis, is in Kerkstraat, the former dwelling attached to the Veerpoort (1600).

From Leerdam take the road past the railway station, following signs to **Geldermalsen**. Cross under the railway, turn left past the windmill, then take the right fork at Buurmalsen towards the town of **Buren**. Do not drive

The old smithy, Buren

into the town, but park just outside. Walk through the arched gateway into this completely enclosed town with its ramparts still intact, upon which stands the town mill. A small gem of a town with a fourteenth-century church, early sixteenth-century Stadhuis, many fine wall houses and a magnificent former Weeshuis (1613) housing the Marechaussee Museum. Historically, the town has had connections with the House of Orange from 1492 to 1795 through the marriage of Anna van Buren to Willem of Orange, who thus became Earl of Buren. In the Culemborgsepoorthuis is the Gelders Boerenwagen Museum, a museum devoted to farm wagons and other items from the past.

Leaving the town, follow the road signs to **Tiel**, the centre of the fruit growing industry of the Betuwe, which lies on the river Waal near the point at which the Amsterdam-Rijn Kanaal enters the river through the Prins Bernhardsluis, the largest inland lock complex in the world. Situated in an area of beautiful villages and fruit farms, Tiel is one of the oldest market towns in the country, known to have a harbour in 435. Growing in importance through the ninth and tenth centuries, the town was fortified in the twelfth century, had its own Mint and became a member of the Hanseatic League. In the town centre are many monuments to these times, although many others were destroyed during World War II. Since then much expansion of trade and industry, particularly in the field of metal-working, has taken place, and Tiel is the site of an important fruit market serving the area. The Grote or St Maartenskerk has a tower dating from 1440, which has been rebuilt after damage in 1944-5. Along the quay a length of the medieval town walls is still to be seen. Many old buildings have been restored since 1945, including the seventeenth-century Waterpoort, which has been completely rebuilt. A local museum is located in the building De Groote Societeit dated 1789, and contains collections relating to the district and its history. Over the centuries much work was done to strengthen and raise the river banks against flooding, and this may be seen by walking along the old walls by the river. Just to the east of the town a bridge nearly $1\frac{1}{2}$km long was built over the river in 1974.

To leave the town, cross the canal beside the motorway then turn right under the motorway and railway, then left immediately, beside the railway through Echteld to **IJzendoorn**. Here turn right through the village to the dyke road, turning left alongside the river through **Ochten** to **Dodewaard**, where the church dates from about 1100. Further along the dyke road, a nuclear energy installation is passed, beyond which the road continues along the river until the town of Lent is reached, at the north end of the bridge across the Waal into Nijmegen.

ROUTE 52   ALONG THE WAAL AND MAAS FROM NIJMEGEN

This route covers the southern part of Gelderland between the Waal in the north and the Maas to the south. The border between Gelderland and Noord Brabant runs along the centre of the river Maas, and the area is divided into two. On the east is the so-called 'Land van Maas en Waal', and to the west the 'Bommeler Waard'. Once again it is an area of pleasant and fertile farmland, with old towns and castles, and quiet roads, set between two major rivers.

Starting from Nijmegen, cross under the railway on the north side of the station, along Weurtseweg, and in **Weurt** turn right just past the church along the dyke near the river, passing beneath the big new motorway bridge, built in 1974. Follow the dyke road past Deest and **Druten**, to the south of which is the village of **Puiflijk** with remains of a thirteenth-century church whose tower has been restored.

On the dyke road past Druten is Huis te Leeuwen, the gatehouse of a seventeenth-century castle, beyond which the road continues to **Beneden Leeuwen**, where there is a memorial to members of the Dutch Resistance army. Still keeping to the dyke road, pass under the end of the Prins Willem Alexanderbrug.

From this point very fine views can be obtained from the dyke road through Wamel and **Dreumel** beyond; the rivers Maas and Waal approach to within 1km of each other. The road eventually arrives at the locks at St Andries, where a canal was first cut in 1599 to connect the two rivers.

Across the locks is **Rossum**, a town on the bend of the Waal. Slot Rossum, an eleventh-century castle, subsequently destroyed and rebuilt in Tudor style in the nineteenth century is now used as the town hall. Beyond this point the dyke road takes a big bend away from the river, so the major road may be taken into **Zaltbommel**, the chief town of the Bommelerwaard, whose defence works still retain much of their original structure. An old Hanseatic town, it originated in the ninth century, and the Grote or St Maartenskerk dates from the thirteenth century, with the tower from about 1500 standing high over the town. In the Markt the Stadhuis and the Waag both date from about 1762, while a short distance to the north is the fourteenth-century Waterpoort. To the east of the Markt is the fifteenth-century Gasthuistoren, restored in 1958, with a clock with moving figures. The local museum is situated in the Huis van Maarten van Rossum, south from the Markt. Of this house only the original gatehouse from 1535 survives.

From Zaltbommel, another dyke road leads west through Zuilichem to **Brakel**, site of a ruined fifteenth-century castle. The ruins lie in the park of the Huis te Brakel and may only be seen across the moat.

*The Gasthuistoren,
Zaltbommel*

Beyond Brakel the dyke road is closed off, so turn south out of the town to signpost 4410, turn right along the major road to signpost 5983, then follow signs to Slot Loevestein. This is a moated castle built about 1360, standing on the point of land between the Waal and the Maas. The existing earth ramparts were built in about 1576, and the only remaining tower from the original building is the round shot tower. The castle is open to visitors. A small ferry (no cars) runs to and from the town of **Woudrichem**, across the Maas. Motorists must return to the road junction at signpost 5983, then turn right across the river, and right again into Woudrichem, whose origins go back to 866. Because of its strategic position it grew in importance, with thriving trade, industry and fishery. The town was fortified in the seventeenth century, and much of the defence works remain. In the old Arsenal is a Fishery Museum, and in the town are other interesting old buildings, including the St Maartenskerk (fifteenth century) and the Water or Gevangenpoort.

South of the town, at signpost 7892, take the road towards Almkerk, crossing straight over the cross roads at signpost 7901 and follow the road to **Dussen**, which lies in an area in which are a number of Oud-Hollandse farms, and an eighteenth-century windmill used for pumping. On the east

Heusden

side of the town is Kasteel Dussen, a sixteenth-century moated castle with gate towers, part of which is used as the local Raadhuis, or Town Hall. From the castle, go through the town to the major road at signpost 3639, turn left and follow the road via Genderen to the cross roads at signpost 8743. Turn right, cross the river Maas by the bridge and follow signs left into **Heusden**, an old fortress town standing on a site of what may have been a Roman outpost. In 1581 the fortifications were strengthened, and ramparts with eight bastions surrounded by moats were constructed. During the nineteenth century, the fortifications were demolished, but in 1968 it was decided to restore and rebuild them, and now the town has regained much of its old appearance, with three windmills on the ramparts. Much wartime damage has also been repaired, including the building of a new Town Hall to replace that which was blown up by the German forces in 1944. A local museum is in the Gouverneurshuis, in Putterstraat, and a museum with a collection of children's toys, dolls and games dating from the past ninety years is in the neighbouring village of **Herpt**.

From here (signpost 1688) a road runs towards the river. Cross by the ferry, and turn right along the dyke road to signpost 1188, where the road ahead is taken through **Ammerzoden**. Kasteel Ammersoyen, a moated stronghold with round towers originated in 1354, and was rebuilt after a fire in 1644. War damage was repaired in the years after 1957, and now the castle is open to visitors. The next village, **Hedel** is the site of a former castle dating from 1300 which now only exists as remains of the walls. A local museum contains much interesting material found in the neighbourhood. Continue to Kerkdriel and along the dyke road to the roundabout thence right to the hamlet of **Alem**, from where the road runs towards the river and a ferry.

Cyclists, and moped riders should be warned that after disembarking the road signs direct cars to the right up the dyke to the road, whilst cyclists and moped riders must use a steep flight of steps. Having got on to the road, turn left and follow through Maren-Kessel to **Lith**, an attractive rural village in an area of open river landscape with high banks and inner dykes, small villages and dyke farms.

Along here the river is very winding, with cut-off portions, many of which form ideal places for wildlife or water sports. Continue from Lith to signpost 6261, then turn left and follow the road to Macheren, thence turning left to **Megen**, a small walled town of which the fourteenth-century Gevangentoren still exists. A number of old dwellings have been restored and the seventeenth-century church and Franciscanen-klooster reflect the importance of the town as a religious centre during the seventeenth century. Return to the road at signpost 6255, turn left and continue through Haren to **Ravenstein**, founded in 1360 with the building of a castle on the Maas. The moat still surrounds the town and the gates date from 1522, when the fortifications were renewed. Restoration has brought back much of the town's old appearance. In common with Megen, Ravenstein was a centre for many religious establishments. The dyke road now follows a winding course via Neerloon and Overlangel to **Grave**, a fortress town in which parts of the early fortifications can still be seen. A number of interesting old buildings exist, including the thirteenth-century Elisabethkerk restored in 1981. Owing to the flooding of the Maas in former times, the town was often cut off from the rest of the country, so work was undertaken to canalise the river and install sluices and locks to control the flow of water. This was started in 1929, and in 1940 and 1942 the dykes were made higher, so the danger to the town and surrounding country is now removed.

During the operations to capture the bridges across the major rivers in 1944, the Maasbrug at Grave was the first of the three bridges required to permit the advance overland from the south. The speed with which American Airborne Troops were dropped in the area enabled this bridge to be taken quickly, unlike the bridges at Nijmegen and Arnhem, where the element of surprise had been reduced. On account of this, the town of Grave was undamaged, and the bridge taken intact. Our route concludes by going across this bridge and returning to Nijmegen.

17 NOORD BRABANT -
DEN BOSCH AND EINDHOVEN

Noord Brabant is the largest Province in the Netherlands, stretching from the Waal in the north to the Belgian frontier in the south, and from Limburg province in the east to the Zeeland delta in the west. The greater part of the province is made up of woodland, heath and peat fen, and is largely 'old' land, not polder. Much of the land is recreational, with several nature reserves, yet some of the most historic towns and modern industrial developments are located here.

In this chapter we shall be looking at the eastern part of the province, including a small part of the extreme northern tip of Limburg.

ROUTE 53   THE TOWN OF DEN BOSCH
Den Bosch is the officially-recognised abbreviation for 's-Hertogenbosch, the historical and cultural centre and capital of the province of Noord Brabant. It was originally a settlement on a high sandhill in the delta formed by the rivers Aa and Dommel, in the wooded estates belonging to the Duke of Brabant, hence the name of the town. However it is probable that there was a Roman settlement before that time. Its first charter was granted in 1185 and the town of Den Bosch grew from then on. The triangular centre is confined on the west by the Dommel, on the north-east by the Aa and on the south by moats along the town walls. Nothing is left of the original walls but most of the massive ramparts from the seventeenth century still exist.

The oldest brick building in the town, the thirteenth-century 'De Moriaan', which now houses the VVV office, stands in the Markt, on the opposite side of which is the Stadhuis, rebuilt in 1670 in Classical style, with a carillon on which recitals are given every Wednesday morning. The Raadskelder or Council Cellar (1529) beneath the Town Hall is now a restaurant. Adjoining the Markt are a number of streets with modern shops, but on looking up it is apparent that the actual buildings are quite old, with some fine façades and gables. Much of this part of the town is a pedestrian precinct. Near the south-eastern corner of the Markt, Kerkstraat leads down towards St Janskathedraal, said to be the most beautiful church in the Netherlands, dating from the early thirteenth century. The sixteenth-century tower is 137m high. In 1561 it was formally created a cathedral, and the whole building is full of interest.

The carillon of fifty bells, the majority of which were cast by the English firm of Gillett and Johnston, is played every Wednesday morning, and there is a very fine organ. To celebrate the town's 800 years' existence in 1985, during which the Cathedral was visited by Pope John Paul II, a complete restoration was undertaken, and the result is quite fantastic. The nearby fifteenth-century Zwanenbroedershuis in Hinthamerstraat contains

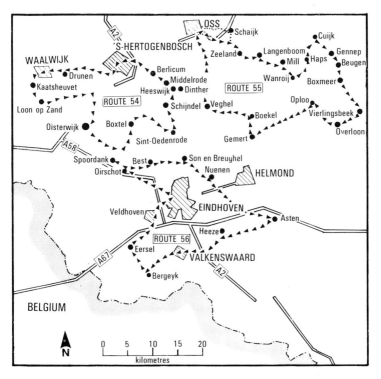

WAALWIJK
's-HERTOGENBOSCH
OSS
Schaijk
Cuijk
Zeeland
Langenboom
Gennep
Mill
Haps
Beugen
Berlicum
Wanroij
Boxmeer
Drunen
Middelrode
Kaatsheuvel
Heeswijk
Dinther
ROUTE 55
ROUTE 54
Oploo
Loon op Zand
Schijndel
Veghel
Vierlingsbeek
Boekel
Oisterwijk
Boxtel
Overloon
Sint-Oedenrode
Gemert
A58
Spoordank
Best
Son en Breuyhel
Oirschot
Nuenen
HELMOND
Veldhoven
EINDHOVEN
Asten
Heeze
ROUTE 56
Eersel
A67
VALKENSWAARD
A2
Bergeyk
BELGIUM

N

0   5   10   15   20
kilometres

collections of religious antiques, music books and religious art. Opposite, the Kerkhof leads to the Museum Slager devoted to works and souvenirs of the artistic family of that name from 1900 to the present day. Continue along Hinthamerstraat, turn right along St Jacobstraat into Bethaniestraat, and on the left is the Noordbrabants Museum, concerned with the art and culture of the Province. At the end of the street, turn right along Hekellaan, leading to Zuidwal, on the old town ramparts. On one of the bastions is a cannon, dated 1511, with a barrel 6 m long, which was never fired because it was not safe. At this point Zuidwal becomes Spinhuiswal. Turn right towards the town again, into St Jorisstraat; on the left is the sixteenth-century Refugiehuis, once a home for religious refugees, and now an arts and crafts centre. At the far end of the street, turn left and immediately right into Postelstraat, where the small private museum, 'De Brabantse Poffer', houses a collection of Brabant curiosities, costumes and local rural crafts. From Postelstraat, turn into Vughterstraat then along Schapenmarkt, right and left into Rozemarijnstraat, which is a narrow alley leading to the river Binnendieze, part of the waterway network which provided the main transport system of the medieval town. At the end of the alley, the river

St Janskathedraal, Den Bosch

disappears underneath an old warehouse. Turn left along Burgemeester Loeff-Plein, then right into Tolbrugstraat. At the end, turn left alongside the Zuid Willemsvaart then right, across the canal on Citadellaan. On the right is the Kruithuis, built in 1621 as a store for ammunition and gunpowder outside the town walls. Its walls are 1 m thick and it now houses an art exhibition.

An interesting way of seeing parts of the old town and its waterways is to take a boat tour from the landing stage on St Janssingel, near the bridge over to Stationsweg leading to the railway station.

ROUTE 54   AROUND DEN BOSCH

This route takes in some of the country to the west and south of Den Bosch, ranging from dune areas to heath and woods, but all pleasant for cycling as well as driving. Leave Den Bosch by taking the Koningsweg south from Stationsplein, turning left across the river then bearing right along Wilhelminaplein. Immediately over the water, take the turning on the right which leads under the railway with the canal on the right. After passing the remains of Fort Isabella, turn right across the canal at the T-junction, then straight ahead for 2km. Turn left at the next T-junction, and follow the minor road towards **Drunen**. Cyclists should turn left after crossing the canal near the old fort, and follow the cycle route alongside for about 8km, then continue into Drunen. Go through the town, a fast-growing place with various industries including shoemaking and the manufacture of

216

**PLACES TO VISIT IN AND
AROUND 's-HERTOGENBOSCH**

Den Bosch
De Moriaan: oldest building, with
VVV office.
St Janskathedraal; most beautiful
church, with carillon.
Zwanenbroedershuis: collection of
religious antiques, books and art
works.
Noordbrabants Museum: collections
of articles and works of art from
province.

Drunen
Lips Autotron: 100 years of motor
vehicles.

Waalwijk
National Shoe and Leather Museum.

Kaatsheuvel
De Efteling: fairy-tale leisure park.

Oisterwijk
Vogelpark: about 3,000 birds from
all over the world.

---

leather goods. Near the far end is the Lips Autotron, a museum dealing
with 100-year history of motor vehicles, containing one of the largest
collections of old and new cars in the world. It includes an 1885 Benz, the
Mercedes belonging to the last Emperor of Germany, and Porsches
belonging to the State Police. In addition, there is a collection of fire
engines and a steam engine, together with films and attractions for
children.

From the Autotron Museum, continue to the windmill. Keep left, take
the next turning left, then right at the next cross roads, across the canal into
Waalwijk, the centre of the shoemaking industry, with the National Shoe
and Leather Museum housed in the former home of a wealthy tanner.

From Waalwijk, turn left at the major road junction, and follow the road
signed to **Loon op Zand** and Tilburg. In about 3km is the entrance to 'De
Efteling', a well-known Recreation Park, started as a family leisure
attraction in 1951. Fairy-tale figures, a steam train running through the
park, many spectacular displays and attractions, are enjoyed by thousands
of Dutch families every year.

From De Efteling, continue south to Loon op Zand, turning left at the
beginning of the dual carriageway. In the town is a fifteenth-century
church, and a moated mansion house with outbuildings on the foundations
of an old castle. From signpost 3270 follow the minor road east, turning left
at the T-junction (signpost 5012) then right towards the car park at 'De
Rustende Jager'.

This is a good place from which to walk or cycle through the extensive
Loonse en Drunense Duinen, an area of sandy heathland and coniferous
woods. The area is open to the public and makes an ideal place for watching
birds and other wildlife, or just for enjoying the peace and quiet of the
countryside.

One of the tableaux at De Efteling family park

From 'De Rustende Jager', continue along the road in the same direction, watching for signs to **Heikant**, **Zwijnsbergen** and **Helvoirt**. **Zwijnsbergen** is a sixteenth-century moated castle which is not open to view, although the estate is open for walking. In **Helvoirt** is a farm, 'De Putakker', dating from 1540, with an old-fashioned well in the yard. The church here dates from the fifteenth century, and concerts of vocal and instrumental music are held.

On the south side of the town, cross the main N65 road at signpost 1026 and take the road to **Haaren**, in what has been called the 'garden of Brabant'. To the south of the village, near the railway, is Kasteel Nemelaer, first mentioned in 1303, the estate of which is open to walkers. Cross the railway to **Oisterwijk**, a pleasant town which was chartered in 1213. The oldest surviving house, originally a brewery, was built in 1633. To the south-east, on the road towards Spoordonk and Oirschot, is the Vogelpark, home of some 3,000 birds from all over the world. To the south of the town are extensive areas of heath and fen, with paths through the woods and beside the water. Much of the area is kept as nature reserves, and in some cases entry permits are required. A pleasant drive through the countryside can be taken by forking left beyond the Vogelpark and following the minor road via Rosephoeve, De Logt, then left at paddestoel 23722 to Lennisheuvel, across the railway at signpost 9820 and past Kasteel Stapelen, now a monastery. In **Boxtel**, the St Petruskerk dating from the fifteenth century has been a place of pilgrimage for the past 600 years, commemorating the miracle of the Holy Blood. In 1393, Boxtel laid its first hard-surfaced street with cobblestones, or *kleien*. Since then, the jealous inhabitants of the neighbouring villages have nick-named the Boxtel men *kleistampers*, or so it is said. The town was also the scene of Wellington's first experience of action against the French, as an officer in the unsuccessful operations by the Duke of York in 1795.

At signpost 9296, cross under the main N2 road, go ahead for about 3km and turn right at the cross roads at signpost 1008. Continue, over the railway, to Olland, thence on to **Sint-Oedenrode**, a rural town in an area with thousands of poplar trees. The wood is used for making *klompen* or wooden shoes. The National Klompen Exhibition is held here every year. The present town hall occupies the former Slot Dommelrode, built in 1605, and inhabited by various aristocratic families before becoming a monastery between 1819 and 1954. On the south side of the town is Kasteel Henkenshage, dating from 1840 but with some medieval portions. In Kerkstraat is the Museum Brabantse Mutsen, a small collection of Brabant country-women's caps and bonnets housed in the restored St Paulusgasthuis, with a pump in front of the door.

From signpost 4800 at the northern end of the town, a straight road runs north through typical scenery for this part of the country, with fields and meadows, oak trees and conifers, and of course the ever-present poplars. In about 4km, the road enters **Schijndel**, a town noted for brewing, hop-growing, klompen-making and hoop making, using the poplar wood. There is an old church, St Servatiuskerk, with a fifteenth-century tower, standing in the market place near a modern town hall. A windmill, 'De Pegstukken', is open to visitors. In addition to three klompen-makers, there is a basket maker in the town, associated with a museum of basketmaking.

The road from signpost 10500 runs towards the canal, and across a bridge just north of the locks, to the twin villages of **Heeswijk-Dinther**, where the Abbey van Berne in Dinther (twelfth century) is the setting for organ concerts. In Heeswijk is the Meierijsche Museumboerderij, or Farm Museum, in a 250-year-old Saxon farm with authentic interior from about 1900. Just outside, at Muggenhoek, *huifkarren* tours are possible in a wagon with driver. Along the road running north, parallel with the canal, is Kasteel Heeswijk, an impressive fourteenth-century building which houses collections of paintings, porcelain, antique furniture, and wrought ironwork. Apart from the immediate surroundings of the castle, the estate is open to the public, and in the area there are a number of other woods and open spaces where walking and picnic places are provided.

From here the road runs through **Middelrode**, and continues into **Berlicum**, with a fifteenth-century brick-built church restored after war damage. Along the road called Loofaert are several fine old farmhouses, the most outstanding of which is Eikenlust, dating from the sixteenth century, with a hexagonal tower and bakehouse. About 1km beyond the town on the right, is Huize te Wamberg, originating in 1620 and standing in the estate of the same name. Signs will direct cars or cycles back into Den Bosch from just beyond the estate.

ROUTE 55   TO THE EAST OF OSS

From Den Bosch, cars can reach **Oss** very quickly along the N50/A50 trunk road, but a much more pleasant route, for both cars and cycles, is along the minor road which runs between the main road and the railway, through the villages of **Nuland** and **Geffen**. To the north lies an area of meadows and polder stretching to the banks of the river Maas, and along the way are some pleasant areas of woodland and the recreation area Geffense Bosjes, with walking and swimming. The town of Oss is one of the oldest inhabited places in Noord Brabant, dating from pre-Christian times, and received its first charter in 1399. Lying near the border between Brabant and Gelderland, for centuries it was involved in the wars with Gelderland. It was maintained as a fortress until a great fire in 1751 destroyed the whole of the historic town centre. The impressive Grote Kerk is built on the site of the former fourteenth-century Willibrorduskerk, destroyed in that fire. Since the end of the nineteenth century, Oss has been very much industrialised and the richly decorated houses in Molenstraat were the homes of notable merchants and industrialists of that time. The most remarkable building is the Villa Constance, former home of the margarine magnates Van den Bergh and Jurgens, later used as the town hall, and now housing the Jan Cunencentrum, a museum containing a permanent exhibition of paintings and works by members of the Romantic and Hague schools, archaeological finds from the area, religious art and costumes. Today the town remains an important industrial centre with many well-known firms having establishments in the area.

To the east of the town, between the railway and the A50 motorway, lies an extensive area of woods, the Gemeente Bos and Herperduin, which may be crossed by cyclists in the direction of **Schaijk**. Motorists should follow the main road south from signpost 1309 to pass under the motorway junction (signpost 11816) and follow the road east to Schaijk. Primarily agricultural, it is rapidly becoming a residential and holiday centre, although there are still many old farmhouses, one being the Armenhof, a restored sixteenth-century building.

From signpost 4620 on the main road, take the road south to the rural village of **Zeeland**, which lies on the edge of the eastern part of Brabant known as Peelland, or simply the Peel. Largely peat bog until the turn of the century, it still contains extensive heath and fen, much of it a nature reserve with public access.

From the eastern side of Zeeland, cross the main road at signpost 7976, turn right at signpost 1057 through Langenboom, thence to **Mill**, and **Sint Hubert** which in the Middle Ages lay on the trade route from the Peel. Both villages are situated in a particularly beautiful part of the country, with sand tracks through the woods on the rising ground surrounded by low-lying fenland. Kasteel Aldendriel to the left of the road through Mill is completely moated, and dates from 1450, and parts of the church date from the fifteenth century. The windmill dates from 1847. In Sint Hubert the mill dates from 1878, and the church has a fifteenth-century tower. Further along the road is **Wanroij**, whose windmill is the only one in the country with three floors. At the end of the village a turning on the right leads to the Recreation Centre De Bergen, which lies on the edge of the extensive and typical landscape of the Wanroijse Peel.

Return from Wanroij, take the road to **Haps**; just before the village, at **Putselaar**, turn left at paddestoel 22833, then take the second turning on the right to the Royal Rose Nurseries, 'Verschuren'. Continue through the village, taking the left fork at signpost 3794, past the windmill and left again at signpost 3793, and follow signs to cross the new A73 motorway into **Cuijk**. A rapidly expanding town situated on the bank of the river Maas, with fine views out over the river towards the Reichswald Forest in Germany. On the other side of the river is a narrow strip of land which lies in the province of Limburg, between the river and the German frontier. Turning south from Cuijk, along the road beside the river, take the left turn off the main road at signpost 7103, just before the windmill, and follow the minor road through Sint Agatha to **Oeffelt**. This sheltered area along the river bank is white with may-blossom in the Springtime. Superb views are obtainable from the bridge over the Maas, which was built in 1955. Cross the bridge to **Gennep** in Limburg, first granted a charter in 1371, and standing at the place where the river Niers runs into the Maas. The Stadhuis is a very fine building from the seventeenth century, and the district museum contains a large collection of archaeological finds and decorative pottery. The scenery in the river valley is particularly attractive.

Returning over the river bridge to Oeffelt, turn left at signpost 4073 and follow the road south to **Beugen**, where a nature area, 'De Vilt', with rich flora and meadow and deciduous woods, surrounds an isolated arm of the river Maas. Beyond Beugen the road comes into **Boxmeer**, formerly an agricultural community which has recently grown into an industrial centre. There was a Roman settlement here, then the town grew around a castle built about 1200. A new castle was built in German Baroque style in the seventeenth century, and since 1896 has been used as a convent under the name of Huize Madeleine. St Petruskerk has been rebuilt since 1944, but contains many of the furnishings and treasures from the former church, whose crypt dating from about 1400 still exists. The Maasheggen, on the flood plain of the river, provides a fine natural area with free walking allowed.

From Boxmeer, follow the road along the river valley to **Vierlingsbeek**, where there is a memorial to those citizens who gave their lives during the last months of the war in 1944. At the end of the village are the remains of an old watermill.

Turn to the right through the village to the station, cross the railway, and follow signs to **Overloon**. This small town was the scene of one of the fiercest tank battles of World War II in 1944, which lasted from 24 September to 16 October, resulting in heavy losses for both the German and Allied (British and American) forces. The full story is told in the Netherlands National War and Resistance Museum, established on the edge of the town where much of the fighting took place. Many items of equipment and vehicles used by both sides during the war are displayed here, and a building houses many documents, photographs, models and other items which explain and illustrate the way in which the Dutch people were overcome and treated during the occupation of their country, and the way in which many of them resisted the occupiers. The main object of the museum is explained as being a warning to future generations of the consequences of racial intolerance if allowed to go unchecked.

In the town itself is a memorial chapel known as the 'Onderduikerskapel' or resistance chapel, for this was one of the greatest centres of the resistance movement during the war. Just on the edge of the town is a British War Cemetery.

Take the road leading west out of Overloon, following signs to **Oploo**. At the edge of the village, bear right, and on the right is an eighteenth-century watermill which is still in working order, as is the nearby windmill, dated 1800. From the road junction north of the village, at signpost 10843, turn left along the road across typical *peel* or fen country, to **Elsendorp**, then continue along the same road to **Gemert**, a town which was once ruled by a German Order of Knights. A number of interesting buildings may be seen, including Kasteel Gemert, dating from 1391. The neighbouring village of **Handel** was a place of pilgrimage, and along the road from Gemert is the unique sight of a series of wayside shrines, originally built in 1696; the ones seen today date from the early eighteenth century onwards. A windmill in Gemert was originally a paper-mill of 1665, transferred from the Zaanstreek in 1907 for use as a corn mill. The road north leads to **Boekel**, a rural village first founded in 1343, in which is a small museum, the 'Drie Kronen', containing a collection of cooking stoves from all provinces of the Netherlands and other European countries. At the cross roads in the centre of Boekel, at signpost 7524, turn left to **Erp**, where the fen country gives way to fields interspersed with poplar-lined pathways. Another 4km brings the road to **Veghel**, a trading and industrial town on the Zuid Willemsvaart. A memorial stands in the town to the American Airborne Forces who captured the bridge over the canal in September 1944.

Travelling north through Vorstenbosch, **Nistelrode** is reached, an old farming township near the nature park De Maashorst. A visitor centre, the Bezoekerscentrum Slabroek, has exhibitions to explain the origins, flora, fauna and use of this area of woodland and heath, and there are waymarked nature trails. To return to Oss, continue along the road through Heesch, and under the motorway.

ROUTE 56 IN and AROUND EINDHOVEN
Eindhoven is easily reached from Den Bosch or Oss via the excellent motorway system. The largest town in the south of the country, it was granted town rights in 1232, and has had an important function in the fields of commerce and transport from earliest times to the present day.

The growth of the town began to accelerate with the growth, of the international firm of Philips, started in 1891 by Anton and Gerard Philips who began to make electric lamps. The firm is now operating in many countries, and has important establishments all over the Netherlands, but the head offices and many other premises remain in Eindhoven. The possibility that the town would become dependent on one company was reduced when, in 1928, the DAF automobile factory was established. Since then, more varied industry has been attracted to the town. Because of the presence of important internationally-known companies, the town has a unique cosmopolitan character, borne out by the excellent shopping precincts in the town, and the great variety of restaurants, etc.

Much of the town is modern, although there are still a few reminders of earlier times. In the centre is the Augustijnenklooster dating from the fifteenth century, just a few minutes walk from the station, and a number of elegant houses dating from th eighteenth and nineteenth centuries. The river Dommel runs through the town, with a tributary, the Kleine Dommel, branching off towards the east side. On this river is a double watermill dating from the twelfth century, lying on Collseweg. Another watermill on Genneperweg on the south side of the town was built about 1249, and has been restored.

From the old to the new, and apart from the modern shopping centres and hotels, office blocks and factories, perhaps the most outstanding building is the 'Evoluon', likened to a flying saucer, a futuristic structure housing an extremely interesting exhibition which explains the achievements and applications of science and technology by means of models, self-activated displays, multi-lingual commentaries, dioramas and other equally fascinating methods. A comfortable restaurant and other facilities are provided, and the whole place requires at least a day to do it justice. Situated near the ring road, on Noord-Brabantlaan, the Evoluon has plenty of parking space, or can be reached by public transport from the centre. A more conventional but no less interesting museum is the Museum Kempenland, a local history museum dealing with Old Eindhoven, pre-history, geology, costumes, farming, and so on. It is housed in the former Antonius van Paduakerk in the district of Strijp, a short distance from the station. In nearby Emmasingel, is the original factory where the Philips brothers started making electric lamps. Just across the river from Stadhuisplein is the famous Van Abbemuseum, containing an outstanding collection of twentieth-century art.

A tour of the neighbouring countryside may be started by leaving the Evoluon, along Beukenlaan, then turning left on to Oirschotsedijk, which runs across the Oirschotseheide and the Wilhelminakanaal to the town of **Oirschot**, which has a history going back before the year 1200. The town centre is a conservation area, and includes a number of typical Noord Brabant farmhouses, many with reed-thatched roofs. St Pieterskerk, restored after war damage has a fine carillon of 49 bells. The Lieve-Vrouwekerk originated in the eleventh century as a chapel. A stone windmill from 1857 stands near the town centre, and an interesting monument is the 'Oirschotse Stoel', an enormous wooden stool symbolising the thriving furniture industry of the town. The Museum 'De Vier Quartieren', contains three rooms devoted to Brabants life, crafts, art, religion and so on from 1795 and another museum, named 'Hand en Span', deals with local farm tools and implements of the period from the middle of the last century to 1940. Just to the north-west is the village of **Spoordonk**, which has a nineteenth-century watermill where the wheel is set between two brick buildings, the whole being preserved.

From Oirschot, take the road east to **Best**, a modern residential and work place set in a landscape noted for its rows of tall poplar trees, leading to the growth of 'klompen-making'. Several makers are open to view, and the first Netherlands Klompenmuseum includes demonstrations of the art or craft of turning a block of poplar wood into a pair of *klompen*. The town hall is notable for its astronomical clock which may be connected to the carillon. St Odulphuskerk dates from the twelfth century, with Gothic additions from the fifteenth century. In the former presbytery garden is one of the largest collections of growing plants, flowers, trees and shrubs in the Netherlands, with more than 1,700 species, opened in 1980 by Prince Claus. Just to the north of the town is De Vleut, Bird and Animal Park, with exotic birds and animals in pleasant surroundings.

From the east of the main road N2, (signpost 811) the road to **Son en Breugel** runs across the Sonse Heide, where a monument by the entrance to the open-air theatre recalls the bravery of an American parachutist, Joe Mann who lost his life while saving the lives of a number of his comrades in 1944. The heath is partly a nature reserve and partly open for walking. The town is formed from two former villages on the banks of the river Dommel. It also lies on the main route from Eindhoven to Nijmegen, and in 1981 a new lifting-bridge was opened over the Wilhelminakanaal to reduce traffic

PLACES TO VISIT IN AND AROUND EINDHOVEN

Eindhoven
Evoluon: exhibition on the evolution of science and technology.
Museum Kempenland: local prehistory, geology, costumes, farming, etc.
Stedelijk Van Abbemuseum: twentieth-century art.

Oirschot
Museum De Vier Quartieren: traditional life in Brabant.

Best
Eerste Nederlandse Klompenmuseum: museum devoted to everything pertaining to *klompen* (clogs).
De Odulphushof: largest collection of growing plants, flowers, trees and shrubs.

Nuenen
Van Gogh-Documentatiecentrum: exhibition relating to the life and work of Vincent van Gogh.

Asten
National Beiaardmuseum: history and working of bells, carillons and clocks.
Natuurstudiecentrum Jan Vriends: collection of birds, butterflies, small mammals, etc.

Heeze
Kasteel Heeze: furniture, paintings and tapestry.

Eersel
Historic village centre.

congestion. The town is a busy commuter town for Eindhoven. Breugel was the birthplace of the painter Pieter Breughel in 1515, and a memorial stone in the Pieter Breughelplein records this fact. The first bishop of Den Bosch was born in Son in 1506. During the airborne operations of September 1944, American forces were landed near Son en Breugel to capture the bridge over the canal. This was destroyed by the occupying forces but rebuilt within two days.

A memorial to the American Airborne Forces lies on the south-eastern side of the town, and from here a road runs south, crossing the Wilhelminakanaal through Nederwetten to **Nuenen**, a dormitory town for Eindhoven and Helmond. The town itself is perhaps best known as the family home of the painter Vincent van Gogh, whose father was the pastor of the church. Vincent lived and painted in Nuenen from 1883 to 1885, and a monument to him stands on De Berg. The Oude Domineeshuis (1764), has been restored to the condition it was in during van Gogh's time and contains his studio. The permanent exhibition of papers, letters, photos and reproductions relating to the painter is in the coach house of a former mansion.

From the centre of Nuenen, take the road south but turn left before the motorway junction, then right across the bridge on the minor road which then turns left across the railway, following signs to Het Broek. Cross the Eindhovensekanaal to **Mierlo**, where there is a British War Cemetery, and continue south to the A67 motorway, then turn left along the minor road to Lierop. In the centre, at signpost 5416, take the road to cross the Zuid Willemsvaart at Sluis 10 and continue to **Asten**. This town has its origins in the year 1200, and is best known for the Eijsbouts Bell Foundry, and the National Beiaardmuseum (National Carillon Museum), which illustrates the history, development and use of bells all over the world. Exhibits and films show the process of moulding, casting and finishing bells of all sizes, and the methods of hanging and ringing bells from the simplest types to the automatic carillons heard in so many Dutch towns. The mechanism of old clocks is also shown, and many exhibits can be operated or heard. In the local foundry memorial bells have been cast for exporting to America, and the former carillon keyboard from Mechelen Cathedral in Belgium, now in the museum, was made in England. Associated with the museum is the Nature Study centre and museum, Jan Vriends.

South of Asten lies an area of waste ground, covering some thousands of hectares. This is the fenland known as *peel*. Partial drainage of the fen commenced by cutting channels, small and large. As the ground became drier, the peat was dug and dried, for use as fuel. This began on a large scale in about 1850. Areas where the peat was not dug remain as heathland, and such an area is the 'Groote Peel', now a nature reserve where the plants of the fenland may be seen in their original state.

The road west from Asten to Someren crosses the canal at the bridge by Sluis 11. Continue towards **Heeze**, passing between the Strabrechtse Heide to the north and the Somerense Heide to the south. Heeze lies in an attractive holiday area among heathland and woods, and Kasteel Heeze lies on the site of a twelfth-century stronghold, later enlarged to become known as Kasteel Eymerick. It now contains many works of art, antique articles and furnishings.

On the south side of the town, just across the railway, is a windmill dating from 1841, which has been fully restored. The road past the mill leads to **Leende**, where by going under the A2 motorway, the road to **Valkenswaard** is reached. This whole area is very picturesque, with heath, woods and lakes, making it a very popular holiday area. Being so near the Belgian frontier, many people travel from Belgium to visit the shops and markets in Valkenswaard, and to attend the various fairs, flower festivals, sporting events and competitions which are held here.

Cross over the main road in the town centre towards **Dommelen**, and on the left of the road is an undershot mill, dating from about 1200, driving two sets of stones. Continue through Westerhoven to **Bergeyk**, one of the oldest places in the area, being set in the middle of a number of archaeological sites. Bronze Age burial mounds have been found, and the results of excavations are on display in the district Museum Eicha. The church was built in 1422, with a separate *klokkenhuis* or bell tower from 1669 in which hangs a bell from 1367.

Turning north again from the town centre, at signpost 5308 take the left fork to **Eersel**, which has one of the most authentic village centres of South Netherlands. Many of the houses, from the eighteenth and nineteenth centuries, are listed for preservation. The chapel of Onze Lieve Vrouw dated from 1464 was closed for worship in 1648, and was then used for a town hall, prison, and shelter for the fire pump. It was reconsecrated as a chapel in 1957. The local museum is housed in the Acht Zaligheden, an old farmhouse, and deals with the typical life and work of a local farming community from 1850 to 1950. Outside the building is a herb garden, and a collection of wild flowers and plants native to the region.

From the edge of Eersel, the A67 motorway runs north to Eindhoven, but a parallel secondary road runs to the suburb of **Veldhoven**. Remains have been found here of reindeer hunters from 9000BC, and of various later occupants until Roman times. Several eighteenth-century houses remain in the town, and the prehistoric finds from the neighbourhood are on display in the local museum 't Slot, housed in a farmhouse of a type not usually found in these surroundings, being built on the foundations of a former castle. To the west of Veldhoven lies an area of heath and woods, with many paths and cycle tracks, and to the north is the increasingly busy Eindhoven Airport. Eindhoven centre may be reached by following signs for Centrum.

18 NOORD BRABANT - TILBURG AND BERGEN OP ZOOM

In this chapter we deal with the remainder of the Province of Noord Brabant, known as Hart van Brabant (Centre of Brabant) and West-Brabant. Apart from a strip of land along the northern boundary formed by the river Maas, and a corner bordering on Zeeland in the north-west, most of the area is woodland, heath, farmland and old estates, and much being devoted to nature conservation and recreation. There are, however, some busy industrial areas.

ROUTE 57   TILBURG AND ITS SURROUNDINGS

Tilburg, at the centre of Hart van Brabant, grew to importance during the industrial revolution, when a group of rural hamlets became a world textile centre. This came about in such a way that the centre still retains much of its 'small-town' character although a number of very modern buildings have been superimposed. Since the decline of the textile industry, diversity has led to a large new industrial estate being developed. Much of the town centre is now a pedestrian precinct the outstanding feature being the twin spires of the neo-Gothic church of 1870. A palace for King Willem II was completed in 1849, just one year after his death, and was later used as the Town Hall, until the completion of the modern Civic Centre. After extensive war damage, the old railway station was replaced in 1965 by a new station complex combined with a new Post Office building, and the whole has become an architectural showpiece.

The town is the site of the Netherlands Textile Museum, containing examples of textiles from all over the world, and spinning and weaving. Daily demonstrations are given. Another museum of considerable interest is the Schrift en Schrijfmachinemuseum, with a massive collection of everything to do with writing and the written word, from Chinese manuscripts to typewriters. Tilburg is a centre for wine importers, and it is no surprise to find a Wine Museum, the 'Maison du Vin', where all aspects of winemaking and bottling are shown.

To the west of Tilburg is very pleasant country, with plenty of opportunities for recreation. From the town centre, go to the ring-road, either Ringbaan-noord or Ringbaan-west, and so to the roundabout Hasselt-Rotonde. Follow signs for **Dongen**, along Rueckert Baan and Dongenseweg, crossing the Wilhelminakanaal and out past the Industrie-terrein. Dongen is a rural community with an urban-industrial character, a good shopping centre, and several small tanneries along the river Donge.

At signpost 10885 turn left, and cross the canal to **Rijen**, the industrial half of the town of Gilze-Rijen. The two parts are separated from north to south by the railway and the motorway, and a military airfield. Through Rijen, turn right at the station and come to the main road at signpost 1308.

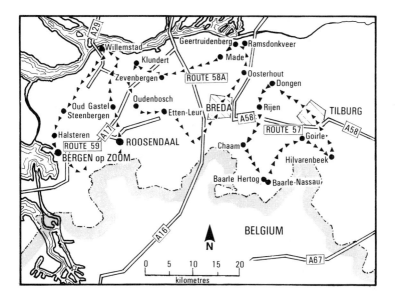

Turn right and continue to signpost 435, then left to **Molenschot** with its sixteenth-century chapel, after which signs to **Gilze** lead along the road at the edge of the woods, screening the airfield. Cross the motorway, and then bear right at signpost 8184 instead of going into Gilze. The route runs through the Boswachterijs Chaam and Ulvenhout, with extensive walking and cycling routes, picnic areas and car parking places, and enters the small town of **Chaam**, a favourite holiday centre with a fifteenth-century church.

From signpost 10507, turn left and take the road to **Baarle-Nassau-Hertog**. This rather complicated name for a small town is typical of the complicated nature of the place, as it lies on a very confusing part of the Dutch-Belgian frontier. Part of it is Dutch and part Belgian. The explanation is that the Dutch municipality of Baarle-Nassau comprises eight Dutch enclaves, seven of which are within Belgian enclaves and one in Belgium. The Belgian municipality of Baarle-Hertog consists of twenty-one Belgian enclaves on Dutch territory. As if that is not enough, there are places where the frontier runs through houses, and in one case through a café. One house has two number plates, one Dutch and one Belgian, because the frontier divides the front door of the house! A settlement existed here before Roman times, and the first written records date from 922.

In the twelfth century, the lands surrounding Baarle were divided, some belonging to the Duke (Hertog) of Brabant, and some to the estates of Breda, in the control of the Count of Nassau. At the Treaty of Westphalia in 1648, the Nassau holdings were given to the Northern Provinces and the

229

Duke's parts of Baarle went to what is now called Belgium. When, in 1843, the frontier between the Netherlands and Belgium was established, the present peculiar situation was unchanged. It is no wonder that the word *smokkelaar* appears locally — it must have been a paradise for smugglers! St Remigiuskerk stands in Belgian territory on the site of a chapel of 980, and the town hall of Baarle Nassau was originally in one of the oldest houses in Baarle, bearing the date 1639.

From the town centre, take the road north-east towards **Alphen**, which will cross and recross the frontier on the way. This is farming country, but in recent years the holiday industry has grown, and several conservation areas are open for walking, cycling and picnics. Alphen has a small local archaeological museum, as old tumuli, or burial mounds, have been found in the hilly heathland of the area. Through Alphen the road continues to **Riel**, where the right turn to **Goirle** should be taken at signpost 1582.

Goirle is a commuter town for Tilburg. In Kerkstraat, is St Janskerk, a new church with an old tower from about 1460; nearby is a windmill (1896), still in working order and is associated with the museum 'Heemerf De Schutsboom'. This covers the cultural and economic life of the Catholic Netherlands during the past century, and also has an eighteenth-century weaver's cottage, nineteenth-century dwelling, old vegetable and herb gardens and beehives.

From Goirle, take the road to **Hilvarenbeek** from signpost 7838. After passing the Jonkers Stillery Museum, and the windmill (1830), the town centre or Vrijthof is reached. This is a unique Frankish market-field which is a conservation area, with an old town pump, several beautiful alleys and small streets, a fourteenth-century church and old houses. The museum, De Doornenboom, has a very fine collection of medical instruments, books and other items from the eighteenth century to World War II, together with archaeological finds from the district from Neolithic and later times.

The dual-carriageway main road, and the parallel secondary road north to Tilburg, pass the entrance to the Beekse Bergen Safari and Recreation Park. Numerous rides, water-amusements and other entertainments can be enjoyed in the Recreation Park on the right of the road, while the Safari Park, on the left, contains more than 800 wild animals, roaming freely; visitors may drive their own cars or ride through in special buses. A bird park and children's farm are also provided.

To return to Tilburg, follow the main road and join the ring road.

From Tilburg, **Breda** may be reached directly either by motorway or by the parallel main road past Rijen. It is a town with a very stormy history, first chartered in 1252. The town walls were extended in the early sixteenth century to the line of the present Singel. In the same century, Breda saw the start of the line of Oranje-Nassau, from which the present Royal Family of the Netherlands is descended. Through the various struggles with French and Spanish invaders, the town was frequently under attack.

In 1879 the old town walls were demolished to allow expansion

Tilburg
Nederlands Textielmuseum: old
machines, tools and samples of
spinning and weaving. Schrift and
schrijfmachinemuseum; writing
implements from pens to
typewriters.

Baarle-Nassau
Unique frontier community with
enclaves.

Goirle
Heemerf De Schutsboom: museum
with traditional dwelling, crafts,
gardens and nearby windmill.

Hilvarenbeek
Vrijthof: unique Frankish town
centre. Museum 'De Doornenboom'
is housed in an old mill, and contains
a collection of old medical
instruments.
De Beekse Bergen: Recreation Park
with associated Safari Park.

northwards. The castle stands on the site of an original building from about 1198, which was reconstructed in its present form in 1696. Since 1828, the castle has housed the Royal Military Academy, which is still in being. Breda has been a garrison town for a long time, and there are other military barracks in the neighbourhood. Many of the interesting old buildings lie close together around the centre of the town.

ROUTE 58   A WALK IN BREDA

Starting from the railway station, go along Willemstraat and cross the canal or former moat, and the large park called the Valkenberg will be seen. This was formerly the garden of the castle, which is situated on the west side of the park. A notable feature is the Spanjaardsgat or Spaniard's Gate, with two towers and a watergate, which formed part of the sixteenth-century fortifications. Before the entrance to the castle, in Kasteelplein, is the National Ethnological Museum. From the end of Kasteelplein, turn left along Catharinastraat, and on the left is the entrance to the Begijnhof, whose buildings date back to 1535. The beautiful herb garden within the courtyard is worth seeing. By the Begijnhof is the Waalse Kerk (Walloon church) built in 1438. Continue along Catharinastraat, bearing right into Veemarkt-straat, passing on the right the Lutherse Kerk dating from 1560, thence into Grote Markt. Turn left to the Municipal and Episcopal Museum, housed in the former Vleeshal (1617). Turn right along Ridderstraat, and right again along Torenstraat to the most noticeable building in the town centre, the Grote or Onze Lieve Vrouwe Kerk, standing on a site of a stone church which existed in 1269. The present building was commenced in 1410, being completed in 1538. The tower, 97m high, was built during 1468 to 1509, to replace an earlier one which

The huge church of St Jan, Oosterhout

collapsed. Fire damaged it in 1694 and it was restored in 1702, having a new set of bells installed in 1723. The church contains many tombs and memorials to the Lords of Breda, the Counts of Nassau, and many other people famous in the country's history. After extensive restoration, the fine pulpit (1640) was placed in position, also the Princes' pew (1663), used by the Barons and Baronesses of Breda (namely the Royal Family of the Netherlands). The fine organ was installed in 1715, but contains parts of the original one from 1533. Fortunately, the church was not damaged during the liberation of Breda in 1944. The town has a good shopping centre, and much of it is a pedestrian precinct.

ROUTE 58A   AROUND BREDA

Breda makes a good centre for exploring the neighbouring countryside of Noord Brabant, and the following route takes in some of the old towns to the north and west, towards the river Maas.

From the station, follow Oranje Singel eastwards, then turn left along Teteringenstraat and Teteringsedijk. Turn left into Kapittelweg, and continue to the ring road (Nieuwe Kadijk). Turn right, and at the next junction turn left into Oosterhoutseweg. The road leads through **Teteringen**, a suburb of Breda which lies on the border between the higher sandy ground with its woods and sand drifts, and the polder landscape nearer the river Maas. In Teteringen there are still farmhouses from the past two centuries, and the town hall is in a former farmhouse dating from 1750. Some pleasant walks are possible in the neighbourhood. The road continues to **Oosterhout**, a very pleasant residential place, with industrial development on the outskirts. The town has a rather unique group of *Slotjes* or little castles, built around the thirteenth century by members of the Order of St John (the Knights Templar). Five of these still exist, and the St Jansbasiliek, which dates from the fifteenth century, has a massive but uncompleted tower. The St Catharinadal, a convent, has occupied a fifteenth-century building since 1647, and the sisters of the community specialise in restoration of old books and manuscripts.

The old main road from Oosterhout runs parallel with the A27 motorway north to **Raamsdonksveer**, which lies between the river Donge and the Bergsche Maas. In the northern part of the town, in the industrial area, is the National Automobile Museum. From the old main road through the town continue towards the industrial area of Dombosch, where signs to the museum will be seen. With much more than just motor cars, there are exhibits of all types of carriage and cart, bicycles and motor-cycles from the earliest days, and motor vehicles from the end of the nineteenth century to the present day, including racing cars.

Cross the bridge south of the industrial area, at signpost 6334, to the town of **Geertruidenberg**, granted town rights in 1213. Lying on a point of land between the rivers Donge and Amer, which flow into the Bergsche Maas, the town was an early trading centre, until the disastrous floods of 1421. The town then became a frontier fortress. Although very small, the old town is very picturesque. The St Geertruidiskerk dates from the fifteenth century, but has parts of a fourteenth-century tower, whilst in the Markt are a number of very fine houses, some from the sixteenth century. The town hall dates from the fourteenth century, and a total of five eighteenth-century stone water pumps together with the ancient lime trees, make the market square a really beautiful sight. Remains of the ramparts and moats can still be seen.

From the town, a minor road runs west to **Drimmelen**, beside the river Amer, the name by which the Maas is known from this point. The town is developing rapidly as a sailing and boating centre, and also has a very picturesque canal. Across the water lies the area known as the Biesbosch or forest of rushes. This is an area of river creeks, mud flats and marshland created by the disastrous St Elizabeth Flood of 1421, supporting unique bird and waterplant life, which has been declared a National Park. Reservoirs in the area supply Rotterdam's drinking water. The 'Biesbosch Bezoekerscentrum' is in Drimmelen, where visitors may obtain information about the area, and from where boat trips may be made into the Biesbosch.

Made, which is part of the same municipality as Drimmelen, is a growing residential town about 2km south, from whence the road west via **Wagenberg** is taken to **Zevenbergen**, standing on clay soil in the polder landscape. Beyond the town the road continues to **Klundert**, lying on the edge of a large industrial area, but itself strategically placed in the past as a fortress town, whose restored defence works are worth seeing. The town hall, in Flemish-Renaissance style, dates from 1621, and a stone near the entrance marks the height of the flood water in February 1953. Turning south from the town centre (signpost 5916), the road runs to a bridge across the motorway; turn left over this, then right, crossing a second motorway

---

**PLACES TO VISIT IN AND
AROUND BREDA**

Breda

Rijksmuseum voor Volkenkunde:
ethnic collections from eastern
countries.

Stedelijk en Bisschoppelijk Museum:
collection of ecclesiastical art and
history of Breda.

Grote Kerk: many historical
monuments and fine organ.

Oosterhout

Historic Market square with St Jans-
basilica and *Slotjes*.

Raamsdonksveer

National Automobielmuseum:
antique cars, carriages, motorbikes
and bicycles.

Geertruidenberg

Historic town centre and ramparts.

Drimmelen

'Biesbosch Bezoerkerscentrum':
history and natural history of
Biesbosch marshes.

Hoeven

Bosbad Hoeven: Recreation Park.

---

bridge to **Standdaarbuiten**, on the river Mark, a town standing in typical polder landscape with dykes and double rows of trees. The church, from 1810, contains a silver Communion Table dated 1685. A short distance from the town is **Oudenbosch**, dominated by the Basilica of Sts Agatha and Barbara, built between 1865 and 1880, a small-scale copy of the church of St Peter in Rome. The front façade was not completed until 1892. A memorial stands here to the Zouaves, the Dutch soldiers who fought during 1860-70 for the Pope and the Papal States during the formation of modern Italy, and a small museum also deals with this aspect of history.

From the centre (signpost 1761) the road south crosses the railway and runs towards **Bosschenhoofd**, where signs direct visitors to the Bosbad Hoeven, a recreation park well equipped with all kinds of facilities for swimming, riding, water sports, and with children's playgrounds and amusements of all kinds. Adjacent to the park is the Volksterrenwacht Simon Stevin, an observatory which is open to the public. From this area, take the road into the nearby town of **Hoeven**, by the windmill on the east side of the town, then follow the road east to **Etten-Leur**, a fast growing community whose industrial expansion has left the town centre of Leur untouched. The twin spires of St Petruskerk, and the Trouwkerkje dating from 1614, together with the St Paulushofje (1681) are of interest, part of the latter now used as a museum showing local costumes and crafts. The town also has a museum dealing with the history of printing. To the south of the town, from signpost 288, runs a road to **Rijsbergen**, across pleasant rural countryside with soft fruit growing as one of the specialities of the area. A growing interest in holiday, recreation and camping is also apparent.

Cross over the main N263 road and follow minor roads via Kaarschot to the bridge across the A16 motorway, and bear left by the Mastbos, a beautiful area of woods with many walking and cycle paths. Towards the northern end of the woods, approaching the suburb of **Ginneken** on the edge of Breda, is the Kasteel Bouvigne, built in the fifteenth century as a country mansion and hunting lodge, whose fine landscaped gardens are open to the public. The return into Breda is through Ginneken, which has a fourteenth-century church.

ROUTE 59   ROOSENDAAL AND BERGEN op ZOOM

Originating as a peat-cutting village in the thirteenth century, Roosendaal is now an industrial and shopping centre for West Brabant, situated among beautiful wood and heath, ideal for holidays and recreation. Its importance is also partly due to its position as a frontier station of the Netherlands railway system, carrying the main line from France through Brussels and Antwerp towards the north. In the former Presbytery of the Abbey of Tongerlo (1762) is the Museum 'De Ghulden Roos', with collections of West Brabants folklore and costumes.

From Roosendaal, a road runs north from signpost 4181, along Gastelseweg, crossing over the A17 motorway, to **Oud Gastel** with a fifteenth-century church tower. It then crosses the river Dintel to **Fijnaart**, in polder landscape with high dykes, noted for fruit growing, and numerous eighteenth and nineteenth century farmhouses breaking the apparently endless horizons.

Cross the A59 motorway to the north of Fijnaart to Oude Molen, then at signpost 4375 turn left, then fork right. The road may be followed across the polder to the dyke road, then turn left to **Willemstad**, one of the best-preserved fortress towns in the Netherlands. The former occupations of cattle breeding and agriculture have been supplemented by water-sport and tourism. The fortress was built in 1565-83 to guard the entrance to the Hollands Diep, leading into the river system of the Maas and Waal, and to Dordrecht. The fortifications, comprising ramparts, moats, high dyke walls, gates and the Fort De Hel are all worth seeing, and because of its obvious strategic importance it should be no surprise to find, built into the old ramparts, modern concrete bunkers and gun positions dating from the German occupation of 1940-4. In the town, the Princehof or Mauritshuis was built in 1623 as a hunting lodge for the Prince of Orange, then from 1626 to 1795 it was used as the Governor's residence. It has been restored and is now the Town Hall. The Arsenal (1793) has a fine façade with three stone gateways. The church, built in 1596, was the first church in the Netherlands built for the Protestant faith, and is worth seeing for its stained glass windows, organ and other features.

The road out of Willemstad to the west, runs past Fort De Hel, thence via Helwijk, to cross the motorway following signs to Heijningen, where there is a memorial to the floods of 1953. Continue on minor roads to cross the river Dintel into **Dinteloord**, established when the Prinslandse Polder was created in 1605. On the edge of the town, at signpost 11018, the main road south is followed across typical polder landscape to **Steenbergen**, which in the fourteenth century was a thriving harbour town on the Steenbergse Vliet. When the harbour silted up, the inhabitants turned to agriculture and cattle breeding. During the sixteenth and seventeenth centuries the town was fortified. The main road continues south to **Halsteren**, with its St Antonius windmill, Town Hall (1633) and St Martinuskerk (fifteenth century). A number of eighteenth-century farmhouses are to be seen in the district, and just to the east of the town, on the edge of an area of woods open to the public, are the remains of Fort de Roovere, part of the old defence line running north from Bergen op Zoom.

The road south leads to **Bergen op Zoom**, an ideal place to stop for a holiday. There are many opportunities to take part in water sport, touring by car or bicycle, or walking in the nearby woods. Lying, as it does, on the motorway system from the ferry port of Vlissingen, Bergen op Zoom tends to be passed by visitors hurrying to get to the rest of the country. This seems a pity, as the town well deserves more attention. The name comes from the fact that in about 1219 a certain Boudewijn, from Bergen, possessed land on the Zoom, a ridge of high ground between the marshland, and the mud flats of the Schelde estuary. So the town became known as Bergen op (ten) Zoom.

The town was well established in 1287, and received a charter in 1365, and with the exception of the harbour area, was enclosed by ramparts, of which the only remaining part is the Lievevrouwepoort. In the fifteenth century, the town had grown in importance and the walls were extended to enclose the harbour area. It kept its place as an important market town until the sixteenth century, when the trade began to be taken by Antwerp. Subsequent struggles with Spain and France led to the strengthening of the fortifications, but in the eighteenth century, industry began to establish itself in the town and surroundings. Since the opening of the Schelde-Rijn canal in 1975, Bergen op Zoom has once more become a channel for international transport.

The Lievevrouwepoort or Gevangenpoort has already been mentioned,

*The Gevangenpoort,
Bergen op Zoom*

and after the extension of the fortifications it no longer functioned as a town gate, so was used as a prison. The Town Hall in the Grote Markt comprises several old houses, which have been combined with one façade. One was rebuilt after a fire in 1397, another was the residence of English merchants until 1480, and the third was purchased by the town in 1516. The 'new' façade was built in 1611. Across the market square is the Grote or St Gertrudiskerk, built in the fourteenth century, replacing an earlier church on the same site. Only the tower remains of the fourteenth-century building. A short distance from the square, in Steenbergsestraat, is the Markiezenhof, the residence of the former marquis of Bergen op Zoom, built in 1485 to 1512. The buildings are grouped around three inner courts and have been used as a military hospital by the French, and a barracks by the Dutch army. After a thorough restoration, it is now used as a cultural centre and municipal museum. In the town are some fine and elegant houses, which were once occupied by English merchants and weavers.

A pleasant route from Bergen op Zoom is by way of the road leading south-east, across the motorway at signpost 10775, via Heimolen to the junction at signpost 4672, near the Belgian frontier. Turn left towards Wouwse Plantage village, then follow signs along winding roads to **Nispen**, a pleasant village with a windmill. Cross over the main N217 road (which is dual carriageway) at signpost 5095, and keep straight on to the next junction. Turn left, then next right, and follow through to Visdonk. Parking places, picnic areas and plenty of walks through the woods can be found in this attractive countryside.

19 LIMBURG; ALMOST ANOTHER COUNTRY

Although Limburg is part of the Netherlands, the atmosphere is so different that it almost seems that you are in another country. Even some Dutch people take their holidays in Limburg because they know it is the one part of the Netherlands where they can feel as if they are in a foreign country without going abroad. Despite a history which, because of the strategic position of the province, has made it an arena for battles, sieges and pillaging from Roman times to World War II, Limburg has managed to preserve its own special character of tranquility and unspoilt nature, a countryside dotted with castles, churches, ruins and picturesque villages. The province is some 150km long, and in one place is only about 5km wide. There are some exceptionally attractive routes through a very varied countryside, ranging from the flat peelland in the north, through the central lakes area, to the hilly wooded country of the south. This is the province which opened the first ever tourist office in Holland, at Valkenburg, and was 'discovered' by the British as a tourist resort in the nineteenth century. Some 20,000 British visitors a year still come to Valkenburg. Limburg is a busy industrial area, yet despite this there is still plenty of open space, and even the industrial cities have something of interest for the visitor. The Roman remains at Heerlen, and the mine museum at Kerkrade are just two such places. Limburg is a very cosmopolitan province, with the biggest variation in dialects and a strong French and German influence.

The Queen's Commissioner to the Province describes the people of Limburg as having the industriousness and precision of the Germans, the *joie de vivre* of the Burgundians, Dutch sobriety and French frivolity. A real mixture, making the province quite unique.

The tour of the province starts at Venray, easily reached by road from Nijmegen via Gennep, crossing the river Maas at Well.

ROUTE 60   NORTH LIMBURG AROUND VENRAY

Venray is, in terms of area, one of the largest municipalities in Holland, covering more than 14,500 hectares, situated in the peaceful *peel* countryside, and consisting of the town of Venray itself and ten other villages, as well as numerous hamlets. More than 6,000 hectares of this is fenland and forest, freely accessible in most cases on foot or bicycle.

The town itself was very badly damaged in World War II, but fortunately most of the treasures of the fifteenth-century St Petruskerk were saved from total destruction. The church contains an outstanding collection of fifteenth and sixteenth-century woodcarvings, in particular a very fine series of statues of the Apostles. There is also a sixteenth-century baptismal font and fine carved seventeenth-century pulpit. This church is one of the largest in Holland, and is popularly called the Cathedral of the

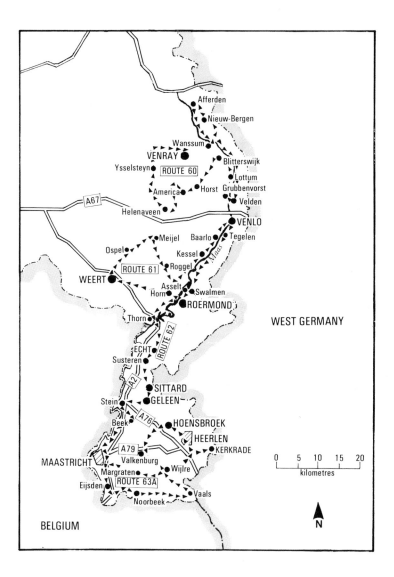

Afferden
Nieuw-Bergen
Wanssum
VENRAY
Ysselsteyn ROUTE 60 Blitterswijk
Lottum
America Horst Grubbenvorst
A67 Velden
Helenaveen
VENLO
Meijel Baarlo Tegelen
Ospel Kessel
ROUTE 61 Roggel
WEERT
Asselt Swalmen
Horn
Thorn ROERMOND
WEST GERMANY
ROUTE 62
ECHT
Susteren
A2
SITTARD
Stein GELEEN
Beek A76 HOENSBROEK
HEERLEN
A79 KERKRADE
MAASTRICHT Valkenburg
Margraten Wijlre
Eijsden ROUTE 63A
Vaals
Noorbeek

BELGIUM

0   5   10   15   20
kilometres

N

Peel, dominating the neighbourhood.

The museum, "'t Freulekeshuus', in Eindstraat, not far from the church, contains a collection of flint tools and other artefacts from prehistoric times, the Bronze age, Roman period and the Middle Ages. In addition there are religious objects, old costumes Guild regalia and livery. A great deal of the collection was discovered within the municipality itself.

Leaving Venray via Stationsweg cross the railway just north of the station, and enter the village of **Oostrum**; at signpost 3948, turn left towards **Geysteren**, turning right again at the cross roads in approximately 300m. This road runs along the southern edge of the Landgoed Geysteren, an estate with a greatly varied landscape of woods, fields and heathland, attractive lanes and a deep little valley. There is an historic chapel in the woods, and two old watermills. Continue through the village to signpost 2708, and turn right following the river as far as **Wanssum**. On reaching the main road, turn left and continue towards **Well**, a distance of about 3km, crossing the river Maas. On reaching the T-junction with the Nijmegen-Venlo road, turn left, and in about 500m turn right again. (Signpost 1253). The road eventually leads to Kevelaer, in Germany, but skirts the area known as the Leukerheide, where a large 'broad' is being developed as a recreation area. In about 3km, at signpost 11958, turn left, still skirting the Leukerheide, and after a further 4½km turn left again, eventually turning right into Nieuw-Bergen. Go through the village and turn right at the major road junction, then in 500m left again along a small road through the *Landgoed Bleijenbeek*, turning left at the T-junction at the end of the road, near the remains of Kasteel Bleijenbeek, destroyed in 1945. Continue to the village of Afferden, with its thirteenth-century parish church.

From here, take minor roads south through Bergen to **Ayen**, where the white St Antoniuskapel, built in the seventeenth century, can be seen. Continue along the road to **Well**, passing the eighteenth-century St Rochuskapel on your way. The castle at Well, built in the fifteenth century, is now in use as a conference and study centre. On reaching the main road, turn left and proceed to the T-junction (signpost 12077).

Turn right and follow the main road to **Arcen**. The remains of a fourteenth-century town gate, known as the Schanstoren, can be seen near the river by the Maashotel.

Continue south through Lomm to **Velden**, keeping to the main road until signpost 865, about 1km after entering the town. Turn right towards the ferry for **Grubbenvorst**, where a short detour to the south may be made after crossing the river to see the picturesque ruins of 'Het gebroken Slot'. The official name of the castle is Kasteel Gribben; it was first built in the thirteenth century, but has been a ruin for hundreds of years. Legend tells that a white lady is doomed to live here for ever on account of her lover's unfaithfulness, and it is said that her ghost can be seen wandering about the ruins. Return to the ferry and keep to the road beside the river to **Lottum**. The sixteenth-century castle, behind the church on the right as you enter the village, was completely restored in 1926, and miraculously escaped severe damage during World War II.

Continue northwards to **Broekhuizen**, with an attractive village centre of cobbled streets and stately old houses, and **Broekhuizenvorst** with an early sixteenth-century church. Here too the streets are set with small cobblestones, in a mosaic pattern. Continuing alongside the river towards **Blitterswijck**, Kasteel Ooyen can be seen on the right of the road, a white building dating from the seventeenth century. In the village turn left at signpost 3291 towards Meerlo, turn left on entering the town and continue to Tienraij, then turn right in the village centre towards **Horst**. In the Kasteelse Bossen, to your left as you approach the main road bypassing the town, is an old castle ruin and a recreation area, reached from the town side of the main road. Cross the main road and turn left at the first major cross roads, which takes you into the town. The fifteenth-century church in Horst, like so many others in this neighbourhood, was totally destroyed in 1944, but has been rebuilt in its original style. In the old town hall is a small museum of antiquities relating to the area.

From Horst follow the road westwards to the small village of **America**, noted for mushroom culture. There is also a large recreation park offering swimming, fishing, pony-rides, midget golf and water-bikes, playgrounds and other amusements. From the park (het Meerdal), proceed south along the main road for about 6km then turn right through the hamlet of Evertsoord to the village of **Helenaveen**, just inside the Province of Noord Brabant. Take the road to the right immediately on entering the village, through the beautiful landscape of the *peel* to **Griendtsveen**. There are several places en route to leave the car and walk around part of this fascinating area. At Griendtsveen, cross the railway and turn right along the road leading to **IJsselsteyn**, passing on the right the huge German military cemetery, where all the German soldiers who died in Holland during World War II are buried. On reaching IJsselsteyn village, turn left and take the main road north for 5km, then turn right at signpost 7952 and follow the road through the woods, entering Venray again in the north west of the town.

ROUTE 61   AROUND VENLO AND WEERT

Venlo is the principal town of North Limburg, and according to legend it was founded in the year AD96. It is a very busy commercial centre, and one of the busiest border crossings in Western Europe. Because it is so close to the Ruhr industrial area of Germany, it is very much an international shopping centre, with more than 80,000 German customers visiting the town every week. The massive town hall, a great sixteenth-century Renaissance-style building with a double outside staircase and two tall turreted towers stands in the centre of the Markt. Until the nineteenth century, Venlo was fortified, but the walls and gates were then demolished and the town began to expand. It has developed as the largest market gardening area outside the Westland district of Holland, and is particularly well known for its salad produce and asparagus.

There is plenty of parking space around the edges of the old town, especially by the river. Apart from the town hall, there are not many old buildings to see but in Grote Kerkstraat, close to St Martinuskerk, is a rather nice seventeenth-century orphanage, and a sixteenth-century patrician house with decorated iron wall-plates, restored in 1921. The Museum Goltzius is the local historical museum, and the Museum van Bommel van Dam, houses a collection of modern art.

From Venlo, leave via Roermondsestraat, south-west towards **Tegelen**, whose name gives a clue to its origin. It was a place where the clay was of perfect quality for making bricks and, more especially, floor and roof tiles. They were made here as long ago as Roman times, and the industry is still functioning in the town. Tegelen is also famous for its Passion Plays, second only to Oberammegau, which are held every five years. The next play is due to be staged in 1990; in the magnificent open-air theatre, 'De Doolhof'. In the town hall is a small museum of local pottery, mostly from the eighteenth and nineteenth centuries, and a small potters' workshop of the period. In nearby **Steyl**, on the western side of the main road, are two particularly interesting places to visit. The first is the Museum Missiehuis Steyl, containing a collection from the 'mission' lands of the Far East and Africa, including anything from butterflies and scorpions to Buddhas and African masks. The second is the Botanische Tuin Jochum-Hof, a most interesting botanical garden with both indoor and outdoor plants, and a tropical house containing cacti, orchids, coffee and banana plants. There are separate herb and heather gardens, and a special section devoted to North Limburg flora. There is also a very interesting 'Prehistoric' garden.

From Steyl, follow the road south again, passing Belfeld, and at Reuver bear right at signpost 5358 towards **Beesel**, and the sixteenth-century Kasteel Nieuwenbroek, a white house, with wings either side of the main building and rather nice *trapgevels*. From here, the road leads south again to join the main road at Swalmen. After about 1km on this road, bear right again to **Asselt**, where, near the river in Pastoor Pinckerstraat, is the oldest known church in the Netherlands, known locally as het Rozenkerkje, or the little pink church. In 1915, the ruins were scattered all over the district but were all brought together by the local people so that the church could be rebuilt in its original state. It is thought that it was once used as a Roman look-out post, and it was known to be a place of worship in the tenth century. In the nearby old coach house is a small museum, with a collection of articles from the Stone and Bronze Ages, Roman and Frankish periods, and the Middle Ages, plus a collection of folk art from Central Limburg. The museum is open on request.

From Asselt take the road to the south of the village, then turn south along the main road towards Roermond. At the first junction, bear right in the direction of Weert, crossing the river Maas to **Hoorn**. Kasteel Horn stands on a mound with a high surrounding wall. The thirteenth-century foundations have been built up over the years, notably in the fifteenth and sixteenth centuries. The castle, once the home of the Counts of Horn, is not open to the public except by special arrangement, but the park is freely accessible.

There are two windmills in the village, both situated in Molenweg. One is an old wooden mill with sixteen sides, and the other is a brick mill, which is the smallest mill in Limburg. Follow the main street through the village to the main N273 road, then turn left and right again in about 500m on to the N68 road leading to **Weert**. Cyclists will find a parallel road alongside. At **Baexem**, the seventeenth-century Kasteel Baexem can be seen on the left, and shortly after this, on the right, there is a very old *standerdmolen* or post mill, dating from 1599, which originally stood in Haelen and was brought to Baexem in 1845.

Continue along the road to **Weert**, situated on the borders of Holland and Belgium and known to exist in the eleventh century, as 'Weerta', meaning a settlement between the water and the moorland. In the early fourteenth century, it was under the control of the Counts of Horn, Lords of Weert, and became a thriving wool and cloth centre. This 'golden age' came to an end with the Eighty Years' War, when Weert became completely isolated; things only began to improve when the Zuid-Willemsevaart was dug in 1825, and with the coming of the railways Weert lost its isolation for ever. It is an attractive town, much of it now pedestrianised. There is a car park near the castle, another a short distance further along near the canal. From either car park it is an easy walk into the Markt, where the St Martinuskerk stands, its tall tower built in the Kempen style, and made taller in 1960. Inside are some fine wall and ceiling paintings, some very attractive carved choir stalls, and the tomb of the last Count of Horn, who was beheaded in Brussels by Count Egmond in 1568. The remains of his fifteenth-century castle which was destroyed in the early eighteenth century can be seen on Biest, leading off Kasteelsingel. These include one of the corner towers, now converted into a private home. In the road leading off Biest, behind the castle (Recollectenstraat), is the Gemeentemuseum De Tiendschuur, with collections concerning the history and folklore of Weert, plus a large natural history department. Another museum, in the former stadhuis, opposite St Martinuskerk, is the Museum of Religious Art (Museum voor religieuze Kunst) Jacob van Horne. Many of the exhibits were obtained from the Franciscan fathers in Weert, whose monastery is situated in the old Kasteel de Aldenborg; given to them by Jacob van Horne. The gateway known as the Paterspoortje, is situated in Biest. There is another museum in Weert, a little further from the town centre, to the south of the railway, in Kruisstraat. This is the Nederlands Tram-Museum, which has a collection of all kinds of objects linked with the tram services, including three full-size tramcars. Weert used to be connected by tramline to Masseik in Belgium, hence the situation of this museum. The old Muntgebouw, or mint, has been fully restored and stands in the centre of the new shopping centre.

Leave Weert by crossing the canal near the Bassin car park, and immediately turn right alongside the canal to Nederweert. This road takes a sharp bend to the left just before reaching the junction with another canal,

with historical and folklore collections.
Jacob van Horne Museum of religious art.
Netherlands Tram museum, with collection of objects related to tramways.
Muntgebouw — sixteenth-century Mint in centre of modern shopping complex.

Kreijel (Nederweert)
Interesting windmill.

Ospel
Peel museum — archaeological and historical museum.
Bezoekerscentrum 'Mijl op Zeven' — Visitor centre in old *peel* farmhouse. Waymarked routes over 'virgin' *peel*.

Hof
Ancient well and boundary stone.

Nunhem
Leudal valley, watermill and visitor centre.
St Servatuskapel and well, where early Dutch Christians were baptised.

Kessel
Massive ruins of tenth-century castle.
'Heksendans' square in village where witches are said to have danced.

Baarlo
Kasteel Erp, park and watermill, and old public wash-house.

and in another kilometre turn right crossing the canal and following in the direction of **Eind**. At the next major road junction, turn sharp left to **Kreijel** (signpost 4359). In this small hamlet is a rather nice *beltmolen*, a small brick mill with a round cap, standing on a mound or 'belt' surrounding the base. Continue straight ahead for a further kilometre, then turn right along the road to **Ospel**. Through this village is the Peelmuseum, which describes with its collections, both archaeological and historical, the history of the *peel* area. About two kilometres further on, through winding country lanes, is the Bezoekers Centrum 'Mijl op Zeven', which is concerned with the natural history of the *peel*, and is situated in one of the old *peel* farmhouses, on the edge of a national nature reserve, one of the finest areas of undeveloped bog and heathland in Holland. There are three waymarked routes over the *peel* from the Visitor Centre, giving an opportunity to examine at close quarters the rare plants, and to see something of the many birds which breed in the area. From here, continue towards **Meijel**, but at the main road turn left then immediately right to the hamlet of **Hof**, north of the village. Here there is an old nineteenth-century pump, built on top of a spring, and known as Willibrordusputje. Close by, area, which is operated by the Staatsbosbeheer. Admission is free, and it is boundary stone, erected at the time of the split between the Seven Provinces and Austria. One side carries the arms of the Seven Provinces, the other the eagle of Austria. Take the road south into Meijel, and continue southwards to **Roggel** passing the St Antonius mill at Nijken, another interesting *beltmolen*. In about another $1\frac{1}{2}$km, after passing the road to Helden on the left, a left fork leads through the town towards Haelen. About 1km outside the town is a parking place beside a cycle path which leads to the Leudal, one of the loveliest little river valleys in Limburg. The old watermill has been fully restored and in the summer months can be seen working as a grain mill. There is a small visitor centre in the building, depicting some of the natural history and archaeological finds from the area, which is operated by the Staatsbosbeheer. Admission is free, and it is possible to explore the area further on foot, keeping to the paths, and walk through the estate to the old St Servatuskapel, standing on a little hill in a grove of high acacia trees. Next to the chapel is a well, now dry, where it is said that St Servatus baptised the early Dutch Christians. From the car park at the beginning of the Leudal, drive south and take the first road on the left, which takes you past Nunhem close by St Servatuskapel before reaching the main N273 road. Turn left and continue past Neer to **Kessel**. Drive into the centre of the town, past the mill, towards the ruins of the castle which stand on a mound by the Maas. This tenth-century ruin is a massive structure, which has gradually been destroyed during many wars over the centuries. In the village is a small square known as De Heksendans, where legend has it that witches used to dance! Surrounding the square are old merchants' houses in rather good condition, particularly the Witte Huis (white house) with decorative wrought ironwork on the door. From Kessel, the riverside road may be followed to **Baarlo**, where Kasteel d'Erp has been restored and is the official residence of the Burgemeester. Nearby is an old watermill, in the castle grounds, together with an old public wash house. These have been restored, and the mill can be seen working when there is enough water in the mill race.

From Baarlo, follow the river road again, past the ferry, to the viewpoint at the sharp bend in the road. Turn left and continue past Kasteel de Berckt, now in use as a monastery for both monks and nuns. The castle is not open to the public, except the chapel for Sunday Mass. Continue to the main road, turn right and in 1km turn right again to Venlo.

ROUTE 62   FROM ROERMOND TO MAASTRICHT
This route takes the visitor through the narrowest neck of Limburg, along the river Maas and the central lakes area, through beautiful historic villages, and offering fine views over the Maas Valley.

Roermond is an ancient town, founded in the thirteenth century, and has a rich history. Once the chief town of the former Gelder district, in the fifteenth century it became a member of the Hanseatic League. This trading association brought much growth and Roermond became famous as a weaving town. Parking is available on Roersingel, near the old stone bridge, and in the Markt. The outstanding feature of the town is the huge Munsterkerk, a beautiful twin-towered Romanesque building founded in 1218. The towers were actually added when the church was restored by Cuijpers in the nineteenth century, but they are so much in keeping with the original building that this is difficult to realise. Inside is the tomb of Gerard van Gelre and his wife Margaretha van Brabant, who both died in the thirteenth century. This lovely abbey church stands in the Munsterplein, a wide open square in the centre of the town, which was once ringed by moats. Now filled in, wide boulevards ring the town in their place.

Despite having suffered a number of serious fires over the centuries, many buildings have survived. On the northern corner of the square, behind the Munsterkerk, at the corner of Pollartstraat, is the Prinsenhof, once the Palace of the Stadhouder or governor of Upper Gelre, but now used as a *hofje*. The building, in Maasland Renaissance style dates from the seventeenth century. Turn into Pollartstraat, passing the district courts in the old episcopal palace (1666) with an old sundial on the left wing, turn left into Heilige Geest Straat then right again into Jesuitenstraat. Here are some of the many 'patrician' houses in the town, with *portes-cochères*, doorways large enough for coaches to enter. Turn left into Swalmerstraat where there are more of these fine houses then ahead to the Markt, with the large Town Hall standing at one end of the square. Just across the street to the north is the Kathedraal St Christoffel, its tower crowned with a gilded statue of the patron saint of the town. Part of the old town defences can be seen at the end of the Buitenop, dating from the mid-fourteenth century. From here, return to the town centre via Roerkade, past the eighteenth-century Maria Theresiabrug, then via Brugstraat and Marktstraat to Neerstraat, where there is an attractive patrician house known as 'De Steenen Trappen' (stone steps) built in 1666. Further along is the Minderbroederskerk, once belonging to the Franciscans, but now a Dutch Reformed Church. Continue along Zwartbroekstraat to Zwartbroekplein then via Kapellerpoort to Andersonweg. At no 2-8 is the local museum, containing historical collections about the history of Roermond, together with collections of the work of some of the local artists. The house belonged to the architect P.J. Cuijpers, who did such a magnificent job restoring the Munsterkerk.

Leaving Roermond via the bridge (Hornerweg), follow the signposts initially to **Horn**, then turn left about 1 km after entering the village towards Beegden, Heel and Thorn. **Beegden** and **Heel** are known for their characteristic farmhouses, some of which are listed buildings. **Thorn** is a magnificent little town, with a superb church and medieval atmosphere. It is said that a pre-Christian tribe built a temple dedicated to the god Thor, and when Christianity reached the town, it was changed into a chapel dedicated to the Virgin Mary, and the town was given the name of Thorn. Certainly, the oldest parts of the tower crypt are very old indeed, and are said to contain the remains of the temple. It is known that the church was founded in 992, as part of an Abbey complex intended for both sexes, ruled by a group of noblewomen, whose abbess had almost the power of a sovereign. Because of their wealth, many treasures were obtained for the Abbey which can be seen today. Most of the buildings were demolished in 1817, after the invasion of the French when the independent abbey was dissolved. Only the church, now used as the parish church, remains. It has the most beautiful baroque interior, with balustraded stairways leading to the sanctuary, once the Canons' choir, and to the 'ladies choir' at the western end of the church. A guide, in English, is available on request, which is very detailed and gives a clear explanation of all there is to see. Normally, on entering the church, visitors are shown some slides to illustrate the history of Thorn. The commentary is in Dutch, but these are worth seeing as the various church treasures are illustrated.

The village itself is often called the 'White village' because most of the houses are white-plastered. The old square behind the church, known as the Wijngaard, has cobblestones set in patterns, attractive old lanterns and, in the centre, an enormous old pump. Some of the houses in the square were once homes for the canons and other officials of the abbey and include the treasurer's house. Walking further into Daalstraat, then left at the end into Beekstraat, there is an old watermill, known to have existed in the fourteenth century. Follow the path alongside the stream back towards the abbey. On the left is a small bridge from where a good view of the houses in the village, backed by the church, can be obtained. Continuing along under the trees, we reach the old gateway into Kloosterberg, one of the original abbey entrances along which is the entrance gate to the old abbey kitchens. The large white house on the right, known as Huis Groenenberg, was the residence of one of the abbesses of Thorn. Turning left on reaching Hofstraat, the original front of the Abbey can be seen and part of the old Abbey court. Opposite is a large farmhouse in typical Limburg style with inner courtyard, known as the House with the Three Balls. Leave Thorn via the main N273 road northwards, and on reaching the motorway turn right and continue to the exit signed **Sint Joost**, where the road to **Echt** is joined. Cyclists go by way of **Wessem** and **Maasbracht** to St Joost. The road crosses the huge lakes area of Central Limburg, formed by the excavation of gravel.

At **Echt**, in the old town centre, is a museum devoted to Carnaval, full of costumes, masks, and all that goes to make a successful carnival procession. In the same square, are the district museum and the geological museum, both with collections of particular significance to the area. Travel south towards **Susteren**, at which point, Limburg is only about 5km wide. It is also noticeable that there are large industrial areas within this part of the province. The town has a very old abbey church, built between 980 and 1050, containing a number of treasures, including a very valuable eleventh-century book, 'de Evangelieboek van Susteren', considered to be one of the earliest books in Holland. Also in the church is some priceless, world-renowned tenth-century silver. Travel south towards **Sittard**, another old town with some evidence of its original walls, and a number of interesting half-timbered buildings, including, in the Markt, which is full of small pavement cafés and has a very continental atmosphere, the old town farm. This attractive ochre-coloured house has two floors which overhang the street, the top floor overhanging the first floor. It seems somewhat out of place beside the more modern buildings of the ninteenth and twentieth centuries. Almost next door is the richly decorated baroque façade of the seventeenth-century church of St Michiel. The Grote Kerk, in nearby Kerkplein contains the original fifteenth-century carved choir stalls and some very fine paintings depicting the life of St Peter, to whom the church is dedicated. The district museum, 'De Tempel', housed in an old Jesuit seminary, has a collection devoted to the history and geology of the area, and items connected with the Jewish liturgy.

Leave Sittard by way of Rijksweg Zuid, leading to the industrial town of **Geleen**, known principally for the Pink Pop festival held here at

The old town farm, the Markt, Sittard

Whitsuntide. It should be noted that many areas of the town are sealed off at this time, making it extremely difficult to follow any pre-planned routes in the area.

As you pass through Geleen, it is possible to pick up the signed ANWB 'Mergelland Route' which takes you to **Stein**. It is worth stopping here for a short while to see the old castle ruins by the canal, near the motorway bridge. Also of particular interest is the archaeological museum, built around the remains of a neolithic tomb. Continue following the signed route, which diverts away from the canal, but not before there is an opportunity to observe the superb view over the valley from high up beside the motorway bridge. There are plenty of parking places and there is a footpath which can be followed above the canal banks. Through **Elsloo** and **Beek**, passing the seventeenth-century castles of Elsloo and Gebroek, the route crosses under the motorway, and immediately on the right is a viewpoint, with a good view towards the Maas Valley. The route then descends into Geulle, and down steep winding roads to the canal valley. Take great care, because there are hairpin bends and very steep hills. The road passes several castles, at Geulle, Bunde (where the canal is crossed), and Borgharen (where the canal is crossed back again), and the route then joins the N2 motorway. On reaching the junction with the N278, the road is followed into **Maastricht** city centre.

There is parking on the Markt and on Wilhelminakade by the river.

ROUTE 63   A WALK AROUND MAASTRICHT

Maastricht is the oldest city of the Netherlands, and the provincial capital of Limburg, with a wealth of old buildings and historic monuments, second only to Amsterdam. It has a marvellous international atmosphere, because of its proximity to the borders of Belgium and Germany, and also because of its excellent communications with other countries, both by road and water in Europe, and by air to all parts of the world. Time is well spent exploring the city, which will certainly take more than a day if you wish to see it in any detail, and while in the area it is worth taking a boat trip on the Maas to the caves and grottoes of St Pietersberg.

Starting in the Markt, notice the seventeenth-century Stadhuis, which has a large twin flight of stairs, said to be incorporated because there were two authorities controlling the city at that time. The tower contains a carillon of forty-three bells, which are played regularly. The interior contains some very fine Gobelin and Brussels tapestries, painted ceilings and stucco work. From the Markt, walk down Grote Gracht and left into Helmstraat, which brings you to the Vrijthof, a large pleasant square in front of the huge cathedral. Tradition has it that the Vrijthof was a sanctuary, but it may have been derived from the German word *friedhof*, meaning cemetery, as it is certainly the site of an old cemetery. Around this square may be seen the Generaalshuis, a neo-classical building constructed in 1809 on the site of a former enclosed nunnery, and the 'Spaanse Gouvernement', home of the Dukes of Brabant since the end of the fourteenth century. On the western side near the cathedral stands the Hoofdwacht, or old military guard house, built in 1773. The beautiful St Servaaskerk is well worth visiting. The treasury is open as a museum, and includes the Pectoral Cross and Key of St Servatius himself, and a most beautiful reliquary. The lovely south porch is a fine example of early Gothic architecture, richly decorated with carved and gilded columns and figures. The earliest part of this great church dates back to the sixth century (part of the crypt) although the main part dates from the eleventh to fifteenth centuries. Next door to the cathedral is St Janskerk, with a fine tower 70m tall. First mentioned in 1218, it has been in use by the Reformed congregation of Maastricht since 1632 and contains a beautiful pulpit, made in 1780, and some fine monuments. From the church, walk along St Servatiusklooster into Bouillonstraat, passing the Wachtgebouw, another old military guardhouse, built in 1770. From here, walk down to Ezelmarkt (donkey market) and Bonnefantenstraat, with the little ''t Huis op de Jeker', built over a stream, on the left, emerging at Heksenhoek or witches' corner. At this point, ascend the city walls and walk along above the city for a short way; at the end on the left is the fourteenth-century chapel of the Nieuwenhof. Walk down Zwingelput and Grote Looiersstraat into Lange Grachtje, where some of the original thirteenth-century walls can still be seen. Continue into Begijnenstraat, where, on the left is the 'Faliezustersklooster', a seventeenth-century convent, and the 'Patervink-

St Servatius cathedral, Maastricht

toren,' part of the fourteenth-century ramparts. Nearby is the access to the sixteenth-century parts of the city walls, with the 'Vijfkoppen' and 'Haet ende Nijt' bastions, with a nineteenth-century gate over the end of Begijnenstraat. The eighteenth-century Pesthuis, once used for plague victims is next to de Helpoort, or Hell's gate, and the wall of Our Lady. Continue along St Bernardusstraat to OL Vrouweplein, where the twelfth-century Basilica of Our Lady stands, a building of great architectural importance, as the western end is unique. This is an enormous wall, flanked by two tall pinnacled towers, much higher than the main roof of the church itself. The treasure-house, open to visitors, contains some valuable relics. Continue along Stokstraat, where there are some very nice seventeenth and eighteenth-century houses, to the St Servaasbrug, originally built in the thirteenth century and restored to its original state after severe war damage. From the bridge it is possible to look across the river and see some of the other fortifications of the city. Walk back across the bridge into Maastrichterbrugstraat and right into Kleine Staat, at the end of which, is the fifteenth-century building known as the Dinghuis, once the home of the Chief Justice, but now the VVV offices. From here, walk down Muntstraat back to the Markt, or divert via Grote Staat and Helmstraat to the Bonnefanten museum, housed in a modern building in 'Entre Deux' shopping centre.

Whilst in Maastricht, we recommend that a river trip is taken to **St Pietersberg**, to the south of the city. It is possible to combine a cruise with entrance to the Grottoes, which are the result of years of excavation for the local marl stone. There are more than 20,000 passages under the hill, which, over the centuries, have been used by the citizens as a refuge during times of war. Old inscriptions and paintings can be seen on some of the walls, and there are remains of some of the emergency provisions stored here during World War II. From the fort on the top of the hill, there is a magnificent view over Maastricht and the Maas valley right into Belgium. These places may only be visited in the company of an official guide, as the caves are real labyrinths and it would be easy to get lost. Nearby are many country walks including a nature trail established by the ENCI cement company, with three different waymarked walks in this very pretty nature reserve known as 'd'n Observant', offering superb views from peaceful surroundings. The casemates *kazematten*, military store rooms and galleries built into old mine workings may be seen at Tongerseweg, near the Tongerseplein. For St Pietersberg and the caves, continue eastwards along the ring road from Tongerseplein to Luikerweg, turn right by the police headquarters and follow the road which leads up to fort St Pieter and the Grottoes.

ROUTE 63A   AROUND MAASTRICHT and THE FAR SOUTH OF LIMBURG

The countryside south of Maastricht is quite different from anywhere else in Holland, with deep river valleys, hills with fine views, many castles, and timber-framed houses, which are rarely seen outside Limburg. By following the ANWB 'Mergelland Route' from Maastricht to Drielandenpunt, near Vaals, you will see some of the loveliest villages and finest views in the province.

Leave Maastricht by way of the John F. Kennedybrug, in the direction of Aachen (Germany), but turn off the road immediately after crossing the bridge, at the first exit, following the signs for **Eijsden**. Keeping to the road beside the river, you will see St Pietersberg on the right, and will also pass the large watersports centre just before reaching Eijsden. Beautiful castles can be seen as you travel along the road towards Sint Geertruid, Mheer and Noorbeek, which twists and turns through the hills and hugs the border with Belgium. Fine views and black-and-white houses are plentiful. **Mheer** has the distinction of having a Neo-Gothic-style church which was the first one to be built by the architect P.J. Cuijpers. Continue along the signed route, along small hilly roads towards **Epen**. By the Hotel 'Ons Krijtland', there is a car park from which there is a superb view into Belgium. A steep hill brings you to Epen, where more black-and-white houses may be seen. It is worth stopping here to look around the village as there are some very fine examples of the half-timbered houses, notably the Dorpshof and the Tiendhof near the church. There are also some attractive watermills and quiet paths to the south of the village. The road now becomes even steeper and twisting, although there is the advantage of many viewpoints offering breathtaking views. The road is shady, as it runs through a thickly forested area, 'Boswachterij Vaals', with plenty of parking places and picnic areas, and several waymarked paths. As you approach the town of Vaals, divert to Drielandenpunt, which is signposted from near Vaalsbroek castle. The road twists uphill — watch for one-way circuits — to a parking place from where it is easy to walk to the point where Belgium, Holland and Germany converge. Unfortunately, the place has become very commercialised, with the Dutch and Belgians each having their own souvenir shops and viewing towers, but it is an experience to be able to stand at the junction of three countries, where there is no artificial border, and it is very difficult, apart from the boundary stone, to tell which country you are in.

Return down the hill to Vaals, and leave the marked Mergelland route, taking instead the main road towards Aachen (Aken in Dutch). On reaching the main N278 road turn left and leave the town. About 1km from Vaals is the small village of **Lemiers** with a tiny twelfth-century church, and further on, **Mamelis** is a pretty hamlet, with stone houses set against a background of trees with the towers of a Benedictine Abbey behind them. Turn left here down a narrow road to **Vijlen**, to rejoin the signed Mergelland Route. This village has the highest standing church in the

Mheer
Neo-Gothic church, first church to be
built by Cuijpers.

Epen
Magnificent black-and-white half-
timbered houses in village. Attractive
watermills and quiet lanes south of
village.

Vaals
Drielandenpunt, where three countries
meet.

Lemiers
Tiny village with twelfth-century
church.

Mechelen
Old watermill in centre of village.
Many old half-timbered houses.

Kerkrade
Mine museum, housed in old abbey at
Rolduc.
Beautiful abbey buildings, dating back
to twelfth century.

Heerlen
Museum Thermae, Roman baths
museum. Twelfth-century St
Pancratiuskerk. Fifteenth-century
Gevangentoren.

Hoensbroek
Largest castle between Rhine and
Maas, dates back to the fourteenth
century.

Hulsberg
Beautifully restored seventeenth-
century monastery.

Valkenburg
Main tourist centre of South Limburg.
Attractions include grottoes, castle
ruins and watermills, all kinds of
amusements including a casino, set in
beautiful country surroundings.
Oldest railway station in Holland
(1853) and seventeenth-century
Spaanse Leenhof.

Margraten
American War Cemetery, containing
dead of all American forces in Holland
during World War II.

Netherlands, as well as more half-timbered houses.

The next village, **Mechelen**, has an old watermill in the Hoofdstraat, and
a little further along the route, at **Wittem**, is a castle which has been
converted into a hotel and restaurant. The route turns eastwards now to
Simpelveld, where the church has a Romanesque tower dating from the
twelfth century, and a large convent and monastery of the Loreto sisters
and fathers. Continue into **Kerkrade**, via the main road, to visit the Mine
museum, which is situated in Rolduc Abbey, very close to the German
border near **Herzogen**. The museum gives an insight into the old and
modern conditions of coalmining in Holland — of which Kerkrade was the
centre — until it ceased after the discovery of the natural gas field. The
Abbey itself is one of the most notable Romanesque buildings in Holland,
and dates back to the twelfth century. The crypt is beautifully carved and
decorated, and contains the remains, in a sarcophagus, of the founder of
the monastery who died in 1112. In Kerkrade itself is a rather nice town

park and Botanical gardens.

From Kerkrade drive directly to **Heerlen**, famous for its Roman remains. The Roman baths were excavated here in the 1960s and 70s, and have been left *in situ* and covered with a huge roof, so that they can be seen as a whole. Next door is the Museum Thermae, with some extremely interesting exhibits, such as coins and statuary, and also a Roman road map. A granite post, in the town centre, marks the spot where two Roman roads crossed, thus making it the ideal place on which to found a town. Other interesting buildings include the twelfth-century St Pancratiuskerk and the fifteenth-century Gevengentoren, both in Kerkplein.

Leave the town via the main Sittard road, and in about 4km turn left at signpost 2854 which brings you straight to the car park for Hoensbroek Castle, a fourteenth-century building set on an island surrounded by a lake and moats and the largest castle between the Rhine and the Maas. Now used as a conference centre, it also houses a museum of guns and shooting equipment and a geological/archaeological museum.

From the castle, take the road to **Nuth** and **Hulsberg**, two more attractive villages with black-and-white timbered houses. At Hulsberg there is also a lovely church and beautifully restored seventeenth-century monastery. Continue to **Valkenburg**, a place which has made the tourist industry its main source of income. The first VVV office opened here 100 years ago, and there is everything that the tourist could wish for including a casino and all kinds of other amusements, surrounded by beautiful countryside. Once the centre of a stone-mining industry, like Maastricht it has many underground passages and grottoes, and these have been exploited for tourist use. There is even a full-scale model coalmine in one of them. Another series has been transformed into Roman-style catacombs. Above the town are the ruins of the highest castle in the Netherlands, complete with a genuine secret passage which leads to one of the grottoes. There are cable cars, bob-sleds, chair lifts and all kinds of other incentives to get you up - or down - the hills. There are several other old castles in the area, and in the town are a number of old houses, including the seventeenth-century Spaanse Leenhof, accommodating the VVV. The railway station is the oldest in the Netherlands still in use, and was built in 1853. The small district museum contains old craft materials and tools, paintings and prints.

The countryside around Valkenburg is really beautiful, with small streams and many working watermills. The Fransche molen (1657) contains an exhibition about the watermills in the district.

Leave Valkenburg and go east, this time along the Geul valley to **Gulpen**, via **Wijlre**, where more castles may be seen. From here, turn west to **Margraten**, where the American War Cemetery is situated. All the American land forces who were killed in Holland during World War II are buried here.

We return to Maastricht by following the main N278 road.

FURTHER INFORMATION

NETHERLANDS BOARD OF TOURISM.
(NBT)
Head Office
Vlietweg 15
2266KA Leidschendam
Netherlands
Tel: 070 705705

Australia
Suite 302,
5 Elisabeth Street
Sydney, NSW 2000
Tel: 02 276921

Canada
25 Adelaide Street East, Suite 710
Toronto
Ontario M5C 1Y2
Tel: (416) 3631577

United Kingdom
25-28 Buckingham Gate
London SW1E 6LD
Tel: 01 630 0451

USA
437 Madison Avenue
New York 10022
Tel: (212) 223 8141

West Coast
605 Market Street, Room 401
San Francisco Cal 94105
Tel: (415) 543 6772

Chicago
225N Michigan Avenue, Suite 326
Chicago, Ill 60601
Tel: (312) 819 0300

VVV TOURIST INFORMATION OFFICES

VVV stands for *Vereniging Voor Vreem-delingsverkeer*, but is always referred to as VVV (pronounced 'Fay-Fay-Fay'). For local information it is only necessary to write to VVV followed by the name of the town. In major towns the offices which bear the sign *i-Nederland* can give information on any region in the Netherlands.

INTERNAL FERRY SERVICES

NOTE All ferries carry foot passengers and cycles. Where reservation is compulsory, this applies only to cars. A telephone booking made the same day or the previous day is usually sufficient except for peak holiday times, when as much notice as possible is advisable.

Wadden Islands (Service all year round)

Den Helder-Texel
Every hour. Journey time: 20 minutes.
No reservations. Tel: 02226 441

Harlingen-Terschelling
Three times daily. Journey time: $1\frac{1}{2}$ hours. Reservation compulsory. Tel: 05620 6111

Holwerd-Ameland
Five times daily. Journey time: 45 minutes. Reservation compulsory. Tel: 05191 6111

Harlingen-Vlieland
Three times daily. Journey time: $1\frac{1}{2}$ hours. No cars.

Lauwersoog-Schiermonnikoog
Four times daily. Journey time: 45 minutes. No cars. Tel: 05193 9050 or 05195 1210

Zeeland (Service all year round)

Zijpe-Anna Jacobapolder
Every half-hour. Journey time: 7 minutes. No reservations.

Vlissingen-Breskens
Every half-hour during the day. Journey time: 20 minutes. No reservations.

Kruiningen-Perkpolder
Every half-hour weekdays, every hour Saturday and Sunday. Journey time: 20 minutes. No reservations.

North Holland-Friesland (Service from early May to mid-September)

Enkhuizen-Stavoren
Three times daily. Journey time: 1 hour 20 minutes. No cars. Tel: 02990 23641.

Enkhuizen-Urk
Twice daily (3 July/August). Journey time: $1\frac{1}{2}$ hours. Reservation compulsory. Tel: 05277 3407

Public Transport

Rail
Nederlandse Spoorwegen (NS)
PO Box 2025
3500HA Utrecht
Tel: 030 359111

Timetables, information, and a number of brochures and leaflets (some free) are obtainable in London from Netherlands Railways, 25/28 Buckingham Gate, London SW1E 6LD Tel: 01 630 1735 (This is the same address as the NBT).

Bus
Information on bus services all over the country, with details of connecting railway stations and a map of routes, is published by Netherlands Railways (NS) and is called *Nationale Buswijzer*. Information on city public transport services (bus, tram and metro) can be obtained by telephoning:
Den Haag: 070 824141
Amsterdam: 020 272727
Rotterdam: 010 546890

Boat Trips

These are a good way to see many parts of the country. Many trips have commentaries in several languages; details are available from the local VVV. A selection is given here.

Alkmaar
Rederij Woltheus Afgesneden Kanaalvak
Alkmaar
Tel: 072 114840
Six-hour cruise to Zaanse Schans. Summer only.

Amsterdam
A number of firms operate cruises along the canals, also around the harbour area. Some start from opposite Central Station. Details from VVV or from signs on quayside.

Arnhem
Rederij Heymen
Kantoorschip

Rijnkade
Arnhem
Tel: 085 515181
Various cruises, during summer months,
including a cruise on the Rhine and
IJssel rivers.

Maastricht
Rederij Stiphout
Maaspromenade 27
6211HS Maastricht
Tel: 043 54151
Various cruises including a round trip
on the river Maas; daily from April to
September.

Rotterdam
Spido-Rondvaart
Postbus 815
3000AV Rotterdam
Tel: 010 135400
Various trips departing from Willemsplein. Rotterdam Harbour tour, and
tour of Delta-works are two examples,
the former going daily all year, the latter
during July and August.

Biesbosch
Boat tours of this area start from several
places, one example being:
Biesboschtours
Biesboschweg 7
Lage Zwaluwe
Tel: 01684 2250
Other tours start from Drimmelen, by
Rederij Zilvermeeuw (Tel: 01626 2609)
and Rondvaartbedrijf 'Avontuur' (Tel:
01682 4097).

STEAM TRAIN LINES

Full details of the following steam train
services are contained in the free booklet
'Stoom op het Spoor' (Holland by
Steam) printed in Dutch and English
and published annually by the ANWB.

Apeldoorn – Dieren
July and August, daily except
Saturdays
NS Stations, Apeldoorn and Dieren
Information: Tel: 01883 – 15919

Goes – Oudelande
July and August, daily except
Mondays. Weekends May, June and
September. Depot, NS Station, Goes
Information: Tel: 01105 – 1295 or 01100
–28307

Haaksbergen - Boekelo
July and August, Wednesdays and
Saturdays
Haaksbergen MBS Depot
Information: Tel: 05427 – 11516

Hoorn – Medemblik
May to mid-October, with special trips
and events.
Tramstation Koepoortseweg, Hoorn
Information: Tel: 02290 – 14862

ANWB

These letters stand for *Algemene Nederlandse Wielrijdersbond*, which means
General Dutch Cyclists Union, founded
in 1883 to uphold the interests of
cyclists. It has grown greatly since then,
and now looks after its members' interests
in the fields of tourism, recreation,
environment, traffic and transport, in
the broadest sense. It has come, therefore, to take an interest in all forms of
transport, motorised or not, on land,
water and in the air. Usually the ANWB
is known as the Royal Dutch Touring
Club, but most Dutch people simply
refer to it as the ANWB (pronounced
'Aah-En-Fay-Bay').

The Head Office is at Wassenaarseweg 220, 2509BA, Den Haag; Tel: 070 264426. In the same building is a shop selling all the publications and other articles from the ANWB, including maps, guide books and so on. They are open from 8.45am to 4.45pm daily except Saturday, when they are open from 8.45am to noon. They are closed on Sundays. The ANWB signposts roads, has road patrols, publishes maps, camp site lists, and so on. There is also a day and night service giving up-to-date information on road and traffic conditions, weather and delays to trains or ferries; tel: 070 313131. Visitors from other countries who are members, at home, of motoring or touring clubs affiliated to the AIT can receive assistance from the ANWB road patrols in the event of breakdowns, on the same terms as at home.

Note: The ANWB does not deal with enquiries from overseas.

YOUTH HOSTELS

Youth Hostels in the Netherlands are under the control of the *Nederlandse Jeugdherberg Centrale (NJHC)*, whose central office is at Prof Tulpplein 4, 1018GX Amsterdam, Tel: 020 264433.

SOME USEFUL ADDRESSES

Afdeling Buitenland van het Ziekenfonds ANOZ
PO Box 9069
3506GB Utrecht
Tel: 030 618881
This is the foreign affairs department of the Health Service, and is responsible for arrangements whereby visitors can receive medical assistance. EEC countries have reciprocal arrangements for free health care;

visitors from other countries should ensure they have adequate insurance. Users of medicines are advised to have copies of their prescription details, in Latin. In case of difficulty, contact the ANOZ as above.

Stichting Gastvrije Fietscampings (GFC)
Postbus 27
4493ZG Kamperland
Tel: 01107 2004
An association of camp sites, through which bookings can be made in advance, or on a 24-hour basis from site to site. Useful for cyclists touring, to ensure a pitch the following night.

Landgoed en Kasteel Campings (LKC)
Paterijstraat 11
8081TA Elburg
Tel: 05250 1394
An association of estate owners who have provided campsites, and in some cases holiday cottages, in quiet country areas. Some of the sites require campers to be in possession of the *Kampeerbewijs* issued by the ANWB (See Chapter 2). Nearly twenty estates participate in the scheme.

Netherlands Reservations Centre (NRC)
PO Box 404
2260AK Leidschendam
Tel: 070 202500
Accommodation in hotels can be booked by post or telephone by individuals through this centre, which does not charge for the service. The Centre will confirm the booking.

Staatsbosbeheer (SBB)
Postbus 20020
3502LA Utrecht
Tel: 030 859111

The State Forestry Service organises guided walks, establishes Information Centres, publishes guides and maps, and has established a number of camping and caravan sites. These include sites with all facilities, and sites with minimum facilities (water and toilets), on which cars may not be parked on the pitches. The latter sites are only available to holders of the *Kampeerbewijs*.

CERAMIC FACTORIES

===

Delft
De Porceleyne Fles
Rotterdamseweg 196
Delft
Tel: 015 560234
Open: Monday to Friday 9am-5pm;
Saturday, Sunday and public holidays
10am-4pm.

De Delftse Pauw
Delftweg 133
Delft
Tel: 015 124743
Open: Daily 9am-4pm (weekends
October to March 11am-1pm).

Atelier de Candelaer
Kerkstraat 13
Delft
Tel: 015 131848
Open: Daily 9am-5pm.

Makkum
Tichelaars Koninklijke Makkumer
Aardewerk en Tegelfabriek
Postbus 11
8754ZN Makkum
Tel: 05158 1341
Open: Monday to Friday 10am-4pm.

CASTLES AND COUNTRY HOUSES OPEN TO VIEW

===

The symbol ★ is used to denote places at which admission is free to holders of the museum card, available from the NBT.

Chapter 4

Den Haag
Binnenhof *Ridderzaal*
Binnenhof 8a
Open: All year, Monday to Saturday
10am-4pm.

Chapter 5

Doorn
★Huis Doorn
Langbroekerweg 10
Open: Mid-March to October,
Monday to Saturday 9.30am-5pm;
Sunday 1-5pm.

Haarzuilens
Kasteel De Haar
Kasteellaan 1
Open: Mid-October to mid-November
and February to mid-August, Tuesday
to Sunday and Bank Holidays, 1.30-
5pm.

Maarssen
Slot Zuylen
Zuilenselaan
Amsterdamsestraatweg
Open: Mid-March to September,
Tuesday to Saturday 10am-4pm,
Sunday 2-4pm; October to mid-
November, weekends only.

Nieuw-Loosdrecht
Kasteel Sypesteyn
Nieuw Loosdrechtsedijk 150
Open: May to mid-September,
Tuesday to Saturday, 10am-4pm;
Sunday 2-4pm.

Zeist
Slot Zeist
Zinzendorflaan 1
Open: July and August, Monday to
Friday 2.30-4pm; Saturday and
Sunday all year, 2.30-4pm.

Chapter 6

Amsterdam
Royal Palace
NZ Voorburgwal 147
Open: June to September, Monday to
Saturday 12.30-4pm.

Chapter 7

Medemblik
Kasteel Radboud
Oudevaartsgat 8
Open: June to August, Monday to
Saturday 10.00am-5pm; Sundays all
year 2-5pm.

Chapter 9

Heerenveen
Crack State
Oude Koemarkt
Open: In use as Town Hall. May be
seen during office hours.

Chapter 10

Leens
Borg Verhildersum
Wierde 40
Open: Easter to October, Tuesday to
Sunday 10.30am-5.30pm.

Slochteren
Fraeylemaborg
Hoofdweg 32
Open: April to September, daily
except Monday, 10am-5pm; October
to December, daily except Monday,
10am-4pm; February to March
Saturday and Sunday 10am-4pm;
closed January.

Uithuizen
*Menkemaborg
Menkemaweg 2
Open: April to September, daily 10am-
5pm; October to January and
February to April, daily except
Monday, 10am-4pm; closed during
January.

Chapter 11

Coevorden
Het Kasteel
Kasteel 31
Open: Monday to Thursday 9am-noon
and 1.30-4pm; Friday 9am-noon.

Chapter 12

Muiden
*Muiderslot
Herengracht 1
Open: All year, Monday to Friday
10am-4pm; Sundays and public
holidays 1-4pm.

Chapter 13

Hoenderloo
St Hubertus Hunting Lodge
Hoge Veluwe National Park
Open: May to October, Monday to
Friday 10am-noon and 2-5pm.

Rozendaal
Kasteel Rosendael
Park 1
Open: June to mid-September,
Tuesday to Saturday 10am-5pm;
Sunday 1pm-5pm.

Vaassen
Kasteel de Cannenburg
Maarten van Rossumplein 1
Open: Mid-April to October, Tuesday
to Saturday 9am-5pm; Sunday 1pm-
5pm.

Chapter 15

Brecklenkamp
Havezathe Brecklenkamp
Jonkershoesweg
Open: In use as Youth Hostel. To
view, contact VVV.

Denekamp
Huis Singraven
Schiphorstdijk
Open: Mid-April to mid-July and
September, Tuesday and Friday
10.30am-4pm, Wednesday 10.30am-
1.30pm; mid-July to September,
Tuesday, Thursday and Friday
10.30am-4pm, Wednesday 10.30am-
1.30pm.

's-Heerenberg
Huis Bergh
Hof van Bergh 1
Open: June to September daily,
conducted tours at 2.30pm March-
June and September to October,
Sundays conducted tours at 2.30pm.

Ruurlo
Kasteel Ruurlo
Open: In use as Town Hall. May be
viewed during summer afternoons.

Heino
Kasteel 't Nijenhuis
't Nijenhuis 10
Open: All year, daily, 11am-5pm.

Chapter 16

Amerongen
Kasteel Amerongen
Drostestraat 20
Open: April to October, Tuesday to
Saturday 10am-5pm; Sunday 1-5pm.

Ammerzoden
Kasteel Amersoyen
Kasteellaan 1
Open: June to August, Tuesday to
Saturday 10am-5pm; February to

June and September to November,
Sunday 1-5pm.

Brakel
★Slot Loevestein
Open: April to October, Monday to
Friday 10am-5pm.

Doornenburg
Kasteel Doornenburg
Kerkstraat 27
Open: July to August, Tuesday to
Saturday conducted tours at 1.30,
mid-April to July and September,
Sunday conducted tours at 2.30pm.

Dussen
Kasteel Dussen
Binnen 1
Open: Mid-July to mid-August,
Monday to Friday 2-3pm; April to
mid-July and mid-August to October,
Saturday and Sunday, 2-4pm. Part
used as Town Hall.

Wijk bij Duurstede
Kasteel Duurstede
Open: Restoration in progress.
Enquire opening times from VVV.

Chapter 17

Heeze
Kasteel Heeze
Kapelstraat 25
Open: March to October, Wednesday
and Sunday, conducted tours at 2pm.

Chapter 19

Hoensbroek
★Kasteel Hoensbroek
Klinkerstraat 118
Open: All year, daily, 10am-5pm.

Valkenburg
Kasteel van Valkenburg
Grendelplein
Open: Ruins on view, Easter to mid-
October, 10am-5pm.

Note: Many of the above buildings are open only for conducted tours. Visitors may have to wait for the next tour to start.

COUNTRYSIDE AND FORESTRY INFORMATION CENTRES

Chapter 9

De Koog (Texel)
*Nature Recreation Centre
Ruyslaan 92
Open: All year, Monday to Saturday
9am-5pm.

Chapter 12

Baarn
*National Forest Centre
Kasteel Groeneveld
Open: All year, Tuesday, Wednesday,
Friday, Saturday, Sunday, noon-5pm.

Chapter 13

Rheden
Veluwezoom National Park
Information Centre
Heuvenseweg 5a
Open: Mid-May to mid-September,
Wednesday to Friday, 10am-5pm;
Easter to mid-May and mid-
September to mid-December,
Saturdays and Sundays 10am-5pm.

Chapter 14

Ossenzijl
De Weerribben Visitor Centre
Hoogeweg
Open: All year, daily, 1.30-4.30pm.

Chapter 15

Hellendoorn-Nijverdal
Noetselerberg Visitor Centre

Nijverdalsebergweg 5
Open: April to September, daily,
10am-5pm; September to April, daily
except Mondays, 10am-5pm.

Chapter 17

Nistelrode
Slabroek Visitor Centre
Erenakkerstraat 5
Open: July and August, daily, 10am-
5pm (Saturday 1-5pm); rest of year
Wednesday to Sunday 10am-5pm.

Chapter 18

Drimmelen
Biesbosch Visitor Centre
Dorpstraat 14
Open: All year, Wednesday to Friday
10am-5pm, Saturday 1-5pm, Sunday
11am-5pm.

Chapter 19

Ospel-Nederweert
Mijl op Zeven Visitor Centre
Moostdijk 8
Open: April to mid-September
9am-6pm.

GARDENS AND ARBORETUMS

Chapter 4

Den Haag
Clingendael Estate
Wassenaarseweg
Open: All year, daily, Japanese garden
open daily from May to mid-June.

Rotterdam
Arboretum Trompenburg
Honingerdijk 64
Open: All year, Monday to Saturday
9am-5pm. (Apply for free tickets to
VVV, Stadhuisplein 19).

Chapter 6

Aalsmeer
★Historical Garden
Uiterweg 32
Open: May to September, Wednesday
and Saturday 1.30-4.30pm.

Leiden
★University Botanical Garden
Rapenburg 73
Open: April to September, Monday to
Saturday 9am-5pm, Sunday 10am-
4pm; October to March, Monday to
Saturday 9am-4pm. Hothouses closed
weekends.

Lisse
Flower Exhibition Park
Keukenhof
Open: End March to mid-May, daily,
8am-6.30pm.

Chapter 8

Almere
De Kemphaan Outdoor Centre
Kemphaanweg
Open: April to October, daily, 10am-
5pm; November to March, Monday-
Friday 10am-4pm.

Chapter 10

Groningen
Prinsenhof Garden
Turfsingel
Open: Mid-March to mid-October,
Monday to Friday 9am-sunset,
Saturday and Sunday, 10am-sunset.

Haren
★Hortus de Wolf
Kerklaan 30
Open: All year, Monday to Saturday
10am-4.45pm; Sunday and holidays 2-
4.45pm.

Chapter 11

Frederiksoord
Horticultural School Garden
Maj van Swietenlaan 15
Open: All year, Monday to Friday
9am-noon and 2-5pm; Sundays
between Whitsun and August 2-5pm.

Chapter 12

Baarn
Canton Park and Peking Garden
Faas Eliaslaan 49-51
Open: All year, Monday to Friday
8.30am-4.30pm.

Hilversum
Blijdenstein Pinetum
van der Lindenlaan 25
Open: All year, Monday to Friday
10am-4pm.

Hilversum
Dr Costerus Botanical Garden
Zonnelaan 1
Open: All year, Monday to Friday
9am-5pm.

Chapter 15

Dedemsvaart
Tuinen Mien Ruys
Moerheimstraat 78
Open: April to October, Monday to
Saturday 10am-5pm, Sunday 1-5pm.

Diepenheim
Rosarium de Broenshof
Grotestraat
Open: All year, daily until sunset.

Chapter 17

Best
De Odulphushof
Hoofdstraat 35
Open: April to October, Sunday 1-
6pm.

Chapter 19

Steyl
Jochumhof Botanical Garden
Maashoek 2b
Open: Easter to October, daily, 11am-5pm.

LEISURE AND RECREATION PARKS

Chapter 3

Middelburg
Miniature Town of Walcheren
Koepoortlaan 1
Open: Easter to September, daily, 9.30am-5pm.

Chapter 4

Den Haag
Madurodam Miniature Town
Haringkade 175
Open: April to June, daily, 9.30am-10.30pm; July and August, daily, 9.30-11pm; September, daily, 9.30am-9.30pm; October, daily, 9.30am-6pm.

Rotterdam
Plaswijckpark Recreation Park
CNA Looslaan 23
Open: Daily, 9am-6pm.

Wassenaar
Duinrell Recreation and Fairytale Park
Duinrell 1
Open: Mid-May to September, daily, 9am-9pm; September to mid-May, daily, 10am-5pm.

Chapter 7

Enkhuizen
Sprookjeswonderland
Wilhelminaplantsoen 2
Open: Mid-May to mid-September, Monday to Saturday 10am-5.30pm, Sunday 1-5.30pm.

Chapter 8

Biddinghuizen
Flevohof
Spijkweg 30
Open: April to September, daily, 10am-6pm; October to March, daily, 10am-5pm.

Chapter 9

Rijs
Sybrandy's Recreation and Bird Park
J.Schotanusweg 71
Open: Easter to September, daily, 9am-6pm.

Chapter 11

Assen
Jeugdverkeerspark
Rode Heklaan 7
Open: Easter to September, Monday to Friday 9am-5.30pm, Saturday and Sunday 1-5.30pm.

Zuidlaren
De Sprookjeshof
Groningerstraat 10
Open: Easter to mid-October, daily, 9am-6pm.

Chapter 13

Oosterbeek
De Westerbouwing Rhine Terrace
Open: March to October, daily, 9am-8pm.

Chapter 15

Slagharen
Shetland Pony Recreation Park
Zwartedijk 39
Open: Easter to mid-September, daily, 9am-6pm; mid-September to mid-October, Saturday and Sunday 9am-6pm.

Hellendoorn

Hellendoorn Recreation and Fairytale Park

Luttenbergerweg 22

Open: Easter to mid-September, daily, 10am-5.30pm; mid-September to mid-October, Saturday and Sunday 10am-5.30pm.

Hengelo

De Waarbeek Recreation Park

Twekkelerweg 327

Open: April to August, daily, 10am-5.30pm; September and October, 10am-5.30pm.

Oldenzaal

Het Hulsbeek Recreation Park

Bornsedijk 100

Open: Daily.

Chapter 17

Kaatsheuvel

De Efteling Leisure Park

Europaweg

Open: End March to mid-October, daily, 10am-6pm.

Wanroij

De Bergen Recreation Park

Campinglaan 1

Open: April to September, daily, 9am-7pm.

Chapter 18

Hilvarenbeek

De Beekse Bergen Recreation Park

Beekse Bergen 1

Open: Mid-April to September, daily, 10am-6pm.

Hoeven

Bosbad Hoeven Recreation Park

Oude Antwerpse Postbaan 81a

Open: Mid-May to August, daily, 9am-7pm; mid-March to Easter and September to mid-October, Sunday, 1-5pm; Easter to mid-May, daily, 1-5pm.

The following is a selection of some of the mills which may be visited. (It does not include those which are officially designated as museums or those situated in the open-air museums.)

Chapter 3

Retranchement

Molenstraat 3

Windmill (1643)

Working: July to August, Saturdays 1-3pm.

Chapter 4

Schiedam

De Noord (1794)

Noordvest 38

Windmill. Distillery mill working every Saturday.

De Vrijheid (1785)

Noordvest 40

Windmill. Distillery mill working Saturdays 10.30am-4.30pm.

Kinderdijk

Complex of eighteen windmills (1740) along the Molenkade

Mill visits: April to September, Monday to Saturday 9.30am-5.30pm. Mill days: July and August. All mills in operation on Saturdays 2.30-5.30pm.

Chapter 7

Schermerhorn

Museum Mill (1635)

Noordervaart Zuidzijde 2

One of a group of 3 polder windmills

Open: May to September, Tuesday to Sunday 10am-5pm; October to April, Sunday 10am-4.30pm.

Chapter 9

Anjum
De Eendracht (1889)
Mounebuorren 18
Windmill. Flour mill still in use, with
exhibits
Open: April to September, Monday to
Saturday, 10am-noon, 12.30-5pm.

Chapter 13

Eerbeek
Oude Oliemolen
Kanaalweg 1
Watermill
Apply to VVV or to mill to visit.

Chapter 14

Hasselt
De Zwaluw
Stenen Dijk
Windmill. Corn mill
To view enquire at VVV.

Chapter 15

Diepenheim
De Haller (thirteenth-century)
Watermolenweg 32
Watermill still used for making flour
Open: Tuesday and Thursday, 1.30-
5pm.

Haaksbergen
Oostendorper watermill
Langelo
Double undershot mill for corn and oil
Open: Wednesday and Saturday, 2-
6pm.

Denekamp
Singraven (1448)
Schiphorstdijk
Watermill. Still in use as flour and saw
mill
Open: April to November, Tuesday to
Saturday 10am-4pm.

Vasse
Bels (1830)
Bergweg 9
Double water mill. Now used as a
restaurant.

De Mast
Denekamperweg 244
Water mill. Formerly an oil mill, then
a corn mill.

Mander
Frans
Oosteriksweg 26
Water mill dated 1870. Now a corn
mill.

The three mills above may be viewed
freely all the year.

Borculo
Het Eiland (1628)
Burg. Bloemersstraat
Double water mill. Now a restaurant
open all week.

Eibergen
Mallum Watermill (1188). With Millers
House dated 1753. Working Saturdays
2-5pm

Chapter 16

Wijk-bij-Duurstede
Rijn and Lek Windmill (1659)
Leuterpoort.
Built on one of the town gates
To visit, apply VVV

Buren
De Prins van Oranje (1716)
Molenwal
Windmill. In use on Saturdays.

Chapter 19

Geysteren
Rosmolen
Rosmolenseweg
Geysterse Bossen
Water mill. Outside only on view.

Baexem

Auroramolen (1599)

Rijksweg

Windmill. Working on Sundays and
may be viewed.

Baarlo

Seventeenth-century watermill

A corn mill

In use: Saturdays 10am-noon.

Nunhem

St Ursula watermill (1773)

Leumolen 3

Contains a museum.

To view if not in use: enquire from
SBB Roermond, Tel: 04750 34251.

Epen

Volmolen

Plaatweg 1

Eighteenth-century watermill

May be seen on working days 9am-
5pm.

Mechelen

Bovenste Molen (1828)

Eperweg 21

Watermill

Valkenburg

Fransche Molen (1657)

Lindelaan 32)

Includes watermill museum

Open: Wednesday to Sunday, 10am-
1pm and from 5pm.

MUSEUMS

Note: Entry fees for museums vary; a
few are free. A museum card, available
from the VVV and NBT, will admit the
bearer to the museums listed here bearing
the symbol ★ free of charge. Admission
to some castles, gardens, etc is also free
with the museum card. If you plan to
visit many museums, it is well worth the
cost. For instance, the Rijksmuseum in
Amsterdam and the open-air museums
at Enkhuizen, Arnhem, and Barger
Compascuum are all in the scheme, and
you will save money even if you only
visit these four.

Since there are literally hundreds of
museums in Holland, only a selection
can be listed here. A useful book listing
nearly 600 museums is published by the
Dutch equivalent of HMSO in the
Hague, and is available from major
VVV offices.

Chapter 3

Brielle

★Trompmuseum

Venkelstraat 4

Open: May to August, daily except
Tuesday, 10am-5pm; September to
May, daily except Tuesday and
Sunday, 10am-5pm. Also closed on
Feast days.

Hellevoetsluis

Nationaal Brandweermuseum

Gallasplein 5

Open: April to October, Monday to
Saturday 10am-4pm; Sunday and
Feast days, 11am-4.30pm; October to
March, Tuesday to Saturday, 10am-
4pm; Sunday and Feast days 11am-
4.30pm. Closed the first two weeks in
October.

IJzendijke

Streekmuseum West-Zeeuwsch-
Vlaanderen

Markt 28

Open: Monday to Friday, 10am-noon
and 1.30-5pm, Saturday and Sunday
2-5pm.

Middelburg

★Zeeuws Museum

Abdijplein 3

Open: June to August, Monday to
Friday 10am-5pm; Saturday and

Sunday 1.30-5pm; May to June and
September, Monday to Friday 10am-
5pm, Saturday 1.30-5pm. Closed on
Ascension Day.

Veere
★De Schotse Huizen
Kaai 25-27
Open: April to September, Tuesday to
Saturday 10am-12.30pm and 1.30-
5pm.

Zierikzee
Stadhuismuseum
Meelstraat 8
Open: May to September, Monday to
Friday 10am-noon and 1.30-4.30pm.
Closed on public holidays.

Maritime Museum *Het Gravensteen*
Mol 20
Open: 1 May to 1 October, Monday to
Saturday 10am-5pm.

Chapter 4

Delft
★Stedelijk Museum Het Prinsenhof
St Agathaplein 1
Open: Tuesday to Saturday 10am-
5pm, Sunday and public holidays 1-
5pm. Closed 1 January, Easter, Whit
Sunday and Christmas Day.

★Museum Huis Lambert van Meerten
Oude Delft 199
Open: Tuesday to Saturday 10am-
5pm; Sunday and public holidays 1-
5pm.

Den Haag
★Mauritshuis
Plein 29 (Korte Vijverberg 8)
Open: Tuesday to Saturday 10am-
5pm; Sunday and public holidays
11am-5pm. Closed 1 January and 30
April.
Note: Due to re-open after restoration
in 1987; check with VVV.

★Rijksmuseum Gevangenpoort
Buitenhof 33
Open: April to October, Monday to
Friday 10am-5pm, Saturday and
Sunday 1-5pm. October to March,
Monday to Friday 10am-5pm. Closed
public holidays.

Panorama Mesdag
Zeestraat 65B
Open: March to November, Monday
to Saturday 10am-5pm, Sundays and
public holidays noon-5pm. November
to February, check with VVV.

Nederlands Postmuseum
Zeestraat 82
Open: Enquire at local VVV.

Dordrecht
★Museum Mr Simon van Gijn
Nieuwe Haven 29
Open: Tuesday to Saturday 10am-
5pm; Sunday and public holidays, 1-
5pm. Free admission on Wednesday,
Saturday, Sunday and public holidays.

★Dordrechts Museum
Museumstraat 40
Open: Tuesday to Saturday 10am-
5pm; Sunday and public holidays, 1-
5pm. Free admission Wednesday
afternoon.

Rotterdam
Toy-Toy Museum Flos and Pieter
Mars
Groene Wetering 41
Open: Daily except Saturday, 11am-
4pm.

★Maritime Museum *Prins Hendrik*
Leuvehaven 1
Open: Tuesday to Saturday 10am-
5pm; Sunday and public holidays,
11am-5pm. Closed 1 January and 30
April.
Museum ship *Buffel* moored nearby is
part of museum.

*Boymans- van Beuningen Museum
Mathenesserlaan 18-20
Open: Tuesday to Saturday 10am-5pm; Sunday and public holidays, 11am-5pm. Closed 1 January and 30 April.

Historic Museums of City of Rotterdam

Delfshaven
*De Dubbelde Palmboom
Voorhaven 10-12

Sack-Carriers Guildhall (*Zakkendragershuisje*)
Voorstraat 12-15
All buildings open: Tuesday to Saturday 10am-5pm, Sundays and public holidays 11am-5pm. Closed 1 January and 30 April.

Schieland House
Korte Hoogstraat 31
Open: Tuesday to Saturday 10am-5pm; Sunday and public holidays, 11am-5pm. Closed 1 January and 30 April.

Schiedam
Stedelijk Museum (with National Spirits Museum)
Hoogstraat 12
Open: Monday to Saturday 10am-5pm; Sunday and public holidays, 12.30-5pm.

Chapter 5

Gouda
*Het Catharina Gasthuis
Oosthaven 9
Open: Monday to Saturday 10am-5pm; Sunday and public holidays noon-5pm. Closed 1 January, 25 December.

*De Moriaan
Westhaven 29
Open: Monday to Saturday 10am-

12.30pm and 1.30-5pm; Sunday and public holidays noon-5pm. Closed 1 January and 25 December.

Schoonhoven
*Nederlands Goud-, Zilver- en Klokkenmuseum
Oude Haven 7
Open: Tuesday to Saturday 10am-5pm; Sunday and public holidays 1-5pm. Closed 1 January and 25 December.

Utrecht
*Rijksmuseum Het Catharijne-Convent
Nieuwe Gracht 63
Open: Tuesday to Friday 10am-5pm; Saturday, Sunday and public holidays 11am-5pm.

Centraal Museum
Agnietenstraat 1
Open: Tuesday to Saturday 10am-5pm; Sunday and public holidays 2-5pm.

*Nederlands Spoorweg Museum
Johan van Oldenbarneveltlaan 6
Open: Tuesday to Saturday 10am-5pm; Sunday and public holidays 1-5pm. Closed 1 January, Easter, Whitsun and Christmas.

*Nationaal Museum van Speelklok tot Pierement
Achter de Dom 12
Open: Tuesday to Saturday 10am-5pm; Sunday and public holidays 1-5pm. Closed 1 January, 30 April, Easter, Whitsun and Christmas.

Chapter 6

Amsterdam
*Amsterdams Historisch Museum
Kalverstraat 92
Open: Tuesday to Saturday 10am-5pm; Sunday and public holidays 1-5pm, 1 May 1-5pm. Closed 1 January.

*Rijksmuseum
Stadhouderskade 42
Open: Tuesday to Saturday 10am-
5pm; Sunday and public holidays 1-
5pm. Closed 1 January.

*Rembrandthuis
Jodenbreestraat 4-6
Open: Monday to Saturday 10am-
5pm; Sunday and public holidays 1-
5pm. Closed 1 January.

*Joods Historisch Museum
Waag
Nieuwmarkt 4
Open: Tuesday to Saturday 10am-
5pm; Sunday and public holidays 1-
5pm.

*Rijksmuseum Vincent van Gogh
Paulus Potterstraat 7
Open: Tuesday to Saturday 10am-
5pm; Sunday and public holidays 1-
5pm. Closed 1 January.

Anne Frank House
Prinsengracht 263
Open: Monday to Saturday 9am-5pm;
Sunday and public holidays 10am-
5pm. Closed 1 January, 25 December
and Day of Atonement.

*Stedelijkmuseum
Paulus Potterstraat 13
Open: Tuesday to Saturday 10am-
5pm; Sunday and public holidays 1-
5pm.

Haarlem
*Frans Hals Museum
Groot Heiligland 62
Open: Tuesday to Saturday 10am-
5pm; Sunday and public holidays 1-
5pm. Closed 1 January and 25
December.

*Teylers Museum
Spaarne 16
Open: March to October, Tuesday to

Saturday 10am-5pm. October to
February, Tuesday to Saturday 10am-
4pm, Sunday 1-4pm. Ascension Day
1-5pm. Closed on public holidays.

Leiden
*Stedelijk Museum De Lakenhal
Oude Singel 28-32
Open: Tuesday to Saturday 10am-
5pm; Sunday and public holidays 1-
5pm. Closed 1 January and 25
December.

*Molenmuseum De Valk
2e Binnenvestgracht 1
Open: Tuesday to Saturday 10am-
5pm; Sunday and public holidays 1-
5pm. Closed 1 January, 3 October and
25 December.

Pilgrim Fathers
Documentatiecentrum
Boisotkade 2a
Open: Monday to Friday 9am-noon
and 2-4pm. Closed 3 October and
public holidays.

Rijksmuseum van Geologie en
Mineralogie
Hooglandse Kerkgracht 17
Open: Monday to Friday 10am-5pm,
Sunday 2-5pm. Closed 3 October and
public holidays. Admission free.

Pijpenkabinet (Museum of clay pipes)
Oude Vest 159a
Open: Sunday 1-5pm.
Occasional demonstrations of
pipemaking when open.

Schiphol
Nationaal Luchtvaart Museum
Aviodome
Open: April to October, daily 10am-
5pm. November to March, daily
except Monday 10am-5pm. Closed 25
and 31 December and 1 January.

Vijfhuizen (Near Haarlem)
*Museum Cruquius

Cruquiusdijk 32
Open: April to September, Monday to
Saturday 10am-5pm; Sunday and
public holidays noon-5pm. October
and November, Monday to Friday
10am-4pm, Sunday and public
holidays noon-4pm.

Chapter 7

Alkmaar
*Kaasmuseum
Waagplein 2
Open: April to October, Monday to
Thursday and Saturday 10am-4pm;
Friday 9am-4pm.

Den Helder
*Helders Marinemuseum Het
Torentje
Hoofdgracht 3
Open: Mid-January to November,
10am-5pm; Saturday and Sunday 1-
4pm. Closed Easter and Whitsun.

*Reddingsmuseum Dorus Rijkers
Keizerstraat 1a
Open: Monday to Saturday 10am-
5pm.

Enkhuizen
*Rijksmuseum Zuiderzeemuseum
Wierdijk 18
Open: Outdoor museum, April to mid-
October, daily 10am-5pm: Indoor
museum 5 April to 20 October,
Monday to Saturday 10am-5pm;
Sunday and public holidays noon-
5pm.

Stedelijk Waagmuseum
Kaasmarkt 8
Open: Tuesday to Saturday 10am-
noon and 2-5pm; Sunday 2-5pm.

Hoorn
*Westfriesmuseum
Rode Steen 1
Open: Monday to Friday 11am-5pm;
Saturday and Sunday 2-5pm.

Koog aan de Zaan
*Molen Museum
Museumlaan 18
Open: Tuesday to Friday 10am-noon
and 2-5pm; Saturday and Sunday 2-
5pm.

Medemblik
Nederlands Stoommachinemuseum
Oosterdijk 4
Open: 1 July to 1 September, Tuesday
to Saturday 10am-5pm; Sunday noon-
5pm. Machines working on Saturday,
Sunday, Tuesday, Wednesday,
Thursday. 11 May to 30 June and 4
September to 20 October, Wednesday
to Saturday 10am-5pm, Sunday noon-
5pm. Machines working on Saturday,
Sunday and Wednesday.

Zaandam
De Zaanse Schans
Kalveringdijk
Open: All year, Monday to Sunday.
Between November and April, houses
and museums open weekends only.

Chapter 8

Ketelhaven
*Museum voor Scheepsarchaeologie
Vossemeerdijk 21
Open: April to September, daily 10am-
5pm. October to March, Monday to
Friday 10am-5pm; Saturday, Sunday
and public holidays 11am-5pm.

Chapter 9

*Aldfaers Erf Village Museums
Consists of five museums, listed
below.
Open: 1 April to 1 November, 9am-
6pm; 1 November to 30 March on
request only.

Farm Museum *De Izeren Kou*
Kerkbuurt 19
Allingawier

Woord en Beeld Kerkje
Meerweg 4
Allingawier

Grocery shop and school
Dorpstraat 52
Exmorra

Carpenters workshop
Buren 5
Ferwoude

't Fugelhus (Bird house)
Buren 8
Piaam

De Waal, Texel
★Wagenmuseum
Hogereind 4-6
Open: 15 May to 15 September,
Tuesday to Saturday 9am-noon and 2-5pm.

Den Burg, Texel
★Oudheidkamer
Kogerstraat 1
Open: May to September, Monday to
Friday 9am-noon.

Den Hoorn, Texel

★Zee en Scheepvaartmuseum
Diek 9a
Open: May to September, Monday to
Friday 1.30-5pm.

Dokkum
★Streekmuseum Het Admiraliteitshuis
Schoolsteeg 1
Open: 1 April to 1 October, Monday
to Saturday 10am-5pm; 1 October to 1
April, Monday to Saturday 2-5pm.

Franeker
Planetarium Eise Eisinga
Eise Eisingastraat 3
Open: April to October, Monday to
Saturday 9am-noon and 1.30-6pm;
October to March, Monday to
Saturday 9am-noon and 2-5pm. 30
April, Ascension Day, Easter Monday

and Whit Monday, 2-6pm. Closed 1
January, Easter, 25 and 26 December.

Harlingen
★Gemeentemuseum Hannemahuis
Voorstraat 56
Open: July to mid-August, Tuesday to
Saturday 10am-5pm; May to July and
mid-August to September, Tuesday to
Saturday 2-5pm.

Heerenveen
★Willem van Haren museum
Van Harenspad 50-52
Open: Monday to Friday 10am-5pm;
Saturday 11am-5pm. Closed Sunday
and official holidays.

Batavus Museum
Industrieweg 4
Open: May to September, daily 2-5pm.

Hindeloopen
★Hidde Nijland Museum
Dijkweg 1
Open: 1 March to 1 November,
Tuesday to Saturday 10am-5pm;
Sunday 1.30-5pm.

Hollum, Ameland
Amelander Oudheidkamer
Herenweg 1
Open: 1 April to 1 November 9.30am-12.30pm and 2-4pm.

Leeuwarden
★Gemeentelijk museum Het
Princessehof
Grote Kerkstraat 9-15
Open: Tuesday to Saturday 10am-5pm; Sunday and public holidays 2-5pm. Closed 1 January.

★Fries Museum
Turfmarkt 24
Open: Tuesday to Saturday 10am-5pm; Sunday and public holidays 1-5pm. Closed 1 January and 30 April.

Makkum
Pottery Museum De Waag

Pruikmakershoek 2
Open: 1 May to 15 September,
Monday to Saturday 10am-5pm;
Sunday 1.30-5pm.

Moddergat-Paesens
*Museum 't Fiskerhuske
Fiskerspad 4-8
Open: 1 March to 1 November,
Monday to Saturday 10am-5pm; also
on official holidays.

Sneek
*Fries Scheepvaartmuseum
Kleinzand 14
Open: Monday to Saturday 10am-
noon and 1.30-5pm.

Vlieland
Municipal Museum Tromps Huys
Dorpsstraat 99
Open: In summer season, Monday to
Friday 10am-noon and 2-5pm.

West-Terschelling
Municipal Museum 't Behouden Huys
Commandeurstraat 30-32
Open: 1 April to 31 December,
Monday to Friday 9am-5pm. 15 July
to 15 September, also open Saturday
and Sunday 2-5pm.

Chapter 10

Bellingwolde
Streekmuseum De Oude Wolden
Hoofdweg 161
Open: Mid-March to mid-October,
Saturday and Sunday 2-5pm.

Groningen
*Groningen Museum
Praediniussingel 59
Open: Tuesday to Saturday 10am-
5pm; Sunday and public holidays 1-
5pm. Closed 1 January and 25
December.

*Noordelijk Scheepvaartmuseum and
Niemeyer's Tabakmuseum

Brugstraat 24-26
Open: Tuesday to Saturday 10am-
5pm; Sunday and public holidays 1-
5pm. Closed 1 January, 5 and 25
December.

Leek
*Nationaal Rijtuigmuseum (Carriage
museum)
Huis Nienoord
Open: April to October, Monday to
Saturday 9am-5pm.

Warffum
Openluchtmuseum *Het Hogeland*
Schoolstraat 2
Open: Tuesday to Saturday.
Conducted tours only, 1.30 and
3.30pm.

Chapter 11

Assen
*Drents Museum
Brink 1 and 5
Open: July and August, Monday to
Friday 9.30am-5pm, Saturday and
Sunday 1-5pm. September to July,
Tuesday to Friday 9.30am-5pm,
Saturday and Sunday 1.5pm.

*Automuseum Assen
Rode Heklaan 3
Open: April to October, daily 10am-
6pm.

Barger-Compascuum
*Openlucht museum 't Aole Compas
Berkenrode 4
Open: Palm Sunday to October, daily
9am-6pm.

Borger
*Museum 't Flint'n Hoes
Bronnegerstraat 12
Open: Easter to September, daily
except Monday 10am-5pm.

Coevorden
*Gemeentemuseum Drenthe's Veste

Haven 5
Open: April to September, Monday to
Friday 10am-12.30pm and 1.30-5pm,
Saturday and Sunday 2-5pm. October
to April, Monday to Friday 10am-
12.30pm and 1.30-5pm, Saturday 2-
5pm.

Diever
Glasmuseum De Spiraal
Moleneinde 6
Open: July and August, Monday to
Friday 10am-noon and 1.30-5.30pm,
Saturday 10am-5pm. September to
December and February to July,
Tuesday to Friday 1.30-5.30pm,
Saturday 10am-5pm.

Emmen
*Oudheidkamer De Hondsrug
Marktplein 17
Open: April to June and September,
Wednesday to Saturday 10am-noon
and 1-5pm, Sunday and public
holidays 1-5pm. June to September,
Monday to Saturday 10am-noon and
1-5pm, Sunday and public holidays 1-
5pm.

Frederiksoord
*Klokkenmuseum
Maj van Swietenlaan 17
Open: May to September, Monday to
Friday 10am-5pm, Sunday 2-5pm.

Hoogeveen
*Museum Venendal
Hoofdstraat 9
Open: Monday to Friday 10am-noon
and 2-4.30pm, Saturday 2-4.30pm.

Orvelte Saxon Village
Open: April to mid-October, Monday
to Friday 9.30am-5pm; Saturday and
Sunday 11am-5pm.

Roden
*Nederlandsmuseum Kinderwereld
Brink 31

Open: March to September, Monday
to Saturday 10am-noon and 2-5pm,
Sunday and public holidays 2-5pm.
September to March, Tuesday to
Saturday 10am-noon and 2-5pm,
Sunday and public holidays 2-5pm.

Ruinerwold
Kachelmuseum
Dr Larigweg 53
Open: Monday to Saturday 10am-
5pm.

Schoonebeek
Museumboerderij
Burg Osselaan 5
Open: Most days. Enquire at local
VVV for opening times.

Schoonoord
Openlucht museum *De Zeven Marken*
Tramstraat 73
Open: Palm Sunday to October, daily
9am-5pm.

Westerbork
Nederlands museum van de Knipkunst
Burg van Weezelplein 15
Open: April to October, daily 10am-
noon and 2-4pm. (Times subject to
revision)

Chapter 12

Amersfoort
*Museum Flehite
Westsingel 50
Open: Tuesday to Friday 10am-5pm;
Saturday, Sunday and public holidays
2-5pm. Closed 1 January, Easter and
25 and 26 December.

Laren
*Singer Museum
Oude Drift 1
Open: Tuesday to Saturday 10am-
5pm, Sunday and public holidays 1-
5pm. Closed 1 January, Good Friday,
Easter, Whitsun, 30 April and 25
December.

Naarden

*Vestingmuseum
Westwalstraat 6
Open: Easter to October, Monday to
Friday 10am-4.30pm; Saturday,
Sunday and public holidays noon-
5pm.

Nijkerk

Nederlands Elektriciteits Museum
Waagplein 2a
Open: 1 April to 30 September,
Tuesday to Saturday 9am-5pm,
Sunday 2-5pm. 1 October to 30
March, Saturday 9am-5pm, Sunday 2-
5pm.

Soesterberg

Airforce Museum Kamp van Zeist
Kampweg
Open: 1 April to 30 November,
Monday to Friday 10am-4pm.

Chapter 13

Apeldoorn

*Paleis Het Loo
Park 1
Open: April to October, Tuesday to
Sunday 10am-5pm.

Arnhem

*Rijksmuseum voor Volkskunde *Het
Nederlands Openlucht Museum*
(National museum of Ethnology)
Schelmseweg 89
Open: April to October, Tuesday to
Friday and Sunday 9am-5pm.
Monday and Saturday noon-5pm.

*Elektrum Museum
Klingelbeekseweg 45
Open: Monday to Saturday 2-5pm.
Closed public holidays.

Bennekom, Nr Ede

*Kijk en Luister Museum
Kerkstraat 1
Open: May to mid-September,

Tuesday to Saturday 2-5pm. Closed
on public holidays.

Elburg

Gemeentemuseum and Nat.
Orgelmuseum
Jufferenstraat 6-8
Open: Monday to Friday 9am-noon
and 2-5pm.

Epe

Veluwe Klederdrachten Museum
Markt 5
Open: Monday to Friday 10am-noon
and 2-4pm.

Harderwijk

*Veluwe Museum van Oudheden
Donkerstraat 4
Open: May to September, Monday to
Friday 9am-5pm, Saturday 1-4pm.
October to May, Monday to Friday
9am-noon and 2-5pm. Closed public
holidays.

Hattem

Museum Hattem and Anton Pieck
Museum
Achterstraat 46-48
Open: June to August, daily except
Sunday 10am-4pm; September to
June, Tuesday to Saturday 10am-4pm.

Otterlo

Rijksmuseum Kröller-Müller
Nat Park Het Hoge Veluwe
Open: April to November, Tuesday to
Saturday 10am-5pm, Sunday and
public holidays 11am-5pm. November
to March, Tuesday to Saturday 10am-
5pm, Sunday 1-5pm.

*It Noflik Ste (Tile museum)
Eikenzoom 10
Open: Tuesday to Saturday 10am-
noon and 2-5pm; Sunday and public
holidays 2-4pm.

Oosterbeek

Airborne Museum

Utrechtseweg 232
Open: Monday to Saturday 11am-
5pm, Sunday and public holidays
noon-5pm. Closed 1 January and 25
December.

Chapter 14

Deventer
★De Waag Museum
Brink 57
Open: Tuesday to Saturday 10am-
12.30pm and 2-5pm. Public holidays
2-5pm.

★Speelgoed en Blik Museum
Brink 47
Open: Tuesday to Saturday 10am-
12.30pm and 2-5pm, Sunday and
public holidays 2-5pm.

★Ruimtevaartcentrum Deventer
(Space museum)
Muntengang 1
Open: Monday to Saturday 10am-
5pm.

Doesburg
★De Roode Tooren
Roggestraat 9-11
Open: July and August, Tuesday to
Friday 10am-noon and 1.30-4.30pm,
Saturday and Sunday 1.30-4.30pm.
September to July, Tuesday to Friday
10am-noon and 1.30-4.30pm,
Saturday 1.30-4.30pm.

Kampen
★Stedelijk Museum Kampen
Oudestraat 158
Open: Easter to mid-October, Tuesday
to Saturday 11am-12.30pm and 1.30-
5pm.

Kamper Tabaksmuseum
Botermarkt 3
Open: Times to be announced.
Enquire at the VVV, Kampen.

Staphorst
★Museumboerderij Staphorst
Gemeenteweg 67
Open: 1 April to 31 October, Monday
to Saturday 10am-5pm. Closed on
public holidays.

Zwolle
★Provincial Overijssels Museum
Melkmarkt 41
Open: Tuesday to Saturday 10am-
5pm, Sunday and public holidays 2-
5pm. Closed 1 January, Easter,
Whitsun and 25 December.

Chapter 15

Borculo
Stormramp Museum and Brandweer
museum
Hofstraat 5
Open: Monday to Friday 10am-noon
and 1.30-5pm, Saturday and Sunday
1.30-5pm.

Tolboerderij De Lebbenbrugge
Lebbenbruggedijk 25
Open: Mid-June to end August,
Tuesday to Saturday 10am-noon and
2-5pm.

Doetinchem
★Museum 't Gevang
Nieuwstad/Heezenpoort
Open: Tuesday to Friday 10am-5pm,
Saturday and Sunday 2-5pm.

Enschede
★Rijksmuseum Twente
Lasondersingel 129
Open: Tuesday to Saturday 9am-1pm
and 2-5pm, Sunday and public
holidays 2-5pm.

★Natuurmuseum
De Ruyterlaan 2
Open: Tuesday to Saturday 10am-
noon and 1.30-5pm; Sunday and
public holidays 2-5pm. Closed 1

January, Good Friday, Ascension
Day, Easter, Whitsun and Christmas.

⋆Textielindustriemuseum
Industriestraat 2
Open: Tuesday to Friday 10am-noon
and 2-5pm, Saturday, Sunday and
public holidays 2-5pm. Closed 1
January, Good Friday, Ascension
Day, Easter, Whitsun and Christmas.

DAF-Automobielmuseum
Janninkcomplex
Haaksbergerstraat/Industriestraat
Open: Tuesday to Saturday 10am-
5pm, Sunday 2-5pm.

Groenlo

Stoomhoutzagerij Nahuis
Winterswijkseweg 49
Open: July and August, Wednesday to
Saturday 10am-noon and 2-4pm.

Hardenberg

⋆Oudheidkamer — Museum
Voorstraat 34
Open: End June to early August,
Monday to Friday 2-5pm.

Hellendoorn

⋆Oudheidkamer *Oals Heldern*
Reggeweg 1
Open: May to September, Monday to
Friday 10-11am and 2-4pm.

Holten

Bos Dierenwereld
Holterbergweg 12
Open: Monday to Saturday 9am-6pm,
Sunday noon-6pm.

Lichtenvoorde

Openluchtmuseum *Erve Kots*
Eimersweg 4
Lievelde
Open: May to October, daily 9am-
5.30pm; October to May, daily except
Monday, 9am-5.30pm.

Oldenzaal

Het Palthehuis
Marktstraat 13
Open: Tuesday to Friday 10am-noon
and 2-5pm; Saturday and Sunday 2-
5pm.

Ommen

Oudheidkamer *de Oord*
Den Oord 7
Open: Mid-June to 31 August,
Monday to Friday 10am-noon and 2-
5pm, Saturday 2-4pm.

Ootmarsum

⋆Los Hoes Boerderijmuseum
Smithuisstraat 2b
Open: April to November, daily except
Monday 10am-5pm.

Winterswijk

⋆Streekmuseum Huize Freriks
Groenloseweg 86
Open: July and August, Monday to
Friday 9am-noon and 2-5pm,
Saturday and Sunday 2-5pm.
September to July, Tuesday to Friday
9am-noon and 2-5pm, Saturday and
Sunday 2-5pm.

Chapter 16

Berg en Dal, Nr Nijmegen

Afrika Museum
Postweg 6
Open: Monday to Saturday 10am-
5pm; Sunday and public holidays 1-
5pm.

Buren

⋆Museum Koninklijke Marechaussee
Weeshuiswal 9
Open: 1 May to 1 October, Tuesday to
Friday 10am-noon and 1.30-4pm,
Saturday, Sunday and public holidays
1.30-5pm.

Het Boerenwagenmuseum
Achter Bonenburg 1

Open: May to October, Tuesday to Sunday 1.30-5.30pm.

Culemborg
Museum Elisabeth Weeshuis
Herenstraat 29
Open: Tuesday to Friday 9am-noon and 2-5pm, Saturday 2-5pm.

Leerdam Z.H.
*Nationaal Glasmuseum
Lingedijk 28
Open: Tuesday to Friday 10am-1pm and 2-5pm, Saturday and Sunday and Ascension Day 1-5pm.

*Museum 't Poorthuis
Kerkstraat 91
Open: May to September, Monday to Saturday 10am-noon and 2-5pm.

Nijmegen
Nijmeegs Museum Commanderie van St Jan
Franse Plaats 3
Open: Monday to Saturday 10am-5pm, Sunday and public holidays 1-5pm. Admission free.

Stichting Velorama
Waalkade 107
Open: March to October, Tuesday to Sunday 11am-5pm.

*Rijksmuseum G.M.Kam
Museum Kamstraat 45
Open: Tuesday to Saturday 10am-5pm, Sunday and public holidays 1-5pm.

*Bijbels Openluchtmuseum
Heiligland-Stichting
Mgr Suyslaan 4
Open: Easter to October, daily 9am-5.30pm.

Tiel
Streekmuseum *Groote Societeit*
Plein 48
Open: Wednesday to Saturday 2-5pm;

Monday 10am-noon and 2-5pm.
Admission free.

Woudrichem N.B
Visserijmuseum
Kerkstraat 41
Open: Mid-April to mid-October, Monday to Saturday 9.30am-4.30pm.

Chapter 17

Asten
Asten Museum
Ostadestraat 23
Open: Tuesday to Sunday 10am-5pm.

Best
Eerste Nederlandse Klompenmuseum
De Platijn
Broekdijk 16
Open: April to October, daily 10am-5pm.

Drunen
Lips Autotron
Museumlaan 100
Open: April to October, daily 11am-5pm.

Eindhoven
Evoluon
Noord Brabantlaan 1a
Open: Monday to Friday 9.30am-5.30pm, Saturday 10am-5pm, Sunday and public holidays noon-5pm.

*Museum Kempenland
St Antoniusstraat 3-5
Open: Monday to Friday 10am-5pm, Saturday and Sunday 1-5pm.

*Stedelijk van Abbe Museum
Bilderdijklaan 10
Open: Tuesday to Saturday 10am-5pm, Sunday and public holidays 1-5pm.

's Hertogenbosch
Noordbrabants Museum
Bethaniestraat 4

Open: Tuesday to Friday 10am-5pm;
Saturday and public holidays 1-5pm.
Admission free.

Nuenen
Van Gogh Documentatiecentrum
Papenvoort 15
Open: Monday to Friday 9am-noon
and 2-5pm.

Oirschot
Museum de Vier Quartieren
St Odulphusstraat 11
Open: Tuesday to Sunday 1-5pm.

Oss N.B.
Jan Cunencentrum
Molenstraat 65
Open: Tuesday to Friday 10am-5pm;
Saturday and Sunday 2-5pm.

Overloon
Nationaal Oorlogs en Verzetsmuseum
Museumpark 1
Open: April to September, daily 9am-
6pm; October to March, daily 9.30am-
5pm.

Waalwijk
*Nederlands Museum voor Schoenen
Leder en Lederwaren
Grotestraat 148
Open: Tuesday to Friday 10am-noon;
Saturday and Sunday noon-4pm.

Chapter 18

Bergen op Zoom
*Gemeentmuseum Markiezenhof
Steenbergsestraat 8
Open: Mid-June to mid-August,
Tuesday to Friday 10am-5pm;
Saturday, Sunday and public holidays
1-5pm. Mid-August to mid-June,
Tuesday to Sunday and public
holidays 2-5pm.

Breda
*Rijksmuseum voor Volkenkunde
Justinus van Nassau

Kasteelplein 55
Open: Monday to Saturday 10am-
5pm; Sunday and public holidays 1-
5pm.

*Stedelijk and Bisschoppelijk
Museum
Grote Markt 19
Open: Wednesday to Saturday
10.30am - 5pm, Tuesday, Sunday and
public holidays 1 - 5pm, Closed 1
January and 25 December.

Raamsdonksveer
Nationaal Automobielen Museum
Steurweg 6
Open: Monday to Saturday 9am-
4.45pm; Sunday and public holidays
11am-4.45pm. Closed 1 January and
25 December.

Roosendaal
*Museum De Ghulden Roos
Molenstraat 2
Open: Daily except Monday 2-5pm.
Closed Easter, Ascension Day,
Whitsun, Christmas and 1 January.

Tilburg
*Nederlands Textielmuseum
Goirkestraat 88
Open: Monday to Friday 10am-5pm;
Saturday 2-5pm; Sunday noon-5pm.

Schrift en Schrijfmachinemuseum
Philips Vingboonstraat 3
Open: Monday to Friday 10am-
4.30pm.

Chapter 19

Echt
*Carnavalsmuseum
*Geologisch Museum
*Streekmuseum
Plats
Open: Monday to Friday 10am-noon
and 2-4pm. Also the first and third
Sunday in each month, 2-5pm.

Heerlen

★Museum Thermae
Coriovallumstraat 9
Open: Tuesday to Friday 10am-5pm;
Saturday, Sunday and public holidays
2-5pm. Closed 1 January, Easter,
Whitsun, Christmas and 30 April.

Kerkrade

★Mijn Museum
Rolduc Abbey
Heyendahllaan 82
Open: May to October, Tuesday to
Friday 9am-5pm, Saturday 1-5pm;
Sundays in July only 1-5pm. Closed
on public holidays.

Maastricht

★Bonnefanten Museum
Dominicanerplein 5
Open: Monday to Friday 10am-noon
and 1-5pm; Saturday, Sunday and
public holidays 2-5pm.

Ospel

Historisch Peel Museum
Casseweg 1a
Open: 1 April to mid-September, daily
10am-5pm. Mid-September to April,
Sunday 10am-5pm.

Roermond

★Museum *Hendrik Luyten-Dr Cuypers*
Andersonweg 2
Open: Tuesday to Friday 10am-noon
and 2-5pm; Saturday and Sunday 2-
5pm.

Sittard

Museum *De Tempel*
Gruizenstraat 27
Open: Monday to Friday 10am-noon
and 2-5pm. Saturday and Sunday 2-
5pm.

Stein

Archeologisch Museum
Schepersgat 6
Open: May to September, daily 4-6pm.
October to April, Saturday and
Sunday 4-6pm.

Steyl

★Missiemuseum
St Michaelstraat 7
Open: April to October, Monday to
Saturday 10am-noon and 2-6pm.
Sunday and public holidays 2-5pm.

Venlo

★Museum van Bommel van Dam
Deken van Oppensingel 8
Open: Monday to Friday 10am-5pm;
Saturday, Sunday and public holidays
2-5pm.

★Goltziusmuseum
Goltziusstraat 21
Open: Monday to Friday 10am-noon
and 2-5pm; Saturday and Sunday 2-
5pm.

Weert

Gemeentemuseum *De Tiendschuur*
Recollectenstraat 5-5a
Open: Daily 2-5pm.

★Kerkelijk Museum Jacob van Horne
Markt
Open: Daily 2-5pm.

Nederlands Tram Museum
Kruisstraat 6
Open: Mid-April to October, Tuesday
to Sunday 2-6pm.

OTHER ATTRACTIONS

Aalsmeer

Flower Auction
Legmeerdijk 313
Open: Monday to Friday 7.30-
11.30am.

Broek op Langedijk

★Broeker Veiling
Voorburggracht 1
Vegetable auction, museum and boat
trips.
Open: May to September, Monday to
Friday 10am-5pm.

's-Heerenberg

Gouden Handen Exhibition Centre
Emmerikseweg 13
Folk art demonstrations and
exhibitions.
Open: Mid-March to end October,
daily 10am-6pm.

Lauwersoog

Expozee
Strandweg 1
Exhibition on Wadden and Lauwerzee
area, tides, landscape and wildlife.
Open: April to September, Tuesday to
Friday 10am-5pm; Saturday and
Sunday 2-5pm.

Lelystad

National Goat Centre
Gelderse Hout 1
Goat farm, with cheese and yoghurt
production. Films.
Open: All year, daily 9am-6pm.

*Information Centre Nieuw Land
Oostvaardersdijk 1-13
Exhibition on land reclamation and
development of IJsselmeer Polders.
Open: April to October, daily 10am-
5pm. November to March, Monday to
Friday 10am-5pm; Sunday 1-5pm.
Closed Sunday.

Otterlo

Hoge Veluwe National Park
Entrances also at Hoenderloo and
Schaarsbergen.
Nature reserve, with Visitor Centre,
and Kröller-Müller Museum of
modern art.
Open: Park open daily from 8am to
sunset.

Rotterdam

Euromast
Parkhaven 20
Tower 104m high with Space-Tower
185m high.
Open: Mid-March to mid-October,
daily 9am-10pm. Mid-October to mid-

March, Mast daily 9am-6pm, Tower,
daily 11am-4pm.

Historic Electric Tram
One run per day, from Central Station
through part of the old city to the
Willemsplein, on one of the old city
tramcars. Booking from the VVV
office at Stadhuisplein 19 or in Central
Station. Tickets include 75 min boat
trip around harbour.
Tram departs daily from April to
September at 1.15pm.

Westenschouwen

Delta Expo, 'Neeltje Jans'
Information Centre
Oosterschelde Flood Barriers
Exhibition, films and tour of flood
barrier works.
Open: April to October, daily 10am-
5pm; November to March, Wednesday
to Sunday 10am-5pm.

Amsterdam

Amsterdam Diamond Centre
Rokin 1
Free tours daily except Thursday,
9.30am-5.30pm; Thursday 9.30-
8.30pm. November to February open
from 11am.

Maastricht

Tours of the Casemates and Fort St
Peter every afternoon, starting at
2.30pm during summer and public
holidays. Enquire from VVV office,
Tel: 043 252121.

St Pietersberg Grottoes
Guided tours of two sections of the
cave system are provided,
full details from VVV, Tel: 043 252121.

Valkenburg

Municipal and Fluwelen Grottoes
Originally used in Roman times for
quarrying stone. Guided tours are
arranged throughout the year, and
details can be obtained from the VVV,
Tel: 04406 13364.

INDEX